Key Concepts in
International
Relations

Recent volumes include:

Key Concepts in Social Research
Geoff Payne and Judy Payne

Fifty Key Concepts in Gender Studies
Jane Pilcher and Imelda Whelehan

Key Concepts in Medical Sociology
Jonathan Gabe, Mike Bury and Mary
Ann Elston

Key Concepts in Leisure Studies
David Harris

Key Concepts in Critical Social Theory
Nick Crossley

Key Concepts in Urban Studies
Mark Gottdiener and Leslie Budd

Key Concepts in Mental Health
David Pilgrim

Key Concepts in Journalism Studies
Bob Franklin, Martin Hamer, Mark
Hanna, Marie Kinsey and John
Richardson

**Key Concepts in Political
Communication**
Darren G. Lilleker

**Key Concepts in Teaching Primary
Mathematics**
Derek Haylock

Key Concepts in Work
Paul Blyton and Jean Jenkins

Key Concepts in Nursing
Edited by Elizabeth Mason-Whitehead,
Annette McIntosh, Ann Bryan and Tom
Mason

Key Concepts in Childhood Studies
Allison James and Adrian James

Key Concepts in Public Health
Edited by Frances Wilson and Andi
Mabhala

The SAGE Key Concepts series provides students with accessible and authoritative knowledge of the essential topics in a variety of disciplines. Cross-referenced throughout, the format encourages critical evaluation through understanding. Written by experienced and respected academics, the books are indispensable study aids and guides to comprehension.

THOMAS DIEZ, INGVILD BODE AND
ALEKSANDRA FERNANDES DA COSTA

Key Concepts in
International
Relations

Los Angeles | London | New Delhi
Singapore | Washington DC

SAGE Publications Ltd
1 Oliver's Yard
55 City Road
London EC1Y 1SP

SAGE Publications Inc.
2455 Teller Road
Thousand Oaks, California 91320

SAGE Publications India Pvt Ltd
B 1/I 1 Mohan Cooperative Industrial Area
Mathura Road
New Delhi 110 044

SAGE Publications Asia-Pacific Pte Ltd
33 Pekin Street #02-01
Far East Square
Singapore 048763

Library of Congress Control Number: 2010943037

British Library Cataloguing in Publication data

A catalogue record for this book is available from the British Library

ISBN 978-1-4129-2847-2
ISBN 978-1-4129-2848-9 (pbk)

Typeset by C&M Digitals (P) Ltd, Chennai, India
Printed in India at Replika Press Pvt Ltd
Printed on paper from sustainable resources

contents

key concepts in
international relations

acknowledgements

There are books that take a longer and books that take a shorter time to write – this one was certainly of the former kind! It all started when David Mainwaring approached Thomas Diez in 2004 about whether he would be interested in writing the International Relations volume for Sage's Key Concepts series. Thomas, about to become Head of the Department of Political Science and International Studies at the University of Birmingham, where he then worked, rather naively said yes, assuming that it was possible to write such a manuscript while being Head. A wrong assumption, it turned out, even despite the fact that David Hudson, who then had just completed his PhD in Birmingham, had agreed to share the burden. Three years later, David H. had taken up a new post at University College London. When Thomas moved to the University of Tübingen in 2009, the manuscript had still not made the desired progress: a clear testimony to the continuing relevance of geographical distance even in the age of electronic communication. Ingvild Bode and Aleksandra Fernandes da Costa joined the effort, and with a bit of pressure from Sage's offices, the manuscript slowly took shape. We clearly need to thank David M. for all his patience throughout the years – we admire his optimism in believing in a manuscript when the authors themselves had given up all hope! We are also indebted to David H., who agreed that we could use the draft concept entries he had written on postmodernism/poststructuralism and development, and work them into our manuscript. He also, of course, played a vital part in getting the project off the ground in the first instance and preparing the initial book proposal. In the final stages, our student assistants, Julian Bergmann, Julia Grauvogel and Signe Scheid, helped us edit the manuscript: they spent an enormous amount of time in front of the computer, making sense of a disparate set of draft concepts, checking the literature, streamlining our formats, and searching for recommendable websites. Last but not least, we need to thank and apologize to our friends and families, who probably cannot hear the words 'key concepts' any more without increasing pulse rates.

Thomas Diez
Ingvild Bode
Aleksandra Fernandes da Costa
Tübingen, June 2010

by an outside force or by a change in one or the other elements composing the system, the system shows a tendency to re-establish either the original or a new equilibrium' (Morgenthau 1961: 168). The consequences of this underlying principle should be considered carefully by statesmen, as it aims to avoid that one of the individual actors can become powerful enough to threaten the survival and the independence of the other actors. Keeping the balance of power in mind, it becomes evident, according to Morgenthau, that statesmen have to be aware of the distribution of power in the international system as well as to get involved in the difficult attempt to measure power (Little 2007: 97).

In neorealism, scholars such as Kenneth Waltz have linked the balance of power directly to the concept of (→) anarchy. In this logic, the balance of power is not a natural principle, but structurally induced by the anarchical system. Since neorealism conceptualizes states as rational unitary actors seeking to maintain their position in the international system, balancing against a rising power becomes inevitable rather than optional. Nevertheless, balancing is a defensive strategy in structural neorealism aiming primarily to secure the survival and independence of states; it is not regarded as a strategy towards outstanding power capacities (Grieco 1997: 170). However, an addition was made by other neorealists, such as Stephen M. Walt, who doubted the assumption of balancing as structural automatism. Walt reached the conclusion that it might be more attractive for weaker states to bandwagon, thus enjoying benefits like protection or preferential trade agreements, than opposing the hegemon directly through balancing. Walt stressed that the decision to balance against a rival depended heavily upon the level of political threat. In particular cases, the strategy of bandwagoning, the neorealist antonym of balancing, might be more conducive.

In the English School, as we have already mentioned, the concept of balance of power is regarded as a fundamental institution to preserve international order (Bull 1977: 107). According to Bull, the balance of power has been constraining the rise of a world hegemon or universal (→) empire and thus 'providing the conditions in which other institutions on which international order depends (diplomacy, war, international law, great power management) have been able to operate' (Bull 1977: 107).

4. EMPIRICAL PROBLEMS

Following the explanatory importance of balance of power in neorealism, the empirical question of 'how to count poles and measure power'

acknowledgements

There are books that take a longer and books that take a shorter time to write – this one was certainly of the former kind! It all started when David Mainwaring approached Thomas Diez in 2004 about whether he would be interested in writing the International Relations volume for Sage's Key Concepts series. Thomas, about to become Head of the Department of Political Science and International Studies at the University of Birmingham, where he then worked, rather naively said yes, assuming that it was possible to write such a manuscript while being Head. A wrong assumption, it turned out, even despite the fact that David Hudson, who then had just completed his PhD in Birmingham, had agreed to share the burden. Three years later, David H. had taken up a new post at University College London. When Thomas moved to the University of Tübingen in 2009, the manuscript had still not made the desired progress: a clear testimony to the continuing relevance of geographical distance even in the age of electronic communication. Ingvild Bode and Aleksandra Fernandes da Costa joined the effort, and with a bit of pressure from Sage's offices, the manuscript slowly took shape. We clearly need to thank David M. for all his patience throughout the years – we admire his optimism in believing in a manuscript when the authors themselves had given up all hope! We are also indebted to David H., who agreed that we could use the draft concept entries he had written on postmodernism/poststructuralism and development, and work them into our manuscript. He also, of course, played a vital part in getting the project off the ground in the first instance and preparing the initial book proposal. In the final stages, our student assistants, Julian Bergmann, Julia Grauvogel and Signe Scheid, helped us edit the manuscript: they spent an enormous amount of time in front of the computer, making sense of a disparate set of draft concepts, checking the literature, streamlining our formats, and searching for recommendable websites. Last but not least, we need to thank and apologize to our friends and families, who probably cannot hear the words 'key concepts' any more without increasing pulse rates.

Thomas Diez
Ingvild Bode
Aleksandra Fernandes da Costa
Tübingen, June 2010

how to use this book

This book introduces the reader to 41 of what we consider to be the key concepts of the discipline of International Relations. While the book is mainly written as a reference source for those that are relatively new to the discipline, we hope that it will also prove to be useful to those who have got some background in International Relations already. We have conceptualized this book to fill a gap between the numerous textbooks, encyclopaedias and handbooks that are already on the market, but which often provide either only very short definitions of the key concepts of the discipline or lengthy treatments in complex style that are not readily digestable to a broader audience. Thus, we have written our entries so that they do provide a substantial account of the concepts and the discussions surrounding them, including references to what we consider the most important literature. Of course, it is on the one hand impossible within the space of a book such as this one to reach the depth of a handbook entry, but on the other hand we hope that our entries will be a useful addition to most textbooks, where space to go into detail on specific concepts is even more limited. As such, this book is not meant to be read from cover to cover, although we would hope that it is still possible to read it in such a way and still find it interesting.

Any choice of concepts for such a book is necessarily biased. We do not even claim to have included a list of concepts that is agreeable to all. However, we would still argue that the concepts that follow are central to the current debates in International Relations. In general, we have agreed to focus on theory concepts, and thus have excluded more empirical phenomena such as non-governmental organizations. We do have five so-called theory concept entries, which are marked as such. These follow a slightly different structure and are supposed to provide the broader context of disciplinary development in which the other concepts are set.

Theory concepts are divided into seven sections: core questions; overview and background; methodologies; empirical application; central criticism; core reading; and useful websites. All other concepts follow a six-part structure. They, too, start with the core questions addressed, followed by definitions, theoretical perspectives, empirical problems, core reading, and useful websites. For each entry, we have identified three core readings, for each of which we have provided a short commentary as a guide to further reading. It should not come as a surprise that the number of useful websites listed differs from concept to concept – it has simply been nearly impossible to find recommendations for interesting websites in relation to some concepts, whereas it would have been unjustifiable to limit our list of websites to, say, three in other cases. We hope that these listings will provide a first starting point for exploring the web as an additional tool for research and learning.

Whenever a concept refers to another concept entry, we have marked this with an arrow (→). However, we have generally used such an arrow only the first time a concept refers to another one, so as to improve readability. A final note on references: References should by no means be seen to be exhaustive. We have tried to strike a balance between an easily readable text on the one hand and including references to the most important works on the other. As our own writing progressed, the bibliography already exceeded the limits that we had set ourselves. We hope that this will prove useful to readers.

Anarchy

1. CORE QUESTIONS ADDRESSED

- What is the main characteristic of the international system?
- To what extent is anarchy a given, or can it be altered?
- What are the consequences of anarchy for state identity and behaviour?

2. DEFINITIONS

The concept of anarchy at its core simply means that there is no superior power within a system that would be able to enforce rules. It was after the First World War that G. Lowes Dickinson (1926) introduced the idea of an 'international anarchy', which, like his contemporary Norman Angell (1910; de Wilde 1991: 64), he saw as the main cause of war, as there is no higher authority that would set limits to hostilities between states (see Schmidt 1998: 444). This does not mean that anarchy always results in chaos and the unrestricted use of violence, since there are other ways through which one may prevent the widespread use of violence than imposing a central form of authority – in the international system, this may be done for instance through (→) international regimes, (→) balance of power or different forms of (→) hegemony. One may question whether under such circumstances, especially in the case of hegemony, we can still speak of an anarchical system, but we suggest treating these instances as mitigations of anarchy rather than as situations in which anarchy has been overcome. After all, in neither regime, balance of power nor hegemony, is there a formal authorization of superior power to an actor above the state.

Indeed, as the neorealist scholar Kenneth N. Waltz has pointed out (→ *Theory Concept: Realism and Neorealism*), effective governments have 'a monopoly on the *legitimate* use of force, and legitimate here means that public agents are organised to prevent and to counter the private use of force' (Waltz 1979: 104, emphasis in original). In anarchical systems, there is no such monopoly on the legitimate use of force. This means that there may well be actors who use force, but apart from very narrowly defined exceptions, for instance in the case of self-defence, such use is not seen as legitimate. The flipside however is that there is no central agency that would ensure peace, uphold order or provide a common infrastructure. The units within an anarchical system have to perform these tasks on their own. This means that an anarchical system is a 'self-help' system (Waltz 1979: 105–7), which results in coordination problems and the (➔) security dilemma: 'in anarchy,' to say the least, 'there is no automatic harmony' (Waltz 1959: 182). This does not mean that there is no hierarchy in anarchical systems (see Donnelly 2006), but as we have already argued, such hierarchy does not constitute the formal authorization to use force legitimately. Historically, there has always been some form of hierarchy within the international system, although the degree of hierarchy has varied between what Adam Watson has identified as the poles of 'independence' and 'empire' (Watson 1992: 23–8).

3. THEORETICAL PERSPECTIVES

The concept of anarchy is, as already indicated, particularly important to neorealism. In their emphasis on the systemic level, neorealists such as Waltz see anarchy as the basic structural characteristic of the system of states, or the international system. 'International politics,' Waltz (1979: 113) thus concluded, 'is the realm of power, of struggle, and of accommodation'. In the view of neorealists, there is no escape from this basic structure of the international system – it induces a struggle for survival amongst states as the constitutive units of the international system and thus decreases the prospects for cooperation and durable peace.

While anarchy on the one hand is therefore closely linked to neorealism, on the other hand many other theories have accepted the idea that the international system is anarchical. They differ from neorealists in their view about the exact consequences of anarchy for the behaviour of states, and the degree to which they think a modification of anarchy is possible.

Neoliberal authors (➔ *Theory Concept: Liberalism and Neoliberalism*) thus accept that states are the main actors of the international system, and that this system is anarchical, but they argue that this does not rule out lasting cooperation between states if states see the benefits of such cooperation (Keohane 1984; ➔ *International Regimes*). They further see anarchy as only one basic feature of the international system, which to them is equally characterized by interdependence, so that states are not mere 'billiard balls' with no ties between them (Wolfers 1962), but are interlinked in a web of dependencies (Keohane and Nye 1977).

English School writers such as Hedley Bull also accept anarchy as a central feature of the international system, but in line with their argument that there is not only an international system but an (→) international society, they see anarchy complemented by societal aspects, which is why Bull (1977) titled his main work *The Anarchical Society*. To Bull, anarchy and society are therefore not opposites, to a large extent because he thinks that states cannot be treated analytically as individuals, and that therefore the society of states is different from domestic societies (Bull 1977: 46–7). Thus, the absence of world government does not mean the absence of common norms, interests, and institutions among states. In fact, some of the core norms of international society, such as (→) sovereignty and non-intervention, are at the same time the foundational features of anarchy, and the function of international institutions is to protect and further develop these very institutions.

Just like Bull, Alexander Wendt, from a social constructivist perspective (→ *Theory Concept: Social Constructivism*), considers anarchy to be more than the structure of a system. Instead, he speaks of 'cultures' of anarchy, and identifies three such cultures, with different underlying norms (Wendt 1999: 246–312): a Hobbesian one, in which enmity persists and which resembles a 'realist' version of anarchy; a Lockean one, in which states act in 'rivalry' but accept the constraints of international law in their actions (close to the 'neoliberal' version of anarchy); and a Kantian one, in which 'friendship' persists between states and in which they form a 'pluralistic security community' (Deutsch et al. 1957; Adler and Barnett 1998; Wendt 1999: 299). Such a pluralistic (→) security community is still anarchical in the sense that there is no centralized rule enforcer akin to a government, but it is maintained by a web of rules and shared values that marks it out as a particularly strong international society, in Bull's terms. In a similar way, Barry Buzan (1991: 177) has envisaged the development of 'mature anarchies' in which anarchy was tamed by an increasing degree of ordered relations between states.

Wendt is also responsible for contributing to International Relations one of the most widely used catchphrases, 'anarchy is what states make of it' (Wendt 1992). In his seminal article with that title, he argued that anarchy is not, as neorealists would maintain, an immutable structure, but that it rather shapes the behaviour of states as much as states can shape anarchy. This formulation of the problem of anarchy has become one of the core examples of the interplay of structure and agency as discussed in social constructivism. In a similar argument, Barry Buzan,

anarchy

3

Charles Jones and Richard Little (1993) argued that while anarchy is a 'deep structure' of the international system, it is differentiated according to functional sectors, and varies over time according to the characteristics of states as its constitutive units as well as their interaction capacity.

A final perspective on anarchy is offered by poststructuralism (→ *Theory Concept: Postmodernism and Poststructuralism*). In line with the view that there is no objective way of knowing, poststructuralists have argued that anarchy is therefore not a mere description, but a discursive construction of reality. This discursive construction works on the basis of inserting an essential differentiation between the 'orderly' inside and the 'dangerous', 'chaotic' outside (Walker 1993). Working with the notion of the 'anarchy problematique', Richard Ashley (1988) showed how this depiction of the international sphere as dangerous and threatening sustains the identity and power of the sovereign state, and how sovereignty and anarchy need to be seen as two sides of the same coin in order to make sense. The pervasive construction of anarchy therefore impoverishes the imagination of political alternatives to the state, which is becoming increasingly problematic in the light of the rise of transnational problems.

4. EMPIRICAL PROBLEMS

The most pressing empirical challenge at least to the realist conception of anarchy comes from (→) globalization and (→) global governance. If there is an increasing web of transnational flows; if there is an increasing number of transnational problems, environmental, economic, or otherwise; and if there is an increasing number of international and sometimes even supranational institutions, often involving non-governmental actors in the decision-making processes – are we then really still living under conditions of anarchy? And if not, which structure replaces anarchy?

The problem as such is not new – in a sense, the concept of complex interdependence suggested by Keohane and Nye (1977) already struggled with a similar challenge. Waltz (1979: 104) himself saw interdependence as an effect of the increasing specialization of states, making them more dependent on the provision of goods by others, and thus also more vulnerable if the supply of goods is interrupted. However, he did not consider this to undermine the basic anarchical logic of the system, as interdependence did not lead to closer bonds between states or the emergence of a hierarchical form of government beyond states. In the case of what was then the European Community with its nine member states, he argued that the choice was between 'slowly becoming one state', in which case a number of small states would simply be replaced with a bigger one in the international system, 'or stubbornly remaining nine' (Waltz 1979: 116). This matches Hedley Bull's view of European integration (Bull 1982).

For many, then, the basic anarchical structure of the international system is astonishingly resilient. It may be adjusted here and there, but in effect its core logic remains (e.g. Buzan 2004: 235). Anarchy, one may say in analogy to Stephen Krasner's treatment of sovereignty, has always been compromised (Krasner 1995), but it none the less remains a core feature of the international system. This view stands in contrast to those authors who emphasize globalizing tendencies, as well as those who think that some form of hierarchical governing structure on a global scale is inevitable (Wendt 2003). From a poststructuralist angle, meanwhile, the emphasis on the resilience of anarchy may well simply be another discursive move to maintain the power of states.

5. CORE READING

Bull, Hedley (1977) *The Anarchical Society: A Study of Order in World Politics* (Basingstoke: Macmillan). Bull's focus is on order more than on anarchy, but he provides an excellent statement on why anarchy is not without order.

Waltz, Kenneth N. (1979) *Theory of International Politics* (New York: Random House). Chapter 6 on 'Anarchic Orders and Balances of Power' provides a foundational elaboration of the neorealist conceptualization of anarchy.

Wendt, Alexander (1992) 'Anarchy Is What States Make of It', *International Organization* 46 (3), 391–425. A classic social constructivist piece: the title says it all!

6. USEFUL WEBSITES

http://www.theory-talks.org/search/label/Anarchy. Interview of the Theory Talks series with Barry Buzan.

http://globetrotter.berkeley.edu/people3/Waltz/waltz-con0.html. Interview with Kenneth Waltz on theory and international politics in Berkeley's Conversations with History series.

anarchy

1. CORE QUESTIONS ADDRESSED

- Why do states balance?
- What are the varieties of balancing behaviour in international politics?
- What is the difference between a realist and a neorealist conception of the balance of power?

2. DEFINITIONS

The balance of power is among the most persistent and most widely cited concepts in International Relations. It is essentially about the idea that hegemonic (→ *Hegemony*) (→) power will always be counterbalanced by a strategic alliance of rivals in order to secure their own survival and (→) sovereignty. Whether the concept goes back to theoretical assumptions made with regard to Italian city-states in the Machiavellian time, or whether it has ancient roots in the considerations of Hellenic and Roman politicians during the Peloponnesian and Punic Wars, is contested within literature (see for instance Haslam 2002; Butterfield 1966). The concept has become particularly relevant to the study of world politics after the Second World War and is widely associated with the (→) realist or neorealist theory of International Relations. To these scholars, the balance of power is 'an intrinsic feature of international politics' (Little 2007: 91).

The concept was introduced to International Relations by Hans J. Morgenthau in his *Politics among Nations* in 1948. He conceptualized the balance of power as an 'actual state of affairs in which power is distributed among several nations with approximate equality' (Morgenthau 1961: 167 n. 1). According to Morgenthau, the balance of power is a natural social principle or 'universal concept' operating throughout history and on the group, national and international levels, aiming to establish, as the name of the concept already suggests, an equilibrium or a balance between components. Further considerations regarding the concept's relevance to the study of world politics have been made by neorealists such as Kenneth Waltz and John Mearsheimer, but also by 'English School' authors (of International Relations) such as Hedley Bull (→ *International Society*).

In neorealism, the balance of power is understood as theory, claiming to 'explain the results of states' actions, under given conditions, and those results may not be foreshadowed in any of the actors' motives or be contained as objectives in their policies' (Waltz 1979: 118). According to Waltz, balance of power theory explains the effects of the anarchical self-help system on the behaviour of states, operating whenever a single state seeks preponderance over the others. In this case the threatened states can either try to counterbalance the rising hegemon by an increase of their national capabilities (internal balancing) or by the establishment of informal or formal alliances (external balancing) (Grieco 1997: 170).

According to English School theorist Hedley Bull, the balance of power can be defined as 'a state of affairs such that no one power is in a position where it is preponderant and can lay down the law to others' (Bull 1979: 101). For Bull, the balance of power is one of five core institutions that maintain order in international society. He distinguishes between balances of power on four accounts. Firstly, he differentiates between a simple and complex balance of power, describing the former as a balance of power made up of only two actors while consequently the latter consists of three or more great powers involved. Secondly, he distinguishes between a general and a local balance of power: the former is conceptualized as the absence of one dominant power in the international system, such as Cold War bipolarity. The latter describes a regional balance of power constellation – Bull exemplarily refers here to the Middle East. Thirdly, he argues that there is a difference between a subjectively and an objectively existing balance of power: 'It is one thing to say that it is generally believed that a state of affairs exists in which no one state is preponderant in military strength; it is another to say that no one state is in fact preponderant' (Bull 1977: 103). Finally, he makes a differentiation between a fortuitous balance of power, resulting in a sudden moment of deadlock within an active conflict, and a contrived balance of power, established according to rational calculations of the actors involved (Bull 1977: 101–5).

3. THEORETICAL PERSPECTIVES

In the classical realist approach exemplified by Hans J. Morgenthau, the balance of power is a central concept of world politics. Since in realism world politics is always power politics, and states as principal actors seek to survive, the struggle towards an equilibrium between great powers comes as a 'natural and inevitable outgrowth of the struggle for power' (Morgenthau 1961: 187): 'Whenever the equilibrium is disturbed either by an outside force or by a change in one or the other elements composing the system, the system shows a tendency to re-establish either the original or a new equilibrium' (Morgenthau 1961: 168). The consequences of this underlying principle should be considered carefully by statesmen, as it aims to avoid that one of the individual actors can become powerful enough to threaten the survival and the independence of the other actors. Keeping the balance of power in mind, it becomes evident, according to Morgenthau, that statesmen have to be aware of the distribution of power in the international system as well as to get involved in the difficult attempt to measure power (Little 2007: 97).

In neorealism, scholars such as Kenneth Waltz have linked the balance of power directly to the concept of (→) anarchy. In this logic, the balance of power is not a natural principle, but structurally induced by the anarchical system. Since neorealism conceptualizes states as rational unitary actors seeking to maintain their position in the international system, balancing against a rising power becomes inevitable rather than optional. Nevertheless, balancing is a defensive strategy in structural neorealism aiming primarily to secure the survival and independence of states; it is not regarded as a strategy towards outstanding power capacities (Grieco 1997: 170). However, an addition was made by other neorealists, such as Stephen M. Walt, who doubted the assumption of balancing as structural automatism. Walt reached the conclusion that it might be more attractive for weaker states to bandwagon, thus enjoying benefits like protection or preferential trade agreements, than opposing the hegemon directly through balancing. Walt stressed that the decision to balance against a rival depended heavily upon the level of political threat. In particular cases, the strategy of bandwagoning, the neorealist antonym of balancing, might be more conducive.

In the English School, as we have already mentioned, the concept of balance of power is regarded as a fundamental institution to preserve international order (Bull 1977: 107). According to Bull, the balance of power has been constraining the rise of a world hegemon or universal (→) empire and thus 'providing the conditions in which other institutions on which international order depends (diplomacy, war, international law, great power management) have been able to operate' (Bull 1977: 107).

4. EMPIRICAL PROBLEMS

Following the explanatory importance of balance of power in neorealism, the empirical question of 'how to count poles and measure power' has to be answered (Waltz 1979: 129). As mentioned above, the majority of neorealist scholars started thinking about the distribution of power in the international system in terms of measurable capabilities, such as military capacities and annual military expenditure of rates of economic growth ('power over resources'). In addition, power has been conceptualized as the ability to induce certain outcomes ('power as control over outcomes'). After the end of the Cold War, the concept of balance of power and thus the neorealist claims about the prospects for temporary peace based upon the stability of a bipolar system have been challenged. Opposing neorealists proclaiming a 'unipolar moment' in world history, authors such as Mearsheimer (2001) argued that the preponderance of the United States after the 1990s cannot be preserved, since the balance of power concept would automatically produce counterbalancing activities. He and other authors, such as John Ikenberry (2008), engaged in the analysis of other regional powers, such as China, India or Brazil, and in particular of the prospects of a peaceful rise of China.

In the English School, the most interesting empirical observation made by Hedley Bull is that although the preservation of international law relies heavily upon the balance of power, the re-establishment of such a power often makes a violation of these principles necessary. According to Bull, a rising power can only be counterbalanced by the threat or the use of force and violence, such as for instance through military interventions, thereby violating existing legal principles, such as non-intervention. In situations like this, the 'requirements of order treated as prior to those of law, as they are treated also as prior . . . to the keeping of peace' (Bull 1977: 109).

5. CORE READING

Little, Richard (2007) *The Balance of Power in International Relations* (Cambridge: Cambridge University Press); provides an analysis of the balance of power concepts used by Hans Morgenthau, Kenneth Waltz, Hedley Bull and John Mearsheimer.

Morgenthau, Hans (1961) *Politics among Nations* (New York: Alfred Knopf), 3rd rev. edn. Introduces the balance of power to the study of world politics.

Waltz, Kenneth N. (1979) *Theory of International Relations* (Reading, MA: Addison-Wesley). Elaborates the concept further for neorealist analysis.

1. CORE QUESTIONS ADDRESSED

- How can the relationship between conflict and war be conceptualized?
- How can international conflict be approached and resolved?
- What distinguishes conflict resolution from conflict management?

2. DEFINITIONS

Conflict has always been an inherent feature of human existence and social development. From a sociological perspective, conflict is conceptualized as a situation in which two or more actors, such as individuals, groups or societies, pursue incompatible goals, including dissent about the distribution, appropriateness and legitimacy of a specific object (Kriesberg 2007: 2; Rittberger and Zürn 1990: 14). Handled appropriately, conflict can induce social dynamics leading to transformations and improvements of existing deficiencies in social relations and institutions. Unfortunately, whenever conflict results in aggression and violence, its consequences for societies can be destructive. In general, we refer to violent conflicts as war when at least one of the conflict parties is a government or aims to assume a governmental role. In addition, many scholars try to distinguish war from other forms of physical violence by specifying a certain number of killed people as a threshold (→ *Peace and War*).

Conflict resolution, on the one hand, refers to an interdisciplinary academic field aiming to analyse the causes and developments of social conflict with a propensity to violence. On the other hand, within this academic subdiscipline the term conflict resolution depicts a particular stage within the life cycle of social conflicts, the exact definition of which is, however, disputed.

In particular against the historical backdrop of the Cold War rivalry and nuclear threat, conflict resolution as a distinct field of study emerged in the 1950s and 1960s, aiming to develop strategies for a regulated and peaceful settlement of social conflicts in general and international conflicts in particular. This might include preventive activities or direct influence, such as attempts of mediation or arbitration. Jacob Bercovitch et al. (2009: 1) characterize the discipline as follows – 'Conflict Resolution is about ideas, theories and methods that can improve our understanding of conflict and our collective practice of reduction in violence and enhancement of political processes for harmonizing interest.' Shifting the focus on the conflict parties themselves, John W. Burton defined conflict resolution as the 'analysis of the underlying sources of conflict situations by the parties in conflict. The term also encompasses the process whereby institutional and policy options are discovered that meet the needs of the parties, thus establishing the basis for a resolution of the conflict' (Burton 1987: 7).

Furthermore and as already indicated, the term conflict resolution refers to a specific situation within an ongoing conflict. Oliver Ramsbotham, Tom Woodhouse and Hugh Miall (2008: 29), for instance, argue that: 'Conflict resolution . . . implies . . . that the deep-rooted sources of conflict are addressed and transformed. This implies that behaviour is no longer violent, attitudes are no longer hostile, and the structure of the conflict has been changed.' Thus, conflict resolution is a stage within the life cycle of a conflict, following the emergence, escalation and attempts of managing a conflict. In conflict management, third-party intervention seeks to de-escalate conflict by providing the conflicting parties with alternative strategies to regulate the conflict through agreements with at least some formality. In contrast, conflict resolution addresses the deep-rooted causes of conflict, and aims at a mutual understanding of the conflicting parties towards peaceful dispute settlement that ultimately transforms the incompatibilities at the heart of the conflict, rather than to merely manage them peacefully. This is reflected in Peter Wallensteen's definition of '[c]onflict [r]esolution as a situation where the conflicting parties enter into an agreement that solves their central incompatibilities, accept each other's continued existence as parties and cease all violent action against each other' (Wallensteen 2007: 8).

In contrast to these rather positivistic conceptualizations of conflict and thus of conflict resolution, critical voices, such as for instance Vivienne Jabri (1996), seek to reconstruct the discursive societal processes reproducing conflict and violence as an inherent feature of human existence and political life. In such views, conflict is closely tied to social and political identity, and the incompatibility at the heart of a conflict is not merely one of goals but of self-conceptualizations (see Diez, Stetter and Albert 2006: 565–7). Such scholars often prefer the term 'conflict transformation' (see also Ramsbotham et al. 2008: 21).

Moreover, the concept of conflict resolution has been questioned from a postcolonial perspective, most prominently stated by Paul Salem in his 'critique of western conflict resolution from a non-western perspective' (1993, 1997). Salem argues that from an Arab–Muslim perspective, the concept of conflict resolution is based on western 'liberal' perceptions and norms about societies and approaches that are not shared everywhere in the world, despite the fact that theorists of conflict resolution argue that their approaches are universally applicable and objective. These approaches furthermore do not take into account traditional models of conflict resolution already existing in these parts of the world, but rather seek to apply western-based concepts.

3. THEORETICAL PERSPECTIVES

In the field of conflict resolution, theory and practice are closely linked, in particular since most of the literature builds upon the empirical observations of analysts, diplomats and other practitioners. Nevertheless, with the expansion of the subdiscipline, a number of crucial theoretical concepts and approaches were introduced.

The most central debate within the academic literature on the management of conflicts lasted until the late 1980s and focused on the question of whether third-party intervention should centre on the settlement of conflicts by reaching formal agreements between the political elites or should rather seek to identify and transform the underlying social relations and misperceptions of societal actors fuelling the conflict. According to David Bloomfield (1995), these dichotomous approaches originate in different conceptualizations of conflict: the first position characterized conflicts as objectively observable and based upon positional differences regarding material interests or power. In consequence, authors in this tradition argued for the enforcement of agreements between formal representatives of the parties to manage the conflict. The second position emphasized that the causes for conflict had their roots in the relationship between the parties to the conflict and were therefore subjective. Consequently, these authors argued in favour of a conflict resolution approach aiming to transform the relationships and perceptions of the parties involved (Bloomfield 1995: 153). With the start of the 1990s, more integrative approaches have sought to reconcile these differences and develop more differentiated models of conflict escalation and third-party intervention by combining elements of both positions (e.g. Fisher and Keashly 1991).

Probably the most influential model analysing the conditions of conflict was introduced to the study of conflict resolution by Johan Galtung in the late 1960s, conceptualizing conflict as a triangle between contradiction, attitude and behaviour. According to Galtung, the notion of contradiction refers to the perceived incompatibility of positions by the actors involved, while the term attitudes implies the perceptions and misperceptions of the parties about themselves and their opponent. The last vertex encompasses the respective behaviour towards the conflict. Regarding conflict as a dynamic process, where attitudes, contradictions and behaviour are constantly changing, Galtung concludes that for a conflict to become pronounced, all three components must be present (Galtung 1996: 72; Ramsbotham et al. 2008: 9–10).

John W. Burton developed an additional theoretical approach towards conflict resolution by differentiating between conflicts about interests and conflicts about needs. Drawing on systems and inter-organizational theory as well as (→) game theory, Burton argues that conflicts about material interests, such as access to resources or disputes about territories, can be solved relatively easily by compromise and negotiations as soon as both parties at least share an interest in reaching a solution for the problem. In contrast, conflicts about immaterial human needs, such as security, identity or recognition, are more difficult to handle, since they are usually based on deep-rooted societal and psychological perceptions and emotions. In these cases the conflict can only be resolved by identifying and addressing the underlying causes (Burton 1990; Burton and Dukes 1990).

Following the identification of particular phases of conflict and the development of specific conflict cycles, of which probably the most illustrative is Friedrich Glasl's nine-stage model of conflict escalation (1982), further theoretical approaches seek to associate specific stages of conflict with respective measures, for instance the hourglass model by Ramsbotham et al. (2008) or the contingency model of third-party intervention by Fisher and Keashly (1991). According to Fisher and Keashly, for instance, it is much more promising to seek a change in the conflicting parties' attitudes towards each other prior to a violent escalation of the conflict. After such an escalation has taken place, the negative experiences have intensified prejudice and misperception in a way that it makes much more sense to force the disputants into formal settlement of the conflict by an agreement in order to stop violence. In this stage of a conflict, Fisher and Keashly argue for formal power-based interventions by third parties (Fisher and Keashly 1991: 34–9).

As this brief overview already indicates, the central question concerning third-party intervention is the question of timing, which was most prominently addressed by theories about the ripeness of a conflict, such as formulated by I. William Zartman or Richard N. Haas. According to Zartman, for instance, the intervention into conflicts cannot be successful, as long as the conflict is not 'ripe for resolution', characterized by a 'mutual hurting stalemate' between the conflicting parties. Zartman elaborates this situation as marked by a recent or impending catastrophe, where both parties involved come to the conclusion that not only can nothing be gained by further escalation of the conflict, but also that leaving the conflict at the current stage would even be worse. Following Zartman, at this moment third-party intervention is more likely to be successful since the parties realize that they need outside assistance (Zartman 1989). What remain unspecified in the works of Zartman are the subsequent questions of how this moment of ripeness should be identified by third parties, as well as the options for third parties to actively create these moments of ripeness (Kleiboer 1994: 109).

4. EMPIRICAL PROBLEMS

The more specific institutions and research centres, such as the Stockholm International Peace Research Institute (SIPRI), the Peace Research Institute Oslo (PRIO) or the Institute for Conflict Analysis and Resolution at the University of Virginia, have been established, and the more academic journals, such as the *Journal of Conflict Resolution*, have spread theoretical considerations, the more influential these theoretical approaches towards the resolution of international conflicts have become to practitioners such as diplomats and government representatives within their daily practice. According to Ramsbotham, Woodhouse and Miall, for instance, the Centre for Intergroup Studies in South Africa successfully applied the theoretical approaches emerging in the field towards the disputes between the system of apartheid and its opponents. Similar efforts have been made during the Middle East peace process and in Northern Ireland (2008: 4). Probably the most systematic attempts to apply in particular Burton's problem-solving approach to practice have been made by researchers identified with the 'Harvard concept', including scholars such as Michael Banks, Chris Mitchell and Edward Burton, offering problem-solving workshops in deep-rooted conflicts of the day, such as the conflict between the Greek and the Turkish communities in Cyprus in 1965 and 1966. The idea behind the Harvard concept consists in the engagement of individuals into these workshops, who play a significant role in the negotiation process, but are not officials of the governments involved, hoping for the development of different personal and communicative relationships between the conflicting parties despite the ones dominant in the official dialogues and statements. In evaluating these workshops it became evident that they had to be adapted to the specific conflict situation at hand, but could indeed contribute towards the establishment of alternative relationships amongst the parties of the conflict. Nevertheless, it proved difficult to assess to what extent these changes affected the official negotiation process (Ramsbotham et al. 2008: 48–9).

5. CORE READING

Bercovitch, Jacob, Victor Kremenyuk and William I. Zartman (eds) (2009) *The Sage Handbook of Conflict Resolution* (London: Sage). Provides a comprehensive overview of themes and theoretical perspectives on conflict resolution.

Ramsbotham, Oliver, Tom Woodhouse and Hugh Miall (2008) *Contemporary Conflict Resolution* (Cambridge: Polity Press, 2nd edn). Introduces concepts, definitions and contemporary developments in the field.

Wallensteen, Peter (2007) *Understanding Conflict Resolution* (London: Sage, 2nd edn). Explores the settlement of interstate and internal conflicts by linking theory to contemporary cases.

6. USEFUL WEBSITES

http://www.sipri.org/. The Stockholm International Peace Research Institute offers research resources and databases for peace and conflict studies.

http://icar.gmu.edu/. Institute for Conflict Analysis and Resolution at the George Mason University, Virginia, papers and reports in peace and conflict studies.

http://jcr.sagepub.com/. Website of the *Journal of Conflict Resolution* (Sage).

http://www.wcfia.harvard.edu/programs/picar/. Program on International Conflict Analysis and Resolution at Harvard University.

http://www.ccr.org.za/. Centre for Conflict Resolution at the University of Cape Town.

conflict resolution

15

1. CORE QUESTIONS ADDRESSED

- What is the link between democracies and peace?
- Are interests, norms or institutions responsible for democracies not fighting each other?
- Why do democracies go to war with non-democracies?

2. DEFINITIONS

Few concepts in International Relations have had such strong policy relevance as the idea of the democratic peace. At its heart is the often-made empirical observation that democracies do not go to war with each other. It is important to be precise here: the claim is not that democracies do not go to war at all. Indeed, democracies may even be more likely to go to war than other states if they are faced with non-democracies (Bueno de Mesquita et al. 1999).

The definitions of the two main components of this concept, democracy and peace, are contested, as one would expect. Those who support the idea of a democratic peace generally assume liberal-western notions. Still, definitions of democracy by authors in the democratic peace tradition differ considerably. Michael Doyle, as one of the earliest authors to take up analysis of the democratic peace, offers a comprehensive definition of four criteria: liberal democracies have a market economy, they are recognized as sovereign, their citizens have juridical rights, and their governments are representative (1983: 206–8). In a minimalist definition, democracy is characterized by regular free elections. Scholars further distinguish between so-called young and mature democracies – the age of a democracy and its degree of stability and establishment are typically used as qualifiers with regard to their peacefulness (Rummel 1997; Russett 1993). This further refinement of definitions resulted from theory-inherent debates about the validity of the democratic peace argument as well as contrasting empirical observations.

Peace is based on the minimum requirement of the absence of war and not on any more demanding structural criteria (→ *Peace and War*). This still leaves the problem of what counts as war, which is often seen as a government-sanctioned militarized dispute between states (thus excluding civil wars, although there are also arguments about the contribution democracy makes to maintaining domestic peace). Some authors require a minimum number of deaths for a violent conflict to be counted as 'war' (→ *Conflict Resolution*). In consequence, a variety of disputes between democracies and non-democracies, such as conflicts about borders or trade issues, have not been considered as challenging the core liberal argument since they never crossed the threshold of war, although the conflict settlement has been characterized as aggressive or violent.

3. THEORETICAL PERSPECTIVES

The core argument of the democratic peace is derived from the German Enlightenment philosopher Immanuel Kant's idea of a 'perpetual peace', which he thought possible to achieve through regulated relations between what he termed republican states. Kant stressed that republics, characterized by division of power and representative governments, are less war prone than non-republics, since in case of war the citizens would have to burden the costs of the military actions: as a result, politicians would never lightly decide to start a war, fearing the public opinion and political consequences. Hence, following Kant, democracies would only enter into violent conflict behaviour as a self-defence strategy. It is this core argument that was taken up in the 1980s by authors such as Michael Doyle (1986) or Bruce Russett (e.g. 1993). In testing these claims, scholars used data from the Correlates of War project, which had been gathering data about military conflicts since the 1960s.

Democratic peace is a distinctly liberal concept (→ *Theory Concept: Liberalism and Neoliberalism*). Theories of democratic peace can be characterized as monadic and dyadic variants depending on their primary (→) level of analysis. Monadic variants place their analysis on the unit level: certain characteristics of the unit, in this case the democratic state, trigger its peaceful behaviour towards all actors of the international system. Dyadic variants, by contrast, do not think the external behaviour of democracies is predefined by way of their internal characteristics. Rather, democracies may act peacefully or may use force in their external conduct – the choice of means depends on their type of interaction partner (Müller and Wolff 2006: 41–3). In explaining war and peace, both variants focus on a particularly liberal form of states' constitution as a necessary condition for their external behaviour. The variants' difference lies in the explanatory importance allocated to democracies' internal characteristics: 'only monadic explanations construe these necessary conditions as also being *sufficient*' (Müller and Wolff 2006: 42, emphasis in original). As has been said in the previous part, the strict monadic variant is largely discredited on empirical grounds. At the same time, the entire distinction between monadic and dyadic research perspectives has been termed 'artificial' and only relevant from a theoretical historical perspective, as in reality most theories of democratic peace contain elements of both (Hasenclever 2006: 215 n. 3).

Liberal scholars have tried to identify the factors that are deemed to contribute to democratic peace. These fall into two major categories: structural-institutional constraints and normative-cultural factors.

The first category, structural-institutional constraints, is broadly based on personal interests. War tends to come at a high cost for individuals and disrupts established economic links. As such, one may assume that citizens are hesitant to support war unless they feel threatened or unless the benefits of war are greater than its costs both in terms of economic losses and threats to their personal lives. In principle, private citizens should therefore be opposed to war unless there is an overriding sense of nationalism (such as in the 'rally-round-the-flag' when nationalist sentiments can drive or at least underpin war efforts) or other ideologies, or an immediate threat to their possessions or even existence. Wars therefore often are increasingly questioned in democracies the longer they run: public support tends to wane as threats seem less imminent and bodies are flown home. The war on Iraq that started in spring 2003 is an example.

Taking citizens' personal preferences as the causal link towards external peaceful behaviour of democracies has met with considerable criticism mainly because there is a difference between broader economic and private interests. Industrial firms may gain from war either directly, if they produce technology that is relevant to war, or indirectly, if the likely benefits of new trade links in the case of victory exceed the cost of war and the disruption it causes. This may be one of the reasons why western democracies tend to also avoid war with non-democracies with which they have close trade links (e.g. China) but are more likely to go to war with non-democracies with which they do not trade heavily (e.g. Afghanistan) or which threaten to interrupt existing trade links (e.g. Iraq).

Beyond personal preferences, arguments following institutional constraints hold that democracies do not go to war with each other because their institutional decision-making prevents them from doing so (Bueno de Mesquita et al. 1999). In a dictatorship, military command is unrestrained by civilian control and should therefore be able to mobilize troops more quickly than in democracies where troop deployment is subject to parliamentary approval and therefore the interests discussed earlier. The idea that democratic political culture is seen to increase transparency also contributes to the institutional constraints argument. As wars are inefficient, under the conditions of complete information that are prevalent in democracies owing to freedom of speech and the press, states should be unlikely to enter into war (Schultz 2001; Fearon 1994).

Yet the institutional constraint *per se* cannot be decisive, as taken on its own it is difficult to see why it would not apply to confrontations between democracies and non-democracies. Only in combination with the arguments about norms or interests do institutional constraints matter.

A second set of causal factors seeks to attribute the democratic peace to the normative-cultural realm. This view is based on the assumption that democracies may incorporate norms that support peaceful behaviour as such (Maoz and Russett 1993; O'Neal and Russett 2001: 53). Indeed, democracies live on mutual respect and the acceptance of pluralism. Their citizens and decision-makers are socialized into peaceful ways of conflict management that are part and parcel of domestic democratic culture. Would they not externalize these norms to the outside world? Again, the problem with this monadic explanation is that if it were true, one would expect democracies not to go to war at all.

However, when taking the dyadic other into account, i.e. looking at cases in which democracies encounter non-democracies, normative-cultural factors gain increased relevance. From a social constructivist background (→ *Theory Concept: Social Constructivism*), Thomas Risse-Kappen argues that the mutual perception countries have of one another either paves the way for peaceful cooperation or violent conflict management (1995: 503–6). The advantage of this argument is that it can explain ambivalences and therefore contains explanatory potential for both positive and negative cases of the democratic peace. In-group recognition, i.e. being part of a collective democratic identity, therefore establishes a level of trust among democracies that leads to peaceful behaviour towards one another (Risse-Kappen 1996). In negative cases, democracies may see their own norms threatened to such an extent that they are willing to protect them even if this means compromising the very norms that are seen as threatened. It is from such a perspective that one can understand Woodrow Wilson's argument in favour of 'making the world safe for democracy' so that democracy can then contribute to a safer world.

4. EMPIRICAL PROBLEMS

There are very few who entirely dispute the empirical correlation of the relationship between democracy and war as specified in its dyadic variant. Some of the arguments put forward against the 'democratic peace thesis' have already been addressed, and in most of these, advocates of the thesis can point to misunderstandings or qualify their arguments. Points of critique have naturally been put forward by other theoretical perspectives to International Relations who frequently introduce rivalling explanations to the empirical findings of democratic peace.

Realist scholar Sebastian Rosato, for example, takes liberal explanations for the democratic peace to task and finds them lacking on several fronts (2003). To him, the idea that democracies externalize their norms, a normative-cultural factor, has been widely empirically disproved, particularly during the period of European imperialism (→ *Empire*). Not only did democracies infringe on democratic norms in their external behaviour, but their existence did not even appear to play a decisive role in their foreign relations (Rosato 2003: 588–9). Instead, Rosato sees the reason behind the absence of major military conflicts between democracies in the post-1945 period in the international system's power distribution. Authors with a background in Critical Theory (→ *Theory Concept: Marxism and Critical Theory*) understand the democratic peace as strictly a means to an end used by powerful industrialized states to better exploit the rest of the world (Barkawi and Laffey 1999). Critical theorists further point to empirical realities such as weapons supplied to unjust regimes by democracies that are intentionally left out of the democratic peace picture.

A further point of critique on democratic peace derives from the very policy relevance of the concept. Liberal research has openly issues practical recommendations to further international peace by spreading democracy as a particularly peaceful form of government. Authors such as Edward Mansfield and Jack Snyder suggested that states in democratization processes are in fact more war prone as this critical phase of change may lead them to use external violence as a distraction from domestic conflict situations (1995). Analysis of the potential correlation between democratization and war proneness is, however, far from being examined in a reliable manner (Hasenclever 2006: 237).

In its most radical form, challengers of the democratic peace dispute whether it is indeed democracy that makes a difference, or whether it is not the case that like-minded states generally are more peaceful to each other than to outsiders (Oren and Hays 1997). The problem is that this is difficult to verify, especially after the end of the Cold War and the fall of communism, as the number of states following a different ideological system than democracy is small. To the extent that dictatorships are not driven by a particular ideology, the argument would not hold for them.

5. CORE READING

Brock, Lothar, Anna Geis and Harald Müller (eds) (2006) *Democratic Wars: Looking at the Dark Side of Democratic Peace* (Houndsmills: Palgrave). Influential compilation of articles on the democratic peace, its criticism and subsequent reaction.

Bueno de Mesquita, Bruce et al. (1999) 'An Institutional Explanation of the Democratic Peace', *American Political Science Review* 93 (4), 791–807. Combines quantitative findings with causal explanations of democratic peace from a structural-institutional viewpoint in a brief and concise manner.

Rosato, Sebastian (2003) 'The Flawed Logic of Democratic Peace Theory', *American Political Science Review* 97 (4), 585–602. Elaborate critique of the 'democratic peace thesis' from a realist perspective.

6. USEFUL WEBSITES

http://www.hawaii.edu/powerkills/BIBLIO.HTML. Extensive bibliography on democratic peace collected by R. J. Rummel, one of its earliest and most influential researchers.

http://www.correlatesofwar.org/. Website of the Correlates of War project collecting data on war since 1963. Also been extensively used in theoretical works on democratic peace.

http://users.erols.com/mwhite28/demowar.htm. Critical article by Matthew White on war between democracies, and links to further reading.

democratic peace

Dependency

1. CORE QUESTIONS ADDRESSED

- What is the centre–periphery model?
- What is the assumed causal connection between dependency and underdevelopment?
- Why were the empirical realities of the 1970s detrimental to dependency theory?

2. DEFINITIONS

Dependency, or *dependencia*, refers to the economically subordinated state of developing countries in relation to the industrial countries as a direct structural result of their integration into the capitalist world market. Dependency originated in Latin America in the late 1960s as a concept in development theory in the context of postcolonialism (→ *Development*). Its theoretical basis can however already be found in the early 1950s thought of Raúl Prebisch, who authored crucial studies on the Latin American economy during his time as the director of the UN Economic Commission on Latin America (ECLA) (Prebisch 1950). It was a critical response to the then-dominant modernization theory, which stressed that underdevelopment is a consequence of endogenous factors within the undeveloped countries, such as weak governance performance. These authors suggested that in order to achieve prosperity the solution for underveloped countries would be to copy the political and economic development processes of Western industrialized countries. According to Theotonio Dos Santos, dependency describes 'a situation in which the economy of certain countries is conditioned by the development and expansion of another economy to which the former are subjected. ... Some countries (the dominating ones) can expand and can be self-sustaining, while other countries (the dependent ones) can do this only as a reflection of that expansion' (1970: 231).

Dependency finds its theoretical foundations in Marxism (→ *Theory Concept: Marxism and Critical Theory*), theories of imperialism (→ *Empire*) and Leon Trotsky's insights into the uneven development of capitalism. It assumes that the capitalist world economy is by necessity hierarchically structured into centre–periphery or metropolitan–satellite relationships, i.e. the world centres of industry and capital and the peripheral economies that depend upon them. Periphery, in this sense, it not merely a term indicating a position within a hierarchical world order but also implies that states considered part of the periphery dispose of considerable structural similarities, which are both social and economic in nature. The centre–periphery structure does not allow for the possibility of developing countries to catch up on industrialized countries, as their exploitation by the centre is an integral part of its design. This hierarchy is assumed to be static – countries cannot change their position themselves, as their development possibilities are entirely defined by the world market: 'no country which has been firmly tied to the metropolis as a satellite through incorporation into the world capitalist system has achieved the rank of an economically developed country' (Frank 1969: 11).

The integration of precapitalist 'third world' countries into the world market thus is not seen, as modernization theorists would have it, as triggering their progress from non-development to capitalist-induced development. Rather, dependency theorists view this integration as the 'development of *under*development' (Frank 1969, our emphasis). With this, dependency brings international power inequalities to the attention of development theorists – the lack of which is viewed as the main deficiency of modernization theory.

3. THEORETICAL PERSPECTIVES

Akin to modernization theory (→ *Development*), dependency does not consist of a coherent theoretical framework but can rather be considered a combination of assumptions, perspectives and concepts attempting to understand how the precise structure of global trade impacts negatively on developing countries. Resulting from this diversity there are wide differences as to what is the precise connection between dependency and underdevelopment. In the course of its history, the concept of dependency was occasionally reduced to a mere buzzword, lacking theoretical lining, but it is frequently credited for reintroducing the long-neglected question of the historical causes of underdevelopment.

Consequently, the theoretical status of dependency is questionable: while some authors, such as Fernando Henrique Cardoso, write cautiously about 'situations of dependency', other authors, mainly those with a stronger Marxist background, sought to engage in formalizing dependency theory through deducing diverse peripheral-capitalist development laws. Dependency theory assumes a causal connection between dependency and the underdevelopment of peripheral countries. Underdevelopment is thus absolute within the existing world capitalist system; it cannot be overcome with dependency in place. Authors expound on this causal connection in two main ways: first, they understand dependency as an exploitation relationship and, second, they refer to structural factors within the world system that have an impact on domestic structures of underdeveloped countries.

Understanding dependency as exploitation can refer to either a direct or an indirect exploitative relationship. Exploitation in its *direct* form is a consequence of, in Marxist terms, unequal exchange or deteriorating terms of trade. Throughout the twentieth century, terms of trade have increasingly moved against primary products, which, following the international division of labour, are frequently exported by developing nations, in favour of technologically more sophisticated goods. This has led to the 'decapitalization' of developing countries. Unequal terms of trade further refer to the different wage structures of workers in the core and periphery. *Indirect* exploitation is a consequence of removing economic surplus on all levels of the economic chain so that it is not available for local reinvestment. Instead, surplus accumulates in the metropolitan centres.

A further causal argument refers to the negative impact of domestic structures on underdevelopment – these structures are, however, also a result of the country's dependency and thus of the world system. Indeed, deficits of the economic and social structure of 'third world' countries, i.e. dependent reproduction, structural heterogeneity or a lacking industry of productive goods, are assumed to be constitutive characteristics of dependent or peripheral capitalism, the capitalism variant found in developing countries.

Looking at these theoretical assumptions, many dependency authors suggest independent development through dissociation from the capitalist world market as the solution for the underdevelopment problem. Frequently, hope is placed in a socialist reorganization of peripheral countries, which would result in changing the current peripheral-capitalist development into independent development. The issue of what happens once socialism has been introduced while the countries remain within a still-capitalist world system is, however, largely neglected by dependency theorists.

Dependency proved the inspiration for the world systems theory which is frequently termed its theoretical successor. The two theories share ontological assumptions yet differ on their analytical levels: while the nation-state had been the crucial unit of analysis of dependency, world systems theory, mainly following the works of Immanuel Wallerstein, assumes that the capitalist world system is the highest possible global authority. Its functional necessities not only subdue the countries in the periphery and semi-periphery, but also those in the centre. As in dependency, the world economy is defined by a single international division of labour. In world systems theory, this is based on regimes of labour control, i.e. wage labour, sharecropping and serfdom/slavery, which differ between countries. The strength of states and their positions in the world capitalist system are inferred from their rank in these labour regimes. In further contrast to dependency, the three-tiered framework is not static – countries may change their position, but only as part of a zero-sum game. If a country rises within the system, it does so at the expense of another country or other countries, which, as a consequence, have to fall. Wallerstein terms this the 'dog eat dog workings of capitalism' (1979: 101).

4. EMPIRICAL PROBLEMS

Ever since the late 1970s, dependency has suffered major blows in terms of its empirical applicability. Increasing awareness of the broad variety of development dynamics in a number of countries within this period led to a crisis of development theory in general. Most theories found they were ill-equipped for explaining these varieties and therefore at a loss at providing policy suggestions for developing countries.

Regarding dependency, the late 1970s and the 1980s saw changes and internal differentiation within the 'third world' which was not easily captured with either the categories of dependency or the centre–periphery model. Especially the enormous industrialization and economic successes of so-called newly industrialized countries (NICs!) such as South Korea, Taiwan, Hong Kong and Singapore, seriously questioned the core dependency assumption and especially the statism of the dependency model. In the face of highly different developmental dynamics, it became obvious that the similarity assumption of the periphery concept was overrated. Dependency was thus heavily criticized for levelling history: as the dependent situation of the countries in the 'third world' was assumed to be caused by the external structural force of the capitalist world market, the specific differences of precapitalist societies had practically no relevance for the postcolonial phase. Especially, but not only, in the wake of the NICs' successes, this proved to be too undifferentiated a viewpoint.

Neither could the categories employed by dependency capture the ethnic-nationalist conflicts and religious-social movements that developed along old conflict lines in places such as Indochina and Iran. This failure highlights dependency's problematic analysis of classes and class conflicts: dependency theorists tended to focus on the oligarchies and the bourgeoisie as the most important actors within a state, while the popular sector appears passive and easily manipulated. As was seen empirically, however, 'there are many events which cannot be explained without introducing them [the popular sector] as active actors' (Cueva 1976: 14). André Gunder Frank, one of dependency's main theorists, who continues to write within the field, has reacted to this criticism by substituting the progressive potential of socialism with that of new social movements based on gender or the environment arising from those marginalized from the global capitalist system (1984, 1998; Griffiths et al. 2009).

Faced with this major criticism, some authors within the field decried the 'death of dependency', which may be seen as illustrating the dogmatic tendencies within the field of developmental theories that tend to jump from one paradigm to the next without allowing for the build-up of cumulative knowledge (Boeckh 1985: 69). Dependency is positively credited with introducing the view of the developed and the underdeveloped world not as two opposite poles within a linear spectrum but rather two interrelated elements of a mutually reinforcing system. While the theory of dependency is thus largely discredited, the concept of dependency it seeks to understand remains a salient feature of many developing societies. Elements of dependency and world-systems theory as well as the broader Marxist bases they are built on continue to remain relevant for authors in the tradition of new Marxism.

5. CORE READING

Cardoso, Fernando Henrique and Enzo Faletto (1979) *Dependency and Development in Latin America*, (Berkeley and Los Angeles, CA: University of California Press). Originally published as *Dependencia y desarrollo en América Latina* in 1971. Standard work of dependency that remains relevant beyond the prime of dependency theory.

O'Brien, Philip J. (1975) 'A Critique of Latin American Theories of Dependency', in Ivar Oxaal, Tony Barnett and David Booth (eds), *Beyond the Sociology of Development: Economy and Society in Latin America and Africa* (London and Boston: Routledge & Kegan Paul), 7–27. Brief overview of the causal connections of dependency theory and its critique.

Wallerstein, Immanuel (1979) *The Capitalist World Economy* (Cambridge: Cambridge University Press). Classic work introducing world systems theory by its main thinker.

6. USEFUL WEBSITES

http://www.rrojasdatabank.info/dev0006.htm. The Róbinson Rojas Archive contains articles on dependency theory and related topics.

http://www.eclac.org/default.asp?idioma=IN. The homepage of the United Nations Economic Commission for Latin America and the Caribbean (ECLAC), whose famous staff economists included Raúl Prebisch, Celso Furtado and André Gunder Frank.

http://utip.gov.utexas.edu/about.html. The University of Texas Inequality Project is a research group concerned with measuring and explaining movements of wage and earning inequalities as well as patterns of industrial change around the world.

(International) Development

1. CORE QUESTIONS ADDRESSED

- Why do states engage in international development efforts?
- Do the international system and economy serve to improve living standards or sustain underdevelopment and poverty?
- How can development be measured?

2. DEFINITIONS

International development can be defined as the processes and policies through which various actors seek to improve the living standards of societies that are not their own. While the general notion of development simply suggests evolution or change and can therefore be good or bad, the concept of international development implies normative notions of positive change or betterment. It also implies purposive activity and policies by actors such as state governments, international organizations (IOs) and non-governmental organizations (NGOs) to achieve these aims. However, it remains a highly contested concept, disputed in debates that have sparked an academic discipline of its own, as well as in a huge sphere of public policy. Not everyone accepts that development is a 'good thing'. Changing and competing definitions of development are fundamentally affected by (1) political events, (2) emerging theoretical challenges, and (3) lessons learned.

The concept of development has been central to the theory and practice of international relations since the Second World War. At the core of international development are a multitude of bilateral as well as multilateral aid programmes involving above all the World Bank and various agencies of the United Nations (UN). The project of international development – the notion of helping poor countries achieve improvements in economic growth and welfare – is a relatively recent concept, despite having many historical precedents, including colonialism. Many scholars trace the emergence of an 'era of international development' to Harry S. Truman's 1949 inaugural address, where he called on the US to make the 'benefits of our scientific advances and industrial progress available for the improvement and growth of underdeveloped areas' (Truman 1949). The process of decolonization was crucial to the formation of this new world view. Moreover, the Cold War meant that both superpowers had a strong interest in securing stability, prosperity and therefore alliances within their spheres of interest.

Development is often portrayed in narrowly economic terms, e.g. as increased productivity, technological development, and growth. The most common way to measure development is to examine individual or country income. The World Bank – controlling for population, inflation and exchange rates – uses gross national income (GNI) per capita to categorize countries as low, middle or high income. While this is very useful as a general proxy for development (and especially so for econometric analysis), few people defend such a narrow definition. Development is a complex and multifaceted set of processes including political, social and human aspects. While international development traditionally focused on development on the state level, analysts now also tend to think in terms of human development where this is a life free from poverty and hunger, with good health, equality and decent work so as to live a meaningful life of fulfilment.

An intuitive way of thinking about development is difference. This forces us to ask: difference between what or who? Difference of what? Income, life chances, power? How should we measure these differences? How do we explain them? And what do we do about them? But some also ask whether these differences are 'real' or whether they are a function of how we re-present the world through our personal and theoretical prejudices. All of these questions – theoretical and empirical – are central to the study of international development.

3. THEORETICAL PERSPECTIVES

It is more common to refer to development studies than to development theory. Development studies is a very multidisciplinary field – as well as political science and economics it includes anthropology, engineering, public health, environmental science – and is often characterized by close links between practitioners and academics. This is partly a consequence of the problem-driven nature of development.

Early views of development in the 1950s and 1960s were strongly informed by the liberalism of economists and then political scientists who, in turn, challenged the field's narrow economism. Modernization theorists argued that while all countries were on the path to becoming developed, or modern, some remained undeveloped because of the internal organization of their society. Traditional societies were seen as backward by dint of having rigid social structures, being largely rural and agricultural, and characterized by hierarchical (often religious) authority and as such had few incentives for innovation. Modernization, i.e. a process of social change 'whereby less developed societies acquire characteristics common to more developed societies', was supposed to ameliorate the situation of these societies in the international economic system (Lerner 1968: 386). All the while, the direction of change and the ways to cross the 'bridge across the Great Dichotomy between modern and traditional societies' was supposed to be purported by more developed societies – in other words, those who had led the way (Huntington 1971: 288). By the 1960s and 1970s structuralist critics, called (→) dependency theorists (related to → *Theory Concept: Marxism and Critical Theory*), countered this value-laden view of the world, arguing that persistent economic stagnation was not a result of domestic organization, but the international system. Solutions such as delinking and import substitution industrialization (ISI) were tried alongside calls in the 1970s for a New International Economic Order which was supposed to originate from the United Nations Conference on Trade and Development (UNCTAD) – then newly founded to address the economic concerns of developing countries (UN General Assembly 1974). Yet the 1980s saw the return of an extreme form of liberal market fundamentalism, the so-called 'Washington Consensus' – a list of ten economic reform prescriptions such as privatization and deregulation devised by economist John Williamson that became enormously influential and served as inspiration for the reform conditionalities of the International Monetary Fund (IMF) and the World Bank. Characterized by simplicity, the 'Consensus' was supposed to be a reliable pathway to successful development, but this never translated into reality (Naím 2000: 89). Nevertheless, the Debt Crisis of the 1980s forced many developing countries to accept the harsh conditions of the IMF's and World Bank's 'structural adjustment programmes'.

There are a number of different challenges to the orthodoxy. Feminists (→ *Theory Concept: Feminism and Gender*) demonstrate the gender bias of development, the role of gender inequalities and the feminization of poverty, and how 'women's work' is undervalued (by the market) but is essential for the reproduction of the economy. Environmentalists highlight the consequences of industrial development for environmental degradation plus the fact that the poor are always the least able to insulate themselves from environmental risks. Many argue that until growth is no longer at the heart of development it can never be sustainable. Post-development and postcolonial scholars, similar to poststructuralists (→ *Theory Concept: Postmodernism and Poststructuralism*), argue that the view of development is a universalizing perspective ignorant of difference and propagating westernization. Thus scholars such as Wolfgang Sachs (1992: 3) argue that 'it is not the failure of development which has to be feared, but its success'. More sophisticated analyses, such as Arturo Escobar's work, applying Michel Foucault's notions of (→) power to international development, portrays development as a (→) hegemonic discourse of power and control (Escobar 1984). Since its inception in the 1950s, this discourse and the practices it enacted have created the 'third world', its underdevelopment and the array of development experts in a subtly imperialist (→ *Empire*) move (Escobar 1995).

4. EMPIRICAL PROBLEMS

The key empirical problems revolve around how to define and measure development and how to bring about development. While GNI-per-capita measures are a good place to start in assessing international development, especially among nation-states, they miss two key problems: (1) the distribution of wealth and (2) whether growth translates into reduced poverty. Measuring inequality is one way of analysing distribution, either between countries or within countries. The so-called Gini index provides one such inequality measure, or more precisely a means to measure the dispersion of a distribution of factors such as income or wealth, which was particularly popular in economics. In Latin America and the Caribbean as well as sub-Saharan Africa, the income share of the richest 20 per cent of the population is at least 18 times that of the poorest 20 per cent (World Bank 2008: 5).

In order to measure absolute poverty levels, the World Bank uses a threshold of US$1.25 a day in 2005 prices. It estimates that 1.4 billion people live on less than that (Chen and Ravallion 2008). Yet many, including the World Bank, accept that poverty is about much more than lack of income. The United Nations Development Programme (UNDP) defines 'human development' as being 'about expanding the choices people have to lead lives that they value. And it is thus about much more than economic growth, which is only a means – if a very important one – of enlarging people's choices' (UNDP 2010).

In 1990, the UN published the Human Development Index (HDI) – an idea devised by Mahbub ul Haq (1995) and economics Nobel Prize winner Amartya Sen (1999). It is a composite index for health, education and standard of living that builds on the measuring of life expectancy at birth, adult literacy rates and school enrolment, and GNI/capita. The inclusion of, but not the total reliance on, income is important because it is seen as a vital means to an end, rather than an end in itself. The HDI figure is calculated by measuring how far away a country is from the 'maximum' levels, and countries can and do have very different rankings on the HDI and the GNI/capita index taken on its own. Notably, however, the HDI lacks indicators on the environment or democracy and participation. The UN's Millennium Development Goals agreed in New York in 2000 are the latest development measures to be devised, and strongly shape international development policy at the time of writing. They consist of eight goals covering poverty, maternal health, HIV, education, etc. with targets and indicators that the international community aims to meet by 2015 (United Nations General Assembly 2000). Progress varies and is monitored through the UN's annual progress reports.

A key area in international development that IR scholars have tended to focus on is the aid regime: why states give aid and to whom. Much of the literature suggests the importance of power politics and self-serving reasons for giving aid (Morgenthau 1962). Liberals argue that foreign aid is a rational way of maximizing a state's utility through building-up trading partners. Recent studies, such as Alesina and Dollar (2000), suggest that donor interests do indeed tend to trump recipient needs. Yet, Lumsdaine (1993: 29) has argued that 'foreign aid cannot be explained on the basis of the economic and political interests of the donor countries alone, and any satisfactory explanation must give a central place to the influence of humanitarian and egalitarian convictions upon aid donors'.

It is important to suspend any notions of development as simply a beneficent process of the wealthy helping the poor. As the political philosopher Thomas Pogge argues, the wealthy have a stronger duty to stop harming the poor in the first place, for example the historical harms caused by colonialism and the continuing 'structural violence' (Galtung 1969) caused by an unequal trading system (Pogge 2002). Hence, in addition to aid, key international processes that impact on development outcomes are trade policy, debt relief, direct and portfolio investment, and migrant remittances. The necessary reform of international structures and institutions is unavoidably tied-up with and stymied by the interests of the wealthy and powerful who set the rules (Payne 2005).

5. CORE READING

Escobar, Arturo (1995) *Encountering Development: The Making and Unmaking of the Third World* (Princeton: Princeton University Press). An influential poststructuralist critique of development as a hegemonic discourse of the 'west'.

Rostow, Walt (1960) *The Stages of Growth: A Non-Communist Manifesto* (Cambridge: Cambridge University Press). A modernization classic that proposes to view the development of economies as consistently following a basic five-stage process from traditional society to the age of high mass-consumption.

Sen, Amartya (1999) *Development as Freedom* (Oxford: Oxford University Press). Summarizes Sen's main ideas on human development and presents freedom as necessarily constituent to development.

6. USEFUL WEBSITES

http://hdr.undp.org/en/statistics/. Offers the most recent UN statistics on human development as well as the annual human development reports highlighting specific topics.

http://www.worldbank.org/. Website of the World Bank.

http://www.imf.org/. International Monetary Fund homepage.

http://www.undp.org/. United Nations Development Programme (UNDP).

http://www.unctad.org/Templates/StartPage.asp?intItemID=2068. United Nations Conference on Trade and Development (UNCTAD).

http://www.un.org/millenniumgoals/. UN website dedicated to its work on the Millennium Development Goals.

http://www.wider.unu.edu/. World Institute for Development Economics Research website at the United Nations University.

Diplomacy

1. CORE QUESTIONS ADDRESSED

- What are the main functions of diplomacy?
- Who can be a diplomat?
- Which factors affect diplomatic negotiation processes?

2. DEFINITIONS

Diplomacy, narrowly defined, refers to the conduct of international relations through state officials who seek to secure the objectives of their foreign policies through negotiation rather than resorting to force, propaganda, or law (Berridge 2002: 1). It has been termed 'the master institution' of international society at least since Renaissance Italy when the network of diplomats and consuls who enjoyed the protection of special legal rules, such as diplomatic immunity, and were permanently resident abroad, began to come into place (Wight 1978: 113; Berridge et al. 2001).

While this definition appears straightforward, scholars continue to disagree on conceptualizations of diplomacy on at least three accounts: the peaceful character of diplomacy, the identity of diplomats, and diplomacy's connection to the state system. First, diplomacy is widely regarded as the opposite to the use of force, yet terms such as coercive diplomacy, coined in the Cold War era to indicate the use of threats or limited force to persuade opponents not to change the status quo in their favour, indicate that the lines are not as clear-cut as presumed (Jönsson 2002; George 1991). Second, authors in the field either classify only the activities of professional diplomats as diplomacy, referred to as narrow diplomacy (Nicolson 1939), or include all actors of statecraft within this term, thereby equating diplomacy with foreign policy – this is also termed broad diplomacy (Kissinger 1994). Some even untie diplomacy from state actors and allow for the possibility of diplomacy on behalf of other social groups (Constantinou 1996).

Third, the origin of diplomacy and its connection to the state system remain a bone of contention. Some authors refer to 'political entities' as represented by diplomats, thereby questioning the link of diplomacy to the modern state system, while others reserve the term for the modern diplomatic system originating initially in fifteenth century Europe whose key features still govern today's diplomatic relations (Hamilton and Langhorne 1995; Nicolson 1939). Authors following a broad conception of diplomacy usually do not restrict its exercise to a specific period and territorial entity, but rather proffer a definition along its constituent functions: representation, as acting on behalf of, and communication, as a logically necessary condition for the existence of international relations (Jönsson 2008). Scholars such as Paul Sharp and Costas Constantinou go so far as to define diplomacy exclusively as representation (Sharp 1999) or as 'a regulated process of communication' (Constantinou 1996: 25). The function of communication is also crucial with respect to 'public diplomacy', which refers to promoting foreign policy objectives through influencing and informing foreign publics (Berridge et al. 2001: 17–18). Postmodern conceptions go still further in their definition of diplomacy, viewing it as an existential aspect of the human condition, as 'mediation between estranged individuals, groups, or entities' (Der Derian 1987: 6) that is necessary because of human alienation.

Adopting a broader definition of diplomacy opens up space for the inclusion of diplomatic actors apart from the state, a development that may be necessary given changes in the exercise of diplomacy since the creation of the United Nations and particularly since the early 1990s. Some of these developments are openly encouraged by states – such as 'paradiplomacy', foreign relations conducted by governmental departments other than the foreign ministry at the regional or local level (Aldecoa and Keating 1999); 'citizen' or 'new diplomacy' offering civil society actors the opportunity to act on a global stage (Hocking 1999;

McRae and Hubert 2001); and 'two-track diplomacy', i.e. informal interaction between members of adversarial states complementing traditional diplomacy (McDonald 1991; Phillips 2005). Others, such as 'celebrity diplomacy', refer to the independent activities of the likes of Bono, frontman of the band U2, who are supposed to have filled gaps created by failed legitimacy and efficiency of state-based diplomacy as single-issue diplomats (Cooper 2007).

Diplomatic studies make efforts to develop functional typologies of diplomacy. Apart from the two functions of diplomacy mentioned above – communication, occasionally also referred to as information exchange, and representation – authors discern three to four additional diplomatic functions: negotiation; the protection of citizens and commercial and legal interests of the sending state in the receiving state; the promotion of economic, cultural and scientific relations; and policy preparation or policy advice (Jönsson 2002: 215; Barston 1988: 2–3; Berridge 1995: 39–44).

3. THEORETICAL PERSPECTIVES

Despite its central status within International Relations, theoretical studies of diplomacy are scarce, as the long-dominant paradigms of neorealism and neo-liberalism have 'bracketed' the study of diplomacy (→ *Theory Concepts: Realism and Neorealism; Liberalism and Neoliberalism*). A systematic discussion of diplomacy in International Relations theory only started in the late 1990s, while the most influential contributions have long come from practitioners of the craft and often include lengthy historical accounts. The English School of international relations (→ *International Society*) constitutes an exception to this observation as it defines diplomacy as one of the five broad institutions international society is made of (Wight 1978; Bull 1977). Following Colin Wight, as long as power remains dispersed between diverse states, the diplomatic function of regularized negotiation is crucial in matters of war and peace (1978). All the while, neither the works of Wight nor Hedley Bull inspired sustained IR analyses on how diplomacy works. Iver Neumann has recently attempted to revive English School perspectives on diplomacy by pointing to the opportunity it offers to perceive of international society as a more 'malleable and reflective phenomenon' (2003: 364).

Negotiation stands out as the function of diplomacy with most theoretical underpinnings, its contributions ranging from descriptive analysis to prescriptive guides aimed at practitioners such as Roger Fisher and William Ury's classic *Getting to Yes* (1981). Early theoretical contributions from the 1960s have a background in (→) game theory (Schelling 1960; Rapaport 1960), a heritage that remains important in many rationalist accounts on negotiation yet has been supplemented with other factors such as, exemplarily, the role of culture in international negotiations and general dynamics of the international negotiation process. While the notion of nationally different negotiation styles was prevalent until the 1980s, it has largely been replaced by a broader understanding of the culture–negotiation link in the context of intercultural communication. Scholars have, for example, pointed to problems in communication deriving from negotiation between 'high-context' and 'low-context' cultures. High-context cultures, such as Japan or Egypt, communicate in a less direct, discreet way, perceive of language as a social instrument and are very much concerned with appearance (Hall 1976: 78–9; Cohen 1997). By contrast, low-context cultures such as the USA or Israel communicate directly and explicitly, emphasize language's informational function and value content over appearance. Being aware of these cultural differences and acting accordingly can facilitate negotiation. When it comes to negotiation dynamics, scholars have further identified a list of factors influencing the negotiation process and its outcomes. Among these are actors' use of tactical instruments or strategic moves such as signals or indices (Goffman 1969) and the importance of timing in negotiations. Scholars either identify characteristic stages of the negotiation process or point to the notion of 'ripeness' indicating that negotiation or mediation (→ *Conflict Resolution*) is likely to produce best results when the conflict parties experience a 'mutually hurting stalemate' or perceive of a negotiated outcome as the best way out (Druckman 1986; Zartman 1985; Rubin et al. 1994).

Ethnographic studies by Neumann and Michael Barnett offer a completely different perspective on the institution of diplomacy. Neumann draws on his experience in the Norwegian Ministry of Foreign Affairs in, for example, theoretically describing the diplomat as 'juggling' three scripts of self – the bureaucratic, the heroic and the mediator – which are in constant conflict with one another (2005). In his analysis of the UN response, or lack thereof, to the 1994 genocide in Rwanda, Barnett illustrates how the diplomatic culture of both national permanent missions and the UN headquarters led its officials to believe they were doing the ethically 'right' thing in not acting to prevent the genocide (2002).

4. EMPIRICAL PROBLEMS

In contrast to theoretical studies, empirical studies of diplomacy abound. Aside from bilateral diplomacy, the dynamics of multilateral diplomacy at the United Nations and other international organizations, such as the particular nature of deliberation associated with international summitry, the growth of group diplomacy, the politicization of the UN's technical agencies and the emergence of the technically informed diplomat specialist have been particularly widely studied (Hamilton and Langhorne 1995: 197–205; Dunn 1996). In line with a broad definition of diplomacy, there has also been a focus on preventive diplomacy, understood as diplomatic efforts to prevent violent conflicts, for example initiated by the UN Secretary Generals within their competence to bring matters that might threaten international peace and security to the Security Council for consideration (Cahill 2000; Ramcharan 2008). Former Secretary General U Thant's role in helping to avert nuclear confrontation during the Cuban missile crisis is given as a prime example of preventive diplomacy.

'Traditional' diplomatic practice has also been criticized under three headings. First, even though the literature points to some of the successes of preventive diplomacy, diplomatic institutions and methods have been termed inadequate in frequently failing or being ill equipped to prevent or end violent conflicts. A second criticism refers to the secrecy of traditional diplomacy, although it may also be that such secrecy, while leading to intransparency, at the same time enhances the quality of argumentation and communicative action among the negotiating parties (Lose 2001; → *Discourse*). Finally, in the age of the communications revolution and major digital advances, certain institutions of traditional diplomacy, such as professional diplomats or resident embassies, have been termed obsolete (Watson 1983).

The extension of diplomatic practice to the realm of non-state organizations continues to be a further point of empirical focus (Cooper 2002). The prime phenomena studied in this context include the crucial involvement of non-governmental organizations in the negotiation process of both the Convention on the Prohibition of the Use, Stockpiling, Production and Transfer of Anti-Personnel Mines and on their Destruction (1997), also known as the Ottawa Convention, and the Rome Statute (1998) that established the International Criminal Court. The involvement and preparation of NGO coalitions who were present during negotiation processes was found crucial in negotiating the successful outcomes in both cases (Anderson 2000; Prince 1998; Barrow 2004; Deitelhoff 2009).

5. CORE READING

Berridge, G. R. (2002) *Diplomacy: Theory and Practice* (Basingstoke: Palgrave, 2nd edn). Presents diplomacy along its main functions and working areas, with a decidedly practical focus.
    Melissen, Jan (ed.) (1999) *Innovation in Diplomatic Practice* (Basingstoke: Palgrave). A collection of analyses on the changing practice of diplomacy.
    Neumann, Iver B. (2005) 'To Be a Diplomat', *International Studies Perspectives* 6 (1), 72–93. Offers an ethnographically derived understanding of the diplomat's nature.

6. USEFUL WEBSITES

http://grberridge.diplomacy.edu/. Homepage of Geoffrey Berridge providing updates of his textbooks on diplomacy and links to research resources for students.
http://www.diplomacy.edu/. DiploFoundation, a non-profit organization specialized in online diplomatic training, research in international relations, diplomacy and internet governance.
http://www.isanet.org/sections/diplomatic-studies.html. Diplomatic studies section of the International Studies Association.
http://www.colorado.edu/conflict/peace/treatment/prevent.htm. Website on preventive diplomacy and conflict prevention by the Conflict Research Consortium at the University of Colorado.

···························· Discourse ····························

1. CORE QUESTIONS ADDRESSED

- Why is discourse an important category in the analysis of international relations?
- How are identities constructed through discourse in international relations?

- To what extent is discourse analysis more than merely a method of International Relations?

2. DEFINITIONS

Discourse has become one of the central analytical concepts in many disciplines of the social sciences, including International Relations. However, when analysts refer to discourse, they often have different things in mind. On one dimension, definitions differ in what they consider discourses generally to be made up of. To some, discourse consists of any written or spoken text in the narrow sense of the word. They accord priority to language as the medium through which we make sense of the world. Others include all activity that produces meaning, including symbols (such as flags) or symbolic actions (such as handshakes). While it cannot be denied that the latter are important in making sense of the international, we should note though that they are not meaningful in and of themselves and first need to be given meaning through language, although one should also note that individual words or phrases also only acquire meaning within their broader discursive context. On the one hand, it is therefore important not to have a version of discourse which is too narrow; on the other hand, we need to pay careful attention to the exact relationship of linguistic and non-linguistic practices (Hansen 2006).

On a second dimension, definitions of discourse differ in their substantive specification of what statements or actions are to be included. A Foucauldian perspective (→ *Theory Concept: Postmodernism and Poststructuralism*), for instance, would consider discourse as all those statements that construct an object of international relations, for example (→) anarchy, in a particular way so that it acquires a specific meaning. Others use discourse for the realm of all text and actions that produce meaning. Often one also comes across the use of the term 'discourse' in a very loose sense as an equivalent of public debate, although this usage is too broad and often not thought through sufficiently to be considered any further here.

Finally, the term 'discourse' can also have normative connotations. Discourse is then seen as an open and free public exchange in which hierarchical power structures are overcome and in which the partners of a conversation take each other and each others' arguments seriously. This understanding is often associated with the work of German philosopher Jürgen Habermas (→ *Theory Concept: Marxism and Critical Theory*).

discourse

3. THEORETICAL PERSPECTIVES

Analyses that use discourse as a central concept share the view of language as a crucial part of social and political life. For some, language is a means to communicate arguments. In this view, the role of language is that of an instrument. Discourse analysts would however usually go beyond this conception of language as an instrument and view language as crucial for our understanding of the world. In this sense, we are not merely using language to express ourselves; rather, we can only make sense of the world from within a discursive context in which we operate. It is important to stress that this does not mean that there is no reality outside discourse – such a claim would be foolish indeed. This reality however cannot be experienced directly (Laclau and Mouffe 1985). Even the deaths of war and the hunger of underdevelopment (→*Development*) are not purely physical experiences; they are constructed in particular ways through discourse by those who experience and those who observe them. It is for instance wrong to deduce from the act that someone whose father or mother was killed by an enemy army that he or she will continue to fight the enemy. The death needs to be interpreted and thus rendered meaningful. Depending on this constructed meaning, it may lead to efforts of revenge as much as to efforts of reconciliation.

For most concepts in International Relations, their discursive nature makes sense more intuitively: (→) anarchy, (→) sovereignty, identity and even the state itself clearly do not simply exist as such but are human constructs that can only be understood from a particular discursive perspective. This also means, however, that such concepts tend to be 'essentially contested' (Connolly 1983). There are always several possible meanings coming out of different discourses, and a core part of politics is therefore the struggle over the meaning of such core concepts. It is instructive in this context to compare Andrew Moravcsik's rationalist account of European integration (→ *Regional Integration*) as *The Choice for Europe* (Moravcsik 1998) to Ole Wæver's discursive analysis as *The Struggle for Europe* (Wæver et al. 1998).

Such core concepts tend to bind different discourses together and therefore fulfil a crucial function in the political debate in that particular meanings are stabilized through them. Europe for instance is such a core term at least in the European context because it not only provides meaning to the project of European integration but also because at the same time it brings with it specific constructions of identity, the economy, society, etc. (Diez 1999, 2001; Wæver 2009). Likewise, different definitions of (→) security accord different levels of importance to the military, welfare or the environment, and fill these terms with different meanings (see e.g. the contributions to Lipschutz 1995). Many discourse analysts refer in this context to the work of Ernesto Laclau and Chantal Mouffe (1985), who call such core concepts 'nodal points'.

Given the permanent contestation of meaning in political and social life, these nodal points, through their binding together of a variety of discourses, fulfil an important function in that they allow the at least temporary stabilization of a political debate around a number of core meanings on which policies can be based. A main task of the discourse analyst is to interrogate or 'problematize' these meanings, in particular if they have become the undisputed norm and have taken on a hegemonic status (→ *Hegemony*). It is in this sense that the discourse analyst partakes in 'critical theory' in a looser sense than the more narrowly defined Critical Theory that builds on specific versions of post-Marxism and the so-called Frankfurt School. One should however stress that this does not mean that the fixation of meaning is always and only a 'bad thing'. We *need* to make sense of the world in particular ways and will therefore always marginalize alternatives in order to be able to act and make judgements. Discourse is enabling us to do so, yet at the same time it is problematic both for ourselves and for those who take views that are marginalized in this process to take meanings for granted and to ridicule or no longer consider alternatives.

Broadly speaking, this understanding of discourse is in line with a poststructuralist approach, to which discourse analysis is central. Yet, discourse plays a core role in other approaches as well, in particular (→) social constructivism, where discourse analysis is often used as a methodology to trace the construction of transnational identities (e.g. on Europe, see Herrmann et al. 2004; Risse 2009) or the socialization of actors into new policy norms (e.g. on human rights, see Risse et al. 1999). In contrast to poststructuralist approaches, discourse analysis in these studies is, however, less bound up with theoretical reflections about the power of language and its epistemological role, and rather used as a methodological tool to capture political and social change.

In the social constructivist use of the term, discourse seems to be similar to a set of ideas (see e.g. Goldstein and Keohane 1993) or a cognitive map that guides foreign policy-makers (see e.g. Axelrod 1976). Cognition however happens within the individual, and ideas are likewise an individualistic concept if, as in Goldstein and Keohane (1993),

discourse

they are defined as beliefs (→ *Ideas and Norms*). Discourse, in contrast, is by definition social (see Laffey and Weldes 1997) – it exists through the articulations of many rather than through the thought of the individual. To be considered meaningful, the construction of a term needs to be recognized and shared by others; and the contestation of meaning takes place in the public sphere.

Social constructivists have also made use of the Habermasian concept of discourse. Rather than utilizing discourse ethics as a form of critique of present communicative structures in international relations, scholars such as Risse (2001) have drawn on Habermas's work to establish a third logic of action besides the logic of appropriateness and the logic of consequentality (→ *Theory Concept: Social Constructivism*). This third logic of action refers to communicative action or the logic of arguing, in which actors do not seek to maximize their interests or act solely according to given rules. Instead, they engage in a debate that is focused on the better argument. This provides a micro-foundation of change in the international order that is not induced by force.

4. EMPIRICAL PROBLEMS

Discourse analysis has been used to analyse a number of empirical problems, some of which are addressed in the entry on postmodernism and poststructuralism. One of its early usages was in the area of (→) foreign policy analysis. In the 1970s, a number of approaches focused on the role of individual perceptions and mindsets in foreign policy decision-making. Among the most prominent was cognitive mapping. In this approach, analysts tried to reconstruct the core concepts a policy-maker uses when taking a decision, and how they were linked in his or her mind so that they resulted in a specific policy utility (Axelrod 1976). In a self-critical reflection on their work in this larger project, Bonham et al. (1987) argued that what they had in fact done was not so much the reconstruction of individual thoughts than of historical 'discursive spaces' in which policy-makers were located. In particular, they found that all they had for their cognitive maps were different forms of text by a policy-maker, but that one could not easily assume that this text would indeed reflect the inner thoughts of the individual concerned and thus rather formed a set of historical articulations that tied into other articulations constructing core issues in similar or competing ways.

The idea that discourse enables and constrains foreign policy was later taken up by Ole Wæver and colleagues in Copenhagen, who were particularly interested in the policy of European Union member states towards European integration (see Wæver 2002; Larsen 1997). They argued that no policy in this context could be articulated legitimately without accommodating the predominant discursive constructions of the two core concepts of 'state' and 'nation'. On this basis, French policy-makers, on the basis of their republican understanding of these two terms, had to construct their European policies within the frameworks of either a Europe of nation-states or a transfer of the French model of the state to the European level, while German policy-makers could more easily advocate a decentralized, federal European Union.

One of the most important issues in discourse analysis in IR has, however, been the construction of identities through representations of *the other* (see e.g. Campbell 1998; Hansen 2006; Neumann 1999; Rumelili 2008). The basic argument here is that identities are not simply given but rely on the construction of an opposition between self and other where the other is different from and often inferior to or threatening the self. The analysis of such discourses particularly seeks to problematize constructions that marginalize or even seek to extinguish the other, but it also questions homogeneous representations of the self, for instance in the form of state identities or identities in so-called 'ethnic' conflicts, as an unproblematic category.

Such studies have had a great impact on International Relations and the way core concepts such as identity are seen today. However, they have not been without criticism. In a seminal article from a sympathetic point of view, Jennifer Milliken (1999) once bemoaned the lack of a common research strategy to the study of discourse. Indeed, our discussion in this entry has shown that the concept of 'discourse' continues to be used in a variety of ways. As the work of Hansen (2006) and of Rumelili (2008) however show, questions of research strategy and methodology have become more central to the analysis than they used to be.

Meanwhile, discourse in the form of communicative action has been used to trace peaceful and egalitarian practices in international relations that are focused on the better argument rather than the wielding of power instruments. Deitelhoff (2009) for instance has demonstrated the impact of arguing in the negotiations leading to the International Criminal Court. Joerges and Neyer (2002) have shown how policy issues tackled through committees involving experts in the European Union have been addressed in a more deliberative fashion with less room for intergovernmental bargaining than other problems.

5. CORE READING

Hansen, Lene (2006) *Security as Practice: Discourse Analysis and the Bosnian War* (London: Routledge). A superb analysis that develops a sophisticated discourse-analytical framework and discusses core methodological issues in order to analyse western policy towards Bosnia.

Risse, Thomas (2001) '"Let's Argue!" Communicative Action in World Politics', *International Organization* 54 (1), 1–39. This piece introduced the notion of communicative action as developed by Habermas and then taken up in a debate about the role of discourse in the *German Journal of International Relations* (*Zeitschrift für Internationale Beziehungen*) to the wider international discipline.

Wæver, Ole (2002) 'Identities, Communities and Foreign Policy: Discourse Analysis as Foreign Policy Theory', in Lene Hansen and Ole Wæver (eds), *European Integration and National Identity: The Challenge of the Nordic States* (London: Routledge), 20–49. The most easily accessible statement of discourse analysis as foreign policy analysis by one of its core proponents.

6. USEFUL WEBSITES

http://www.discourseanalysis.net/. Interactive and interdisciplinary website for all those working with discourse analysis.
http://extra.shu.ac.uk/daol/. Online journal for discourse analysis research.
http://www.discourses.org/resources/websites/. 'Discourse in Society' offers links to interdisciplinary forums and journals dedicated to the study of discourse.

Empire

1. CORE QUESTIONS ADDRESSED

- What are the differences between empire and Empire?
- What are the main theoretical explanations for imperialism?
- Why does empire continue to be of interest?

2. DEFINITIONS

While the age of empires has passed with the process of decolonization in the twentieth century, the notion of empire and its associated terms continue to be a well-used currency in International Relations. There are three main understandings of empire. First, and most traditionally, empire may denote a composite of territories and peoples of vast extent, usually created by conquest, stretching far beyond the 'homelands' of the rulers. Said rulers – who may be a single person, a societal elite or a nation-state – are in possession of absolute sovereignty and directly administer and often economically exploit different communities from an imperial centre (Watson 1992: 6). The existence of imperial and subordinate societies implies that there is a core to the empire as well as a periphery. This first understanding also contains an aspiration to universality: empires, such as ancient Rome, entailed, in strong delimitation to 'barbarians' outside imperial rule, a promise of economic and cultural prosperity for their citizens. Empire, in this view, can also be defined as the effective control imposed by the imperial society over subordinated societies (Doyle 1986: 30). While territorially bound, it is not so much the territory formally covered by its (annexed) regions that defines an empire, but rather the places over which it is able to exercise control. Empire thus denotes sovereignty relations on a somewhat diffuse scale.

A second understanding of empire distances itself from formal rule, or rather the direct physical control of territories outside its own. Rather, especially since the end of the Second World War, empire is conceived of as informal, exercised by countries exerting less direct influence to protect their interests and those of their 'friends' and by acting as 'police' in regional conflicts (Howe 2002). In such an understanding, empire can also carry normative connotations, as empires are important to safeguard world order under (→) anarchy. This understanding of empire was frequently assigned to the role of the United States of America (USA) in world politics. Since the beginning of the so-called unipolar moment, the USA was in economic, military and cultural terms by far the most powerful country of the world (→ *Theory Concept: Realism and Neorealism*). Ole Waever's notion of three European empires also fits into this understanding. Building on the work of Alan Watson within the 'English School' of International Relations (→ *International Society*), Waever applied empire as a metaphorical analogy to indicate diffuse power relations beyond national sovereignty.

On this basis, he discerns three European empires that are in interplay with each other and may develop in differing directions: the European Union with its centre in Brussels, the Russian sphere of influence, and a Turkish formation centred on Ankara loosely extending to five Turkish-speaking republics of central Asia and Azerbaijan (Waever 1997b: 67–80).

A third understanding views Empire as a deterritorialized, decentred form of rule, combining both nation-states and supranational entities, which encompasses the entire world, and not only manages territories and peoples but also effectively 'creates' them (Hardt and Negri 2000). Instead of denoting competition between several imperialist powers, Hardt and Negri's *Empire* is the idea of a global Empire that determines and structures the entire world. Its influence encompasses formal (i.e. military) and informal (i.e. economic and cultural) influence.

It is important to distinguish empire from the terms imperialism and colonialism that are often associated with it. Imperialism as a concept is much newer than empire, having been widely used only since the end of the nineteenth century. In a first contrast to empire, it refers to a process, not an object. Generally, imperialism may be defined as a state policy targeted at creating and upholding big political units, directly, by enlarging its territory, or indirectly, by seeking to dominate other states politically, economically or militarily. To separate imperialism from colonialism is yet another challenge, as they are often used synonymously. One could say that while imperialism refers to the administration of territories without significant settlements, colonialism involves the transfer of people to settle in a new territory while subjugating the native population. The terms imperialism and colonialism thus originally stem from different historic periods, with colonialism frequently used to describe settlements in places such as North America, and imperialism denoting for example the 'scramble for Africa' in the late nineteenth century. However, this distinction is not upheld throughout the literature, and continued to diminish as usage of colonialism for both scenarios increased – mostly because what was understood by the term 'colonies' changed drastically in the late nineteenth century and authors used colonialism instead of imperialism in order to distance themselves from Marxist undertones. Today, colonialism is mostly used in strictly political terms: it implies a system of rule by one group over the other, where the first group claims exclusive sovereignty over the second. This sovereignty is often, but not necessarily, exercised at a long distance (Howe 2002: 30).

3. THEORETICAL PERSPECTIVES

While the concept of empire has been around for two millennia, classical theories of imperialism originate from the early twentieth century. Generally speaking, theories of imperialism may be subdivided into political and economic theories of imperialism. Of the two strands, economic theories of imperialism have been decidedly more influential. They commonly share Marxist assumptions (→ *Theory Concept: Marxism and Critical Theory.*)

The first author to present an economic theory of imperialism was John Hobson in 1902. Notably, his work has a clear normative impetus: to enlighten the general public and encourage change in British policy. For Hobson, the empire is neither desirable nor profitable for its citizens. Starting with discrediting elite consensus at the time, i.e. that the possession of colonies is useful and indeed vital for a prosperous national economy, Hobson offers two main explanations for the expansionist tendencies of the leading capitalist countries. First, while the nation at large does not benefit from imperialist policies, there are sectional interests in society such as manufacturers of export goods and the military services that derive considerable private gain from colonial expansion. These 'economic parasites of imperialism' use their societal influence and existing sentimental tendencies to further support imperialist policies. This dual process eventually leads to 'an interested bias towards imperialism throughout the educated circles' (Hobson 1988: 46, 51). Second, and more important for the explanation of imperialist tendencies of capitalist countries, is the income derived from foreign investments.

Following Hobson, capital export is the necessary result of undamped competition: the accumulation of capital in the hands of a few, i.e. 'oversaving', leads to overproduction as the productive force exceeds effective consumption. In this situation of underconsumption, it becomes virtually impossible to profitably invest accumulated capital at home. Hobson thus discerns the capital owners' desire to access new markets in search of profit as the 'economic taproot of imperialism' (1988: 71). Ultimately, imperialist policies are therefore not only a serious waste of societal means, but they are also politically detrimental on two accounts: domestically, they impede societal reforms and foster militarist tendencies and authoritarian types of government. Abroad, they produce a state of constant rivalry between different empires.

This point, as many others, was taken up by two further classical theorists of imperialism writing with an explicitly political objective in mind:

Rosa Luxemburg and Vladimir Ilyich Ulyanov, a.k.a. Lenin. Luxemburg viewed imperialism as resulting from the very functioning of capitalist accumulation (1971). While capitalism in its initial stages was able to tap into non-capitalist milieus within its own societies, to further accumulation at the stage of underconsumption, capitalism is structurally dependent on non-capitalist milieus in order to have access to cheap labour, commodities and non-capitalist consumers. In this process, capitalism takes root in the previously non-capitalist milieus. Lenin follows this reasoning: imperialism is seen to develop because of the inherent structural inefficiencies of capitalist markets – in this view economic crises caused by falling profit rates in capitalist countries can only be resolved through the development of new capitalist markets, in other words, coercive territorial expansion. Akin to Hobson, Lenin is explicitly critical of imperialism because not only does it create the possibility to reap 'super-profits' through exploitation, but it also helps capitalist countries to 'export' their economic mishaps to weaker states, 'bribing' the domestic labour force and putting off revolution (2000). From here, Lenin goes a step further, as the title of his work suggests: true to historical materialism, imperialism is inevitably the highest and last stage in the development of capitalism, indicating the system's imminent collapse (→ *Theory Concept: Marxism and Critical Theory*). Moreover, this also means that by definition only capitalist countries could be imperialist. The main contribution of Lenin, Luxemburg and also Nikolai Bukharin consists in providing an explanation for why capitalist states of the First World War era were willing to use force to achieve their economic objectives – in stark contrast to the liberal assumption (→ *Theory Concept: Liberalism and Neoliberalism*) that international free trade would lead to world peace (Linklater 2009: 121). All of their answers point to the structural demands of the capitalist world economy.

Luxemburg's and Lenin's contemporary Joseph Schumpeter (1951) adds a different understanding of imperialism to the debate. Starting from a liberal viewpoint, which regards free trade as the vital interest of each individual, he concludes that imperialism as a historical phenomenon of that time is caused by chauvinistic elites seeking to secure power and political influence through territorial expansion. Imperialism is thus due to an 'objectless' and irrational psychic disposition of aristocratic elites, an innate drive to conquer. Schumpeter consequently argues that imperialism is detrimental to the development of free and thus efficient capitalist markets. Instead of being the highest stage of capitalism, imperialism is an anachronism in the development of capitalism, a historical relic of precapitalist times.

After Schumpeter, theories of imperialism received some recognition and expansion in the works of (→) dependency and world systems theorists, and fully re-entered international relations discourse throughout the 1990s following the cultural turn. Drawing on Michel Foucault's analysis of power, Michael Hardt and Antonio Negri's 2000 *Empire* is the most influential contribution to this renewed debate. Hardt and Negri deconstruct the state-centric image of world order and the notions tied to it, mainly sovereignty and identity, and subsequently reconstruct them in the 'new Empire'. The all-encompassing imperial order, not limited to time and space, follows this reconstruction of conventional inside/outside parameters of sovereignty and identity: it progressively includes the entire globe, and, in terms of identity, turns its people into a multitude by universally including all. The Empire's creation of the multitude, i.e. the mass of people living in the confines of the Empire, through its dissolution of 'old' identities, carries within it the possibility to overthrow its control. The multitude may be able to use the Empire's communicative channels and structures of control to organize itself through absolute democracy. In other words, global revolution becomes possible through the new global subject of the multitude.

4. EMPIRICAL PROBLEMS

Empires have been analysed from every possible angle: their rise and fall, their power mechanisms, their importance in the progress of human history, their consequences, and even their moral value. Classical theories of imperialism have been the subject of theoretical and empirical criticism from early on – most critics question the theorists' reduction of the reasons for imperialist expansion to the existence of partial economic interests. Economic interests are always influential with regard to state policy – not only in the case of imperialist policy. Explaining imperialism with the existence of economic interests alone is thus hardly satisfactory. In this context, David Landes suggested that the pursuit of imperialist policies is far more likely if there is a power imbalance (Landes 1961). Further, perceiving the role of the state in international politics as that of a mere executor of big corporate interests is frequently deemed too simple an argument. The historical record with regard to sectional interest groups 'capturing' or gaining leverage on the state is at least ambiguous. Classical theories of imperialism imposed a further limit on their explanatory

empire

power by focusing their analyses on only one particular period of history (c. 1873–1917), instead of providing a general theory of capitalist international relations (Teschke 2008: 168). Notwithstanding this, elements of imperialism theories have resurfaced in the context of globalization critiques: globalization, in this sense, is an ideological project of imperialists, the new international capitalist class composed of transnational corporations and international finance (Petras and Veltmeyer 2001).

Hardt and Negri's *Empire* has generated a plethora of critical response of its own – there has been discussion with regard to all of its key arguments, and mainly the claim of dissolving national sovereignty. Frequently, critics found the Empire's existence unconvincing with a look at empirical reality. Especially with regard to the war on Iraq, it was suggested that we are not witnessing the growth of a new imperial power of global sovereignty but rather 'the repetition of a more familiar imperialist power that the United States is attempting to claim' (Passavant 2004: 2). US international conduct following 9/11 thus triggered renewed discussion on imperialism in the old sense of the word, with some authors such as Ignatieff (2003) and Münkler (2005) arguing normatively for the necessity of an empire to safeguard world order, and others strongly criticizing imperialist tendencies. In contrast to the processes of deterritorialization and the creation of global multitude which are presumed to change international relations (according to Hardt and Negri), other authors pointed to the continued prevalence of nation-state identities and their central roles in capitalist development (Harvey 2005; Panitch and Gindin 2004). Hardt and Negri responded to this critique with their book *Multitude: War and Democracy in the Age of Empire*, stressing that Empire is a 'tendency of global political order' rather than a state that has already been reached (Hardt and Negri 2004: xiii).

Conventional theories of imperialism have further come under attack from postcolonial theorists who claim they are missing out on the discursive quality of imperialism, mainly how practices of representation reproduce a logic of subordination that endures even after former colonies have gained independence. With the help of Foucault's insights on the connection between knowledge and (→) power, authors such as Edward Said deconstructed the negative portrayal of non-European peoples in literary texts and historical sources to understand how this reflected and reinforced imperialism (Said 1979). This poststructuralist critique (→ *Theory Concept: Postmodernism and Poststructuralism*) extended the focus of theories of imperialism beyond the economic and political to the cultural realm, thereby adding a third dimension to the analysis.

5. CORE READING

Hardt, Michael and Antonio Negri (2000) *Empire* (Cambridge, MA: Harvard University Press). Central theoretical work that re-invigorated debate on theories of imperialism.

Wolfe, Patrick (1997) 'History and Imperialism – A Century of Theory: From Marx to Postcolonialism', *American Historical Review* 102 (2), 388–420. Provides a concise summary of both classical and more recent theories of imperialism with a focus on Marxist variants.

Doyle, Michael W. (1986b) *Empires* (Ithaca, NY: Cornell University Press). A comprehensive theoretical account on the history and analysis of empires from the ancient world until the twentieth century.

6. USEFUL WEBSITES

http://www.marxists.org/archive/lenin/works/1916/imp-hsc/. Lenin's *Imperialism, The Highest Stage of Capitalism* includes links to others of his works.

http://www.rosalux.de/cms/index.php?id=4892. The website of the Rosa Luxemburg Foundation maintains a section on its website on the 'American Empire' and offers an overview of other sources that publish on 'Empire'.

http://www.globalpolicy.org/empire.html. The independent Global Policy Forum, monitoring and scrutinizing global policy-making, with an 'Empire' section on its website offering resources on the debate on empires and the 'American Empire'.

Theory Concept: Feminism and Gender

1. CORE QUESTIONS ADDRESSED

- What are the three different generations of feminist International Relations?
- Why is the personal political?

- What makes gender an important analytical category in international politics?

2. OVERVIEW AND BACKGROUND

Feminism only began to properly engage in International Relations from the mid-1980s onwards when the context of the postpositivism, or fourth debate, opened up space for feminist works. Feminist International Relations is commonly distinguished into three waves or generations that build on, yet go beyond, other theories in the field (Sylvester 1994).

Preceding the fourth debate, the first wave of liberal feminism followed a decidedly empirical focus in calling attention to the under-representation and subordination of women in international relations in general and in positions of power and influence within international relations in particular (Tickner 2001). This under-representation also translated into academia and was perceived by liberal feminists as a vicious cycle: because there were not more women in IR academia, women were not on the IR agenda (Steans 2006). In contrast to later waves, liberal feminists have a rationalist background and follow the epistemological and methodological prescriptions of positivism. Topics such as income inequalities between men and women and human rights violations targeted at women are analysed by way of quantitative studies, and liberal feminists suggest that women's equality can be achieved by removing obstacles that denied them equal opportunities (Tickner and Sjoberg 2007: 189).

The second wave of the late 1980s, also termed *standpoint feminism*, was part of a general disputation of conventional International Relations, pointing alongside theories such as constructivism and postmodernism to the omissions and exclusions of the discipline. Second-wave feminism introduced people as agents to world politics and conceives of knowledge as socially situated, focusing on the specific contribution female knowledge and practice, coming out of the specific life experiences of women, can make to the transformation of international politics.

The breakthrough feminist contribution to International Relations, Cynthia Enloe's *Bananas, Beaches and Bases* (1989), falls within this second wave. Enloe draws attention to the many different roles women play in world politics, which, as they are not part of formal politics, have remained all but invisible in the discipline. This omission is however not due to women's insignificance in world politics but rather represents a choice of the discipline's neorealist and neoliberal mainstream

(→ *Theory Concept: Realism and Neorealism; Theory Concept: Liberalism and Neoliberalism.*) Enloe concludes that despite women's roles' informality, they are an integral part of international relations and thus need to be taken into account in scholars' quest towards understanding it. This constitutes an extension of the feminist credo 'the personal is political' to the international realm. Broader feminism from the 1970s pointed to two detrimental effects of separating between public and private spheres within a state: first, the separation assigns gender-specific connotations to the spheres, implying a hierarchical order in which the public, allegedly male, sphere trumps the female, private sphere. Second, and in line with Enloe, by being assigned the private realm, women are made invisible; their action and organization are excluded from what is worthy of politics, in other words, what is political (Elshtain 1981). As boundaries between the public and the private therefore reinforce patriarchal power structures, the personal had to be politicized, which is what feminists have been trying to do. On the international level the separation between domestic and international politics further obscures the prior gendered division between public and private spheres (True 2009: 247).

Feminist International Relations therefore seeks to undermine the common separation into different (→) levels of analysis by demonstrating how each level both is based on the image of the rational man and excludes women and femininity (True 2009: 248; Tickner 1992). Sylvester demonstrates this argument by analysing how the provision of national security, the core value of (→) realism, is an exclusively male domain. Being assigned to the comforting domestic roles of caring, women are by definition the object of protection by men and the state, rather than the subject with control over the conditions of their protection (Sylvester 1992: 28). This critique extends to the very model of the rational actor that pervades International Relations theory: feminists perceive of the rational actor as the masculine actor, stemming from a context of gender inequality that depends on the daily female provision of basic needs and care. Conceptualizing international actors as rational thereby again denies subjectivity to the plethora of actors who cannot be conceptualized in this way – including women (True 2009). This viewpoint has also met with criticism by other feminist authors arguing that drawing attention to the exclusion of women from the rational actor spectrum reproduces a problematic understanding of the feminine.

The main contribution of second-generation feminism was to integrate gender as a central analytical category into the study of International

Relations and its subfields such as foreign policy and the international political economy. Second-wave feminism was thus concerned with the 'gendering' of world politics. Gender refers to the social production of masculinity and feminity through life settings leading to experiences from birth that provide men and women with different worldviews. Taking gender seriously thus implies a complete reconceptualization of what international relations is 'all about'. Standpoint feminists therefore sought to uncover the masculine hegemony institutionalized in the social and political context of International Relations and the discipline's key concepts such as sovereignty.

Second-wave theorists were theoretically closely connected to Critical Theory, social constructivism and New Marxism. (→ *Theory Concept: Marxism and Critical Theory; Theory Concept: Social Constructivism.*) Critical feminism developed during the second wave and is still prevalent in feminist IR. It is set in the tradition of historical materialism, yet attributes significance to both material and ideational factors. Gender, as a social relation, is sought to work and produce inequality in much the same way as class structures. Critical feminists therefore combine researching global gender inequality with an interest in capitalism, trying to answer the key question of what role gender inequality plays and how it is reproduced (Steans 2007). Analogous to Critical Theory, scholars normatively aim for emancipation in their theorizing and actively promote the causes of universal human rights and women's interests in world politics. This becomes evident in their research interests, which include tracing the growth and development of women's networks and movements and their influence on international agenda-setting (Joachim 1999).

Finally, the third wave of feminism gave the category of gender a poststructuralist turn by focusing on the discursively constructed meaning of 'gender'. (→ *Theory Concept: Postmodernism and Poststructuralism.*) Scholars in this tradition turn towards uncovering gender discourses in International Relations, literally re-telling stories and narratives (Shepherd 2008). They thus emphasize the role that gender plays in the construction of boundaries on many levels and focus on how 'men' and 'women' are reproduced as meaningful categories through the practice of international relations, from their representation in debates about war or development to their construction in media representations of military exercises. To a poststructuralist feminist, there are no such things as women's interests – what we term women's interests is discursively produced. They therefore remain sceptical of emancipation and metanarratives such as universal human rights, as universalist claims are thought to emanate from a particular background – the universal is always particular. Instead of looking at possibilities for emancipation, poststructuralist feminists seek to identify structures of empowerment (Steans 2006).

While there are discernible different strands of feminism, all promote gender-sensitive knowledge in International Relations and closely examine the workings of gendered power. Their objectives are thus interrelated; they only depart from different ontological points, seeking to gain different kinds of knowledge.

3. METHODOLOGIES

True to the critical project, feminist methods of the second and third wave are clearly normative in nature: they seek to uncover how the very core concepts, such as power, war and security, employed in International Relations are themselves gendered (Tickner 1988; Sylvester 1992; Enloe 1996). Akin to critical theorists, feminists are thus concerned with problematizing and uncovering the construction of knowledge in the discipline. As the range of feminist scholarship in International Relations increased, scholars also began to formulate specifically feminist, commonly interpretivist, methodologies (Ackerley et al. 2006). Owing to their research interests, feminist works were at the forefront of postpositivism and apply methods associated with constructivism, poststructuralism, and postmodernism, such as deconstruction, discourse analysis and genealogy. Gender itself is understood as a transformative category: once its constructed nature is understood, the way it works can be transformed at all levels (True 2009: 253).

In the second wave of feminist International Relations, theorists also maintained that women's standpoint at the margins of world politics allows them a more critical understanding of the subject in comparison to realist perspectives (True 2009). This epistemological advantage is supposed to derive from an outlook less biased by global power relations: feminists approach International Relations 'from below' (Tickner 1992). This stance has however been met by criticism in later generations. First-wave feminists, in contrast, have used traditional positivist methods, as we have already argued above.

4. EMPIRICAL APPLICATIONS

From its very introduction to International Relations, it has been the central concern of feminist scholars to address the empirical neglect of women and gender relations through the enquiry into the empirical realities of women's experiences and their integration into theoretical perspectives. Studies containing empirical feminist viewpoints on international relations are thus manifold. Feminism's most decisive contributions to the study of International Relations stem from the application of gender to the international division of labour, international security and security discourses as well as international organizations. Feminists such as Saskia Sassen and Elisabeth Prügl concentrate on women's places as the 'intimate others' in economic globalization, as a cheap source of labour in the service of a masculinized corporate elite in urban centres (Sassen 1991; Prügl 1999). Other authors point out the ways in which international security and international thinking about war is inherently masculinized (Whitworth 2004; Tickner 1992). Carol Cohn, for example, argues in her famous article 'Sex and Death in the Rational World of Defense Intellectuals' that the masculinized culture and language of the defence community contributes to separating war from human emotion (1987). As an example of third-wave feminism, Laura Shepherd (2006) has traced the way in which gender was constructed in the legitimization of the US-led intervention in Afghanistan in response to 9/11, where the plight of women served as a core pillar in the justification of the war on terror.

5. CENTRAL CRITICISMS

Feminist International Relations has triggered two main points of controversy, both referring to gender as a category. First, a westernized, 'universal' concept of gender applied to 'third world' women may distort feminist explanation in again excluding other forms of oppression by levelling cultural, historical and geographical differences. If gender is indeed socially constructed, surely it cannot be the same in all parts of the world. Feminist authors of the third wave have countered this criticism in paying closer attention to a plethora of gender discourses from the local to the global levels (Miller 2001; Baines 1999; Prügl 1999) and in including constructions of class, nationality and race in analysing complex global power relations (Whitworth 1994, 2006; Chan-Tiberghien 2004). Second, feminists such as Sylvester have themselves criticized the feminist standpoint position at the margins, which is supposed to guarantee a more critical look at International Relations. Pointing to their socially constructed nature, to her, 'all places to speak and act as women are problematic' (Sylvester 1994: 12). Instead of claiming a universal moral 'high ground', Sylvester therefore sees the strength of feminism in providing a multiplicity of perspectives and voices to question the discipline's hegemonic knowledge (True 2009: 256).

6. CORE READING

Enloe, Cynthia (1989) *Bananas, Beaches and Bases: Making Feminist Sense of International Politics* (London: Pandora Press). Classical early work of feminist International Relations placing the personal narratives of women all over the world as firmly part of international security politics.

Steans, Jill (2006) *Gender and International Relations* (Oxford: Polity). Provides a brief and concise overview of feminist International Relations and its main fields of application.

Whitworth, Sandra (2004) *Men, Militarism and UN Peacekeeping: A Gendered Analysis* (Boulder, CO: Lynne Rienner). A feminist account of UN peacekeeping operations, exploring the detrimental impact of soldiers' 'hypermasculine' militarized identities on maintaining peace.

7. USEFUL WEBSITES

http://ftgss.blogspot.com. Blog of the Feminist Theory and Gender Studies Section (FTGSS) of the International Studies Association.

http://www.un.org/womenwatch. United Nations Inter-Agency Network on Women and Gender Equality website.

http://www.cddc.vt.edu/feminism. Feminist theory website hosted by the Center for Digital Discourse and Culture at Virginia Tech University; contains research materials and links to other websites.

https://journals.sfu.ca/thirdspace/index.php/journal/index. *Third Space*, journal of feminist theory and culture.

Foreign Policy Analysis

1. CORE QUESTIONS ADDRESSED

- How can we explain foreign policy decisions?
- How can the analyst contribute to the improvement of foreign policy?
- What are the implications of foreign policy for identity?

2. DEFINITIONS

Foreign policy in its traditional definition is the policy of a state towards external actors and especially other states. In contrast particularly to neorealism (→ *Theory Concept: Realism and Neorealism*), it therefore does not primarily look at the international system as such but offers an 'inside-out' perspective to understand the decision-making process *within* a state that produces policies directed *beyond* the state (→ *Levels of Analysis*).

This traditional definition has become more problematic over time, in particular in the light of (→) globalization and (→) regional integration. On the one hand, this has made it more difficult to draw clear boundaries between what is to be counted as 'domestic' and what is 'foreign'. In the setting of the European Union, for instance, many policy decisions are no longer taken purely within the member states, but have direct effect across the whole of the Union. The EU has also added an additional layer of foreign policy in that such policy is now conducted both on the member state and on the EU levels. On the other hand, non-state actors have increased their influence over foreign policy so that human rights, for instance, have become a field in which states and a network of national and transnational NGOs closely cooperate (and compete) with each other (Risse et al. 1999b).

None the less, the state remains at the heart of foreign policy. The focus on decision-making processes within the state is therefore still useful, even though one needs to take into account that the overall picture is a lot more complex.

3. THEORETICAL PERSPECTIVES

For classical realism (→ *Theory Concept: Realism and Neorealism*), foreign policy was a cornerstone in the study of international relations. In the words of Walter Lippmann (1943), foreign policy was 'the shield of the republic'. For realists, the task and the art of the statesman were to guide the 'ship' of the state through the 'rough sea' of the international system so that it was not conquered and life on board was well. Foreign policy was to guard the predominantly geopolitically defined interests of the state and maintain the balance of power through masterful diplomacy. The writings of the former United States Secretary of State, Henry Kissinger (e.g. 1957, 1994), can be seen as outstanding examples of this tradition, although his record in office is more contested (e.g. Hitchens 2002).

When International Relations as a discipline became more and more interested in explanation on the level of the system (→ *Levels of Analysis*) in the 1960s and 1970s, foreign policy analysis increasingly developed as a separate subdiscipline with its own discussions. These continued to be related to the debates in International Relations as a whole, but developed their own dynamic. For analysts of foreign policy, a focus on the properties of the system to explain particular outcomes such as war was insufficient. The task was to open up the 'black box' of the state and see how foreign policy decisions were arrived at.

One of the most influential works written during that period was Graham Allison's *Essence of Decision* (1971). In explaining the decisions by the United States and Soviet Union governments during the 1962 Cuban Missile Crisis, which brought the world to the brink of the Third World War, Allison argued that the prevailing 'rational actor model' to account for policy decisions was insufficient to offer a convincing answer to the question of why such decisions are taken. He proposed two additional models that analysts would have to consider: the 'organizational behaviour model' and the 'government politics model'. Broadly speaking, Allison alerted the discipline with these two models to the significance of bureaucracies. On the one hand, he treats these as machineries that operate on the basis of often unwritten codes and rules, the so-called 'standard operating procedures', that allow them to make sense of events and respond within known practices. On the other hand, the notion of a machinery is misleading to the extent that there are also different interests, for instance between different government departments such as those concerned with foreign policy, trade and defence, which lead to what is known as 'bureaucratic politics'. Both aspects undermine the rationality of the decision-making process.

The importance of Allison's work cannot be underestimated. During the 1970s in particular, there followed a variety of attempts to explain foreign policy through an inclusion of factors that constrain rationality. In addition to the workings of a bureaucracy, scholars focused primarily on psychological and cognitive factors. Among the former, the effect of stress under heavy time constraints plays a particularly important role, but also the question of personalities in interpersonal relationships among policy-makers (e.g. de Rivera 1968; Kinder and Weiss 1978). It was, however, the latter, cognitive factors that proved to be of particular importance not only for foreign policy analysis but also for the further development of the discipline as a whole.

The study of cognition tries to understand the way people think and arrive at decisions. The main argument of cognitive approaches is that it is important to recognize that foreign policy is ultimately made by individuals; that these individuals have to understand events in specific ways before they can react to them; and that they will have developed specific ways of thinking both to make sense of events and to devise possible responses. Two projects pursuing such an approach have become particularly famous. Robert Jervis (1976) argued that all events need to be 'perceived' by policy-makers and that the analyst has the task to distinguish between (correct) perceptions and 'misperceptions'. A group around Robert Axelrod (1976) developed the method of 'cognitive mapping' through which they tried to distil from interviews, speeches and other texts the core concepts with which a policy-maker works, and how they are interlinked in his or her thinking to lead to the assessment of the utility of possible policy actions. Similar concepts had been put forward earlier, for instance by Ole Holsti (1962, 'belief systems') and Alexander George (1967, 'operational code').

A strong motivation behind such approaches was not only to explain particular foreign policy decisions, but also to make them better by highlighting the biases and blind spots within a policy-maker's mind. Cognitive maps, for instance, could serve as an instrument for self-reflection. Alas, in the end, the complexity of such maps and the time therefore involved in drawing them meant that their success in the world of practitioners remained limited.

These attempts to include cognition in the analysis did however ultimately open the door to other approaches that came to the fore from the 1980s onwards under the umbrella of constructivist and reflectivist approaches (→ *Theory Concept: Social Constructivism; Theory Concept: Postmodernism and Poststructuralism*). On the one hand, the focus on cognition fed into attempts to explain foreign policy at least in part through the importance of ideas in the policy-making process. In the work of Goldstein and Keohane (1993), for instance, ideas are defined as 'beliefs held by individuals' and therefore can be seen as cognitive concepts (→ *Ideas and Norms*). On the other hand, a number of people from Axelrod's group later reflected on their work and argued that in fact, they had not really mapped a decision-maker's 'inner thoughts' but rather a (→) discourse in which the decision-maker had been participating. To infer from this map that these were what the decision-maker actually thought, would be an untenable assumption (Bonham et al. 1987). This led to studies of foreign policy from new angles, including more critical approaches that focused on the problematization of core assumptions and practices within foreign policy discourses rather than the explanation of individual policies (e.g. Campbell 1998), although the latter was still pursued even from discursive perspectives (e.g. Larsen 1997; Wæver 2002).

Many foreign policy analysts nowadays combine different factors in their explanation of foreign policies. One of the first to provide a comprehensive matrix of variables influencing foreign policy decision-making was James Rosenau (1967, 1980). Later, notions such as that of a 'foreign policy system' (Clarke and White 1989) also tried to integrate different approaches within a coherent framework. The advantage of such overarching approaches is that they intuitively make sense – it seems unlikely that actors act only according to rational criteria in a given situation or that they only give in to their feelings. However, there is a trade-off with parsimony, and many crucial insights in foreign policy analysis would not have been possible without the more radical approaches that emphasized one factor over others.

4. EMPIRICAL PROBLEMS

An interesting empirical problem that also further illustrates the development of foreign policy analysis is the relationship of foreign policy and identity. In the classical realist account of foreign policy, the identity of a nation (and that of others) was given and had to be defended through foreign policy. With the rise of cognitive and psychological approaches, authors such as Kenneth Boulding (1959) stressed the role of national stereotypes in decision-making, and argued that images of one's own identity and that of other nations often lead to misjudgements and consequently misguided policies, and eventually possibly war. Clearly, such images were important aspects of cognitive maps and misperceptions. Following this argument, a great number of scholars pursued the problem of the impact of 'enemy images' in conflict and war.

It was David Campbell (1998) who offered a more radical reformulation of the relationship between foreign policy and national identity. For Campbell, national identity was no longer a given as in classical realist thought. Instead, foreign policy served in part at least to construct such an identity through the representation of an 'other' without which national identities (and identities in general) would be meaningless. Campbell saw the institutionalized, state-centred form of foreign policy analysis as part of a broader practice of foreign policy that was 'foreign policy' to the extent that it represented something or a group of people as 'foreign', as 'alien' to the nation, in other words, it 'made' something 'foreign'. This construction of the 'foreign' did not have to be directed at other states or actors in the international realm, but could also take place domestically, within the confines of state borders, in the representation of minorities and other socially marginalized groups. Campbell's work provides a very different perspective on foreign policy that questions from a theoretical perspective the difference between the state and the international that we already problematized in the introduction to this entry.

5. CORE READING

Allison, Graham and Philip Zelikow (1999) *Essence of Decision: Explaining the Cuban Missile Crisis* (New York: Longman). A classic that develops alternatives to the rational-actor model in foreign policy analysis; this is a revised and updated edition, the original appearing in 1971.

Campbell, David (1998) *Writing Security: US Foreign Policy and the Politics of Identity* (Minneapolis: University of Minnesota Press, 2nd edn). This book is not normally seen as part of the canon on foreign policy analysis, but it does deliver a radical reformulation of foreign policy from a poststructuralist perspective that has had an impact throughout International Relations.

Clarke, M. and B. White (eds) (1989) *Understanding Foreign Policy: The Foreign Policy Systems Approach* (Aldershot: Edward Elgar). An attempt to draw various strands of foreign policy analysis together in a systemic theory.

Recommended is also the journal *Foreign Policy Analysis*.

6. USEFUL WEBSITES

www.fpa.org. Home of the US-based Foreign Policy Association.
http://www.brookings.edu/foreign-policy.aspx. The foreign policy portal of the US thinktank the Brookings Institution.
http://www.fpri.org/. Home of the US-based Foreign Policy Research Institute.
http://fpc.org.uk/. Home of the UK thinktank the Foreign Policy Centre.
http://fpwatch.blogspot.com/. A blog devoted to foreign policy.

Functionalism

1. CORE QUESTIONS ADDRESSED

- How can we best achieve lasting peace?
- How can the power of states be constrained?
- What role does expertise play in international/global governance?

2. DEFINITIONS

Functionalism is an approach that is used in different areas, from sociology to architecture. Despite their differences, all functionalists – as the name suggests – emphasize the function of an entity. Thus, in sociology, functionalists explain the existence of social structures with societal needs. In architecture and design, functionalists became known for the slogan that 'form follows function', rather than, for instance, criteria of beauty.

In International Relations, functionalism became largely associated with the work of David Mitrany during and after the Second World War. Like many of his contemporaries, Mitrany considered nationalism and the political organization of societies in nation-states to be the main problem behind Europe's war-torn history. In order to achieve peace, he advocated the rise and spread of functional organizations where international problems would be tackled by those affected by and having expertise about them. He thus followed the functionalist slogan in that he considered the territorial state not to be the adequate form of political organization to address many problems under conditions of increased interdependency. Instead, different problems needed different instruments, and it would be up to those involved in providing a solution to a problem to decide on the concrete institutional framework in which such a solution would be formulated and implemented: 'That trend is to organize government along the lines of specific ends and needs, and according to the conditions of their time and place . . . ' (Mitrany 1966: 54).

3. THEORETICAL PERSPECTIVES

Functionalism as an approach in International Relations is not only central to the study of international integration (→ *Regional Integration*).

Functionalism stands in the liberal tradition (→ *Theory Concept: Liberalism and Neoliberalism*) and follows the conceptualization of politics as a result of the struggle to satisfy individual and societal needs. Therefore, the focus lies on cooperation between a variety of actors across national boundaries, caused by common interests and needs within an interdependent global system. Functionalism does not treat the nation-state and therefore the international system as an ontological given, and instead is seeking ways to overcome the organization of politics in sovereign states. The central point within the functionalist argumentation remains the so-called 'spill-over'. 'Spill-over' is an effect whereby the cooperations and decisions made with regard to a specific issue area have unintended implications for another issue area. The reduction of greenhouse gases for environment protection purposes, for example, always implicates economic consequences for affected industries. Because of interdependence between issue areas, 'spill-overs' cannot be avoided, leading automatically to a deeper cooperation. Furthermore, and again following the liberal tradition of International Relations, functionalists believe in the possibility of achieving peaceful progress by overcoming the cost–benefit calculation of egoistic individuals through reason and morality. Consequently, most scholars consider functionalism as composed of a rational-technocratic element as well as of a normative component, while pointing out that functionalism emphasizes the role of experts and technocrats and assuming that public welfare might be better and more efficiently provided by functional institutions rather than by national governments (Conzelmann 2006: 145; Rosamond 2000: 31–4).

The most immediate opponent of functionalism is federalism. Federalism rejects the assumption of effective and efficient international institutions created only according to functional requirements by postulating the idea of a territorial entity, composed of nation-states as constituent political units and a central government authority. Within a federal state, power is constitutionally divided between the units and the central authority, often according to the principle of subsidiary and national security considerations.

Behind the functionalism–federalism controversy stand two very different strategies towards peace. While the classical federalist emphasizes the need for constitutional processes on a high politics level, supported by a broad federalist movement, functionalists argue that such a strategy will not work because the nation-state is too tied up with the identities and interests of political actors and the public. Thus, integration ought to focus on low politics, 'undercover' so to speak, from where technical linkages and the realization that integration is good will lead integration processes to 'spill over' into other areas, including, ultimately, high politics.

It was Ernst B. Haas (1968) who advanced the theory of functionalism by focusing on the socio-scientific explanation of existing integration processes among states, as for instance the European integration process. His theory of neofunctionalism seeks answers to questions such as why states start to build up cooperation through integration, if different phases of integration can be distinguished, and by which mechanisms economic integration is followed by political integration, creating a 'political community' (→ *Regional Integration*). Furthermore, he emphasizes the specific role of supranational institutions for the success of an integration process (Haas 1968: 16).

4. EMPIRICAL PROBLEMS

There are two main strands of criticism of functionalism. The first strand focuses on the notion that social needs are objectively given and can be met through technocratic expertise. Against this, critics argued that societal demands should be considered as political issues and therefore as highly conflictive. Consequently, when we think of needs and goods in competition with each other, the postulated mechanism of appropriate institutional design resulting from functional requirements appears less evident. More fundamentally, further critique challenges the assumption that public representatives, experts and people in general act rationally. This undermines the idea of 'expert' solutions to problems of transnational governance. A second strand of criticism sees functionalism to be driven too much by normative concerns, and argues that it is insufficiently 'scientific': not only did scholars attest that functionalism, especially in the classic version of Mitrany, has a lack of methodological concerns, but also his approach appears to have a poor prediction record, especially if the European integration process is considered, which resulted rather from regional tendencies than functional requirements. Additionally, although certain tendencies of the globalization process might have weakened the state's capacities of shaping and influencing, certain outcomes in politics remains valid. People's loyalty towards the nation-state appears not to be diminished by the creation of functional transnational institutions (Rosamond 2000: 38–42).

functionalism

65

5. CORE READING

Haas, Ernst B. (1964) *Beyond the Nation-State: Functionalism and International Organization* (Stanford: Stanford University Press). Elaborates functional explanations for transnational integration processes such as the integration of the European Union.

Mitrany, David (1966) *A Working Peace System* (Chicago: Quadrangle Books). Introduces the basic functional arguments with regard to the establishment of international institutions.

Taylor, Paul (1968) 'The Functionalist Approach to the Problem of International Order: A Defence', *Political Studies* 16 (3), 393–410. As the title suggests, a rebuttal of some of the criticisms of functionalism, including responses to the charge that it is not practicable and does not work.

6. USEFUL WEBSITES

http://globetrotter.berkeley.edu/people/Haas/haas-con0.html. Interview with Ernst B. Haas in the 'Conversations with History' series by UC Berkeley.

Game Theory

1. CORE QUESTIONS ADDRESSED

- What are the most important components of game theory?
- Why might game theory be useful for the social sciences in general and International Relations specifically?
- What are the main cooperation problems as identified by game theory?

2. DEFINITIONS

Originating in mathematics, game theory has been applied to the social sciences since John Von Neumann and Oskar Morgenstern's 1944 classic *Theory of Games and Economic Behavior*. It provides a formal modelling approach for so-called 'problematic social situations' in that it depicts strategic choices of and interaction between agents, or players as they are referred to in game theory (Colman 1982). Those players, being rational, seek to maximize their benefit within a situation while considering the interaction of their own strategies with those the other agents involved are likely to choose. Players thus act according to 'strategic rationality'; they 'choose courses of action based on preferences and expectations how others will behave' while being aware of their alternatives (Snidal 1985: 39). In International Relations and political science in general, the interdependent, goal-seeking players of game theory are usually nation-states.

In their essence, the models of game theory are 'highly abstract representations of classes of real-life situations' (Osborne and Rubinstein 1998: 1). Social situations are reduced to their most fundamental characteristics and thereby classified as a certain type of game. Classes of games contain a number of assumptions (i.e. who are the players, what are their strategies and what are their pay-offs?) and predictions (i.e. what is the outcome of the game?). These assumptions and predictions are depicted in the form of matrixes that denote the strategy of each player in relation to the strategy of the other player and the expected pay-offs. Although games can involve a varying number of players and strategies, in its simplest and most commonly used form, game theory uses 2 × 2 matrixes, detailing respectively two strategy options for two players. These strategies are usually labelled 'cooperate' (C) or 'not cooperate'/ 'defect' (D). Models further establish a preference order for each player – outcomes are ranked from best to worst, or from highest to lowest pay-off for the respective player. The matrix structure of game theory further presumes rather stable preferences on the part of the players – confronted with comparable choices, the players are assumed to behave consistently. The predictions regarding the outcome of the game are related to so-called 'Nash equilibria' within games. Players are in an equilibrium if a change in strategies by any one of them would lead that player to earn less than if they remained with their current strategy. In other words, a Nash equilibrium characterizes an interactional outcome in which no player regrets their choice after having seen the other player's choice. Because in this situation no player has the incentive to unilaterally change their action, it is a stable situation. The equilibrium thus denotes the predicted outcome of the game. Classes of games differ in the number of equilibria they contain.

Through understanding the problematic dynamics inherent to social interaction, game theory seeks to provide an explanation for the optimal decision within an interdependent decision situation. Game theoretical approaches point to the problems possibly hindering cooperation in illustrating that the individual optimum within a problematic social situation frequently does not coincide with the collective optimum, also termed the 'Pareto optimum'. The outcome of a game is Pareto optimal, sometimes also termed Pareto efficient, if there is no other outcome that leaves at least one player better off but leaves no player worse off; in short, a state in which each player has a strategy that does best regardless of the other player's choice. In contrast to the Nash equilibrium, the Pareto optimum does not relate to a predicted likely outcome of the game but rather to the optimal collective outcome. Indeed, a Nash equilibrium is often not Pareto optimal, implying that the players' pay-offs can all be increased. Keeping this difference in mind, game theory is considered a helpful tool in explaining why international cooperation sometimes fails although it would be in the interest of all players or states to cooperate.

The type of games that are most relevant to political science and International Relations are so-called mixed motive games: the players' interests are in partial conflict with each other, and as such, the realization of one player's gains is neither always at the other's expense (this would be termed a zero-sum game) nor do their preferences always exactly coincide (this would be a pure coordination game). The players are thus constantly torn between conflict and cooperation.

Further prerequisites that differentiate types of games include the possibility of communication and if a game is played just once ('one-shot game') or repeatedly ('iterated game'). In contrast to one-shot games, players in iterated games follow a strategy previously determining which move is to be chosen for which situation. 'Tit for tat' is an example for such a strategy in an iterated game: here, a player initially cooperates and on the next move replies with the same move (cooperate or defect) the other player made on their previous move (Alker 1996: 303). Iterated games demand a more complex strategy than one-shot games and are susceptive to factors such as the 'shadow of the future' cast by a credible threat of future retaliation (Dal Bó 2005).

3. THEORETICAL PERSPECTIVES

Game theory is closely associated with rationalist theories of International Relations, such as neoliberalism (→ *Theory Concept: Liberalism and Neoliberalism*) and has been connected to a variety of its subfields such as military-strategic political analysis, the study of negotiation (→ Diplomacy), international political economy and (→) international regimes.

Scholars differentiate between four kinds of social situations marked by ideal types of cooperation problems that are used to explain actors' choices in International Relations; these are associated with a typical scenario description: assurance games (e.g. Stag Hunt), coordination games (e.g. Battle of the Sexes), collaboration games (e.g. Prisoner's Dilemma) and suasion games (e.g. Rambo Games). There are two 'prototypical' cooperation problems inherent to these situations: a collaboration problem, present in the assurance game and the collaboration game, and a coordination problem, present in the coordination and the suasion game (Stein 1983). In contrast to collaboration problems, coordination problems typically contain distributional conflict on account of actors' asymmetrical interests.

Game theory involving a collaboration problem has been applied to the negotiation of the General Agreement on Tariffs and Trade (GATT) and the Strategic Arms Limitation Talks (SALT), and is able to explain why international cooperation sometimes fails although it would be in the interest of all players. The Prisoner's Dilemma as an illustration of a collaborative problem is used for modelling arms races but also to illustrate decision-making in collective security actions and global resource management. Game theory involving coordination problems has been applied to negotiation processes. Thomas Schelling, for example, expounded on a series of negotiation or bargaining techniques that can be expected of the two players in coordination problem situations (1960). Schelling's work points to the mainstream usage of game theory: knowledge of the situational structures permits finding or rather deducing 'uniquely rational solutions to problems of choice' (Bennett 1995: 26, emphasis in original).

Looking closer at the two ideal types of cooperation problems, the collaboration problem is characterized by 'situations in which equilibrium outcomes are suboptimal' (Martin 1992: 769). Collaboration problems are present in the assurance game and the collaboration game and contain an element of uncertainty with respect to the player's preferences. Both describe situations in which the collective optimum is not reached because it is individually rational to defect. The more problematic is the collaboration game, usually illustrated by the Prisoner's Dilemma as the most widely studied game in International Relations literature. The name derives from a story where two conspirators are arrested and interrogated separately, left with the choices of remaining silent or implicating the other. While the sentence for both would be only minor if they both maintained silence, the sentence the silent one would receive if the other implicates him would be major. In the matrix in Figure 1, the countries A and B each have two strategies, namely arm (defection) or disarm (cooperation). The matrix below depicts the players' – Country A and Country B – possible strategies and preference orders, while those for Country A are left in each cell (4 = best option, 1 = worst option). The model assumes that both countries would most like to gain an advantage over the other country (arm while the other disarms); would least like to disarm while the other's arms; and would prefer mutual disarmament (3/3) to an arms race – this is the game's Pareto optimum.

		Country B	
		Cooperation	Defection
Country A	Cooperation	3/3 P	1/4
	Defection	4/1	2/2 N

Figure 1   *Prisoner's Dilemma and arms negotiations*

Each player has a dominant strategy to defect in a single game. The resulting Nash equilibrium is dominated by an alternate outcome (2/2 N), while the collective optimum (3/3 P) can only be reached by cooperation. Mutual cooperation would be more beneficial for both players than mutual defection, but there is an incentive not to stick to the cooperative agreement while the other party remains in it. To solve the dilemma situation, both players have to mutually adjust their strategies, thereby moving away from the suboptimal outcome but also rejecting their dominant strategy (Martin 1992: 769). If it is played as an iterated game, the cooperative move (3/3) could also be individually rational because of the 'shadow of the future'.

In contrast to collaboration problems, situations with coordination problems usually contain asymmetrical preference orders that lead to distributional conflict. The first type, the coordination game, has two possible outcomes one of which is preferred by each of the players. Either equilibrium is preferred by both players to any of the non-equilibrium outcomes – both have a dominant strategy to cooperate. The problematic social situation contains little incentive to defect from the resulting cooperative agreement (common aversion to defect), while conflicts over the precise mode of operation might be obstacles. The coordination problem may be solved through an institution that defines the rules and norms of cooperation. Finally, suasion games are useful to analyse situations with pronounced asymmetrical interests of the players. These asymmetries derive either from differential capacities and dependencies of the players or from differential attributions of utility. Either way, they are frequently expressions of an asymmetrical distribution of power as one player is pursuing a dominant strategy regardless of what the other player is doing. Suasion games are illustrated with variants of the Rambo Game: two flatmates have a dispute over cleaning the flat, with one player having high preferences for not cleaning and the other for cleaning (cleaning equals cooperation). Further, the flatmate who has a preference for not cleaning, the Rambo, would also prefer not having the cleaning done at all to them cleaning. The Rambo's preference order (defection as the dominant strategy) determines the game's outcome, leaving the other player dissatisfied. A solution to this kind of social situation is difficult as the Rambo has a high incentive to defect, and it can only be imagined if the Rambo's preference order could be changed through either issue-linkage or side-payments.

Most game theoretical models applied to international relations take unitary nation-states as their main 'players'. Newer developments in game theory, most notably the models by Bueno de Mesquita, criticize this unitary concept and instead propose to look at the preferences of individual decision-makers within countries. In his so-called expected utility model, Bueno de Mesquita follows this methodological individualism, forecasting how players will interact on an issue at hand and who will concede to whom, by looking at how each player perceives their relationship with each other player, what proposals the players make to each other, and how willing the players are to take risks (1981, 2002, 2009; Feder 2002). The computer-based model, dependent on expert inputs based on intensive interviews, is designed to predict policy decisions and outcomes and has been found to be able to successfully predict diverse cases such as the 1984 successors of Ayatollah Khomeini in Iran, earning Bueno de Mesquita the nickname of 'the new Nostradamus'.

There have also been innovative applications of game theory outside the rationalist framework, for example by Jon Elster, who combines game theory with Marxism to explain the micro-foundations for the study of class struggle, social structure and social change (2003: 36), and Hayward Alker, who, in going beyond positivist knowledge, claims to include verbal accounts and the construction of narratives in the study of Prisoner's Dilemma scenarios (1996).

game theory

4. EMPIRICAL PROBLEMS

As game theory has been around for more than 50 years, it has received its fair share of criticism – mainly in relation to how it portrays or rather simplifies reality, the logical errors it contains, and the specific understanding of rationality it implies.

The oversimplification of game theoretical models is, perhaps, the most frequent criticism it encounters. Game theorists find themselves accused of 'squeezing' the world into a rather static matrix that will necessarily disregard information that may be relevant to understand the situation such as details about the context of interaction, insights into the personalities and behaviour of decision-makers, understandings about the diplomatic or foreign policy process, issues that may be linked to the issue in question, differing perceptions of the players and so on. Bringing in these dimensions, as well as more than two players, would necessitate the usage of advanced mathematical models – something that has only been done by social scientists in a small number of studies as it requires elaborate mathematical knowledge. Steven Brams points to a number of other 'pitfalls' inherent to the logic of conventional game theory in International Relations, such as mis-specifying the rules. Brams suggests that game theory is wrong in assuming that players choose strategies simultaneously or independently of each other – instead, 'game-theoretical models should propose rules of play that reflect how players think and act in the strategic situation being modelled' (2000: 1). From a poststructuralist and a communicative action angle, game theory has been criticized for perpetuating the construction of realist discourse. (→ *Theory Concept: Postmodernism and Poststructuralism; Theory Concept: Marxism and Critical Theory.*) Portraying wars and conflicts as strategic games which are to be won and lost forecloses perceiving of cooperation as an action possibility (Hurwitz 1989; Müller 1995).

5. CORE READING

Bueno de Mesquita, Bruce (2002) *Predicting Politics* (Columbus, OH: Ohio State University Press). Offers ways of predicting political outcomes through using computerized game models, by one of the most important authors of game theory.

Colman, Andrew M. (1982) *Game Theory and Experimental Games: The Study of Strategic Interaction* (Oxford: Pergamon Press). Provides a concise and readable survey of ideas relevant to game theory including political and philosophical applications.

Hurwitz, Roger (1989) 'Strategic and Social Fictions in the Prisoner's Dilemma', in James Der Derian and Michael J. Shapiro (eds), *International/Intertextual Relations: Postmodern Readings of World Politics* (New York: Lexington Books), 113–34. A poststructuralist critique of the most widely used game theoretical scenario in International Relations.

6. USEFUL WEBSITES

www.gametheory.net. Provides resource materials to educators and students of game theory.

http://homepage.newschool.edu/het/schools/game.htm. Game theory section of the *History of Economic Thought* website.

http://plato.stanford.edu/entries/prisoner-dilemma. Article from the *Stanford Encyclopedia of Philosophy* provides varieties of the Prisoner's Dilemma.

Global Governance

1. CORE QUESTIONS ADDRESSED

- What is governance on a global scale?
- What are the differences between governance and government?
- What kind of new governance mechanisms are there and which functions are they assumed to perform?

2. DEFINITIONS

The concept of global governance denotes a system of rule on the global scale, composed of formal global governmental institutions as well as informal non-governmental mechanisms. Global governance can thus be performed by a number of actors: by states within multilateral cooperation agreements such as the G8; by intergovernmental organizations such as the United Nations or (→) international regimes such as the Climate Change Regime; and by non-state actors, either in cooperation with states or by themselves, for instance through international campaigns such as the International Campaign to Ban Landmines (ICBL) or through public–private partnerships such as the Global Fund to Fight

AIDS, Tuberculosis and Malaria ('the Global Fund'). The concept of global governance therefore implies a perceptible shift in authority, reflecting the fact that the Westphalian state system is no longer the only source of authority and (→) power in contemporary world politics.

In 1992, UN Secretary-General Boutros Boutros-Ghali initiated a Commission on Global Governance, aiming to 'identify the major challenges confronting humanity at the turn of the millennium and to think about ways in which these challenges could be met' (Wilkinson 2005: 9). The report, which drew widespread attention to the concept of global governance, defines it as: 'the sum of many ways individuals and institutions, public and private, manage their common affairs; [. . .] a continuing process through which conflicting or diverse interests may be accommodated and co-operative action taken' (the Commission on Global Governance 2005: 26). Moreover, the report acknowledges the changing nature of authority and the emergence of new sources of authority by other actors, concluding that the best way to meet the challenges of the twenty-first century is to harness the potentials of these new actors under the guidance and supervision of the UN system (Wilkinson 2005: 9).

Fundamental to the understanding of global governance is the distinction between governance and government. James Rosenau argues that while both terms refer to a system of rule, only the notion of government implies activities that are backed up by formal authority to ensure the implementation of policies and the observation of law (Rosenau 1992: 3). International Relations, and social sciences as a whole for that matter, have been accustomed to identifying government with the state. Governance, by contrast, implies 'the capacity to get things done without the legal competence to demand that they be done' (Czempiel 1992: 250). Rosenau goes on to take a rather 'positive' stance on governance, defining it as a system of rules that always requires the acceptance of a majority. In contrast, government functions can also be performed against widespread opposition. Therefore, he concludes, it 'is possible to conceive of governance without government – of regulatory mechanisms in a sphere of activity which function effectively even though they are not endowed with formal authority' (Rosenau and Czempiel 1992: 4–5). Critical perspectives to International Relations have connected the Foucauldian notion of governmentality to the government – governance debate as an alternative way of thinking about governing, or, in other words, of thinking about relations of power. Governmentality, the 'conduct of conduct' in Foucault's words, examines subtle ways by which societies and populations are governed. If the notion of government is directly connected to the state and the notion of governance is all about governing beyond the state, governmentality is concerned with examining the rationalities and technologies of governing – within this system of thought, the state is rather an effect of practices of governing and just one actor to examine. Governmentality assumes that the acts of governing always involve 'particular representations, knowledges, and expertise regarding that which is to be governed' (Larner and Walters 2004: 496). The practice of governing thus involves the production of truth about those governed, and examining these very practices opens up critical insights into the constitution of both the governed and the governing.

3. THEORETICAL PERSPECTIVES

Theoretical applications of the global governance concept generally stem from liberal approaches to International Relations. (→ *Theory Concept: Liberalism and Neoliberalism.*) For realist scholars, the very 'idea of a realist theory of international governance is a contradiction in terms' (Gilpin 2002: 237) as it would indicate a situation in which the defining (→) anarchical nature of the international system no longer exists. Thus, the realist stance on international governance is, if existent, by necessity critical. This relates especially to the pivotal problem of power and its abuse that to realist minds lacks sufficient attention in the global governance debate. Referencing Hedley Bull, Robert Gilpin concludes that a system of global governance would thus be ultimately controlled and dominated by the world's most powerful state, the global hegemon USA, creating a dangerous system of tyranny to which the balanced state system within anarchy is infinitely preferable (Gilpin 2002: 246–7).

In contrast, liberal authors see global governance as a means of governing in situations of global interdependence in the absence of a world state or another global political body. Liberal research on global governance continues within its long-established tradition of analysing the interaction of states and actors such as international institutions. Here, global governance speaks to the question of world order and is cast as an alternative to the hierarchical concepts of (→) hegemony (Mearsheimer 2001) and a world state (Höffe 2007) deemed empirically inappropriate. Instead, global governance refers to a network of global institutions and actors, which aims to fulfil central governance tasks on a global scale without being backed up by a central global authority. It seeks to fill an explanatory omission in accounting for a changing global order in proffering how anarchy can be overcome without resulting in a hierarchical type of government either by a hegemon or a world government (Holsti 1992: 55–6). Authors within the liberal tradition have moreover been concerned with the effectiveness of global governance and how it may be increased, paying special attention to how networks of different actors may contribute to solving global problems. This idea of network governance has been particularly prominent in relation to global environmental problems. Liberal accounts of these network institutions, such as the so-called public–private partnerships (PPPs), contain (→) functionalist reasoning in that they see their emergence as being connected to governance gaps on the global scale, i.e. deficiencies in global public policy-making, which they aim to close.

Most theoretical approaches to global governance imply normative notions in that they are concerned with how the world is governed and how it might be governed instead (Wilkinson 2007: 344). This vein is particularly explicit in critical IR perspectives on global governance. Both Marxist and feminist approaches, for example, consider the issues of power and structural constraints within global governance (Callinicos 2002). (→ *Theory Concept: Marxism and Critical Theory; Theory Concept: Feminism and Gender.*) Drawing attention to the role of the World Bank and the International Monetary Fund (IMF), Marxist scholar Paul Cammack thus perceives of global governance as a capitalist project aimed at the 'global imposition of the social relations and disciplines central to capitalist reproduction' (2005: 156). Feminist scholars point to possibilities of using the structures and processes of global governance for the sake of emancipation (Steans 2007).

4. EMPIRICAL PROBLEMS

While more 'traditional' types of global governance, such as governance by international organizations or regimes, have been around since the end of the Second World War, new global governance mechanisms, such as PPPs, only emerged at the beginning of the new millennium. PPPs are spread out throughout all issue-areas of world politics, with a concentration on health and environmental issues – the Global Fund or the Forest Stewardship Council are primary examples. Authors distinguish four broad forms of public–private partnerships according to their functions: norm- and standard-setting PPPs, advocating PPPs, service-providing PPPs and norm-implementing PPPs (Börzel and Risse 2005; Kaul 2006; Reinicke and Deng 2000).

As has been alluded to before, new governance mechanisms are supposed to help close governance gaps that resulted and result from the (→) globalization process. Kaul, Grunberg and Stern (1999: xxvi–xxvii) identify four of these gaps: a jurisdictional, an operational, an incentive and a participatory gap. The operational governance gap is generally identified as the most explicit of the four. It is supposed to originate from a discrepancy between the amount of information and policy instruments available to a 'traditional' governance institution and those which would be needed in order to fulfil its governance function. Following the assumption that neither states nor conventional international organizations are able to tackle the closure of these gaps on their own and the resources and capabilities of non-state actors such as transnational corporations and non-governmental organizations are needed. This perceived need justifies their access to international governance institutions. Kaul even argues that the inclusion of non-state actors could not only help to fill these operational gaps but also that the global governance process would become more transparent and democratic by including different types of actors representing different types of interests and opinions (2006: 257).

Beyond liberals' positive take, the effectiveness and legitimacy of these new types of governance mechanisms remains disputed. The increased influence of non-state actors on world politics comes with considerable risks attached: on a functionalist level, the more players are involved in a 'game', the higher the coordination costs. Many authors do not agree with liberal scholars' hope for a more democratic global governance through the influence of non-state actors on a more fundamental level. Critics state that most of these new non-state actors are themselves neither democratic nor legitimate. Rather, they represent a specific patronage while not bound to democratic accountability, such as government representatives (e.g. Keohane 2005: 128ff.). Owing to the fact that most new types of global governance mechanisms have only been created in the early 2000s, and evaluations of their performance are tentative, questions of legitimacy and effectiveness remain unanswered.

5. CORE READING

Rosenau, James and Ernst-Otto Czempiel (eds) (1992) *Governance Without Government: Order and Change in World Politics* (Cambridge: Cambridge University Press). Early influential collection of articles on questions of global governance and world order from the 'big names' in the field.

Wilkinson, Rordon (ed.) (2005) *The Global Governance Reader* (London: Routledge). Comprehensively compiles diverse and important contributions in global governance literature from the early 1990s to the late 2000s.

Kaul, Inge, Isabelle Grunberg and Marc A. Stern (1999) *Global Public Goods. International Organizations in the 21st Century* (Oxford: Oxford University Press). Early liberal contribution to the study of PPPs in global governance.

6. USEFUL WEBSITES

http://www.gppi.net. The Global Public Policy Institute, a European thinktank aiming to develop innovative approaches to effective and accountable governance.

http://www.globalgovernancewatch.org. A joint project of the American Enterprise Institute (AEI) and the Federalist Society for Law and Public Policy Studies which offers legal resources, commentaries, and academic papers related to global governance.

http://www.cfr.org/thinktank/iigg. International Institutions and Global Governance Program at the Council on Foreign Relations (CFR) which aims to identify the institutional requirements for effective multilateral cooperation in the twenty-first century.

Globalization

1. CORE QUESTIONS ADDRESSED

- What defines the contemporary globalization process?
- How does globalization relate to 'fragmegration' and localization?
- What are the central debates in the globalization context?

2. DEFINITIONS

The term globalization became very popular after the end of the Cold War as a 'catch-all' concept describing the widespread perception of the world as merging into a shared global economic and social space, a process caused by information technologies and an increased degree of interdependency. Terms such as global markets or global problems became part of professional and day-to-day conversations of scientists, politicians, businessmen and journalists (Scholte 2005: 51; Held et al. 1999: 1–3).

Despite the concept's omnipresence, the matter of its definition is still the object of controversial discussions. Debate mainly turns around the dual desire of remaining true to globalization's comprehensive nature and aiming for a precise definition (Scholte 2005: 51). Definitions thus fall in broad or narrow categories. Broadly defined, globalization is 'a process (or set of processes) which embodies a transformation in the spatial organisation of social relations and transactions – assessed in terms of their extensity, intensity, velocity and impact – generating transcontinental or interregional flows and networks of activity, interaction, and the exercise of power' (Held et al. 1999: 16). This comprehensive conceptualization allows for the inclusion of different scopes and densities of globalization in various regions of the world at different times. It does not level globalization into a process occurring at the same time and in the same way all over the world. In contrast to this broad definition, Robert Gilpin narrowly defines globalization as a worldwide process of economic integration resting on political foundations: it is 'the increasing linkage of national economies through trade, financial flows and foreign direct investment (FDI) by multinational firms' (2000: 299). Consequently, Gilpin argues in favour of strong political regulations correcting market failures and especially financial flows, thus keeping the process of globalization under political control.

The antonym of globalization as an integrative, boundary-eroding process is the concept of localization, which 'derives from all these pressures that lead people, groups, societies, governments, institutions, and transnational organizations to narrow their horizons and withdraw to less encompassing processes, organizations or systems' (Rosenau 1997: 81), thereby strengthening existing boundaries or replacing them with political entities on a smaller scale, such as cities or regions. The intertwined processes of globalization and localization, or integration and fragmentation, produce a 'mismatch between the extension of transnational activities and a lag in governing capacity of states' (Rosenau 1997: 81). James N. Rosenau coined the neologism 'fragmegration' to capture this phenomenon, while Roland Robertson spoke of 'glocalization' (Robertson 1995).

globalization

79

3. THEORETICAL PERSPECTIVES

Theoretical debates about globalization mainly turn around the origins and the consequences of the contemporary globalization process, especially concerning the capability of states to act, solve national and international problems or provide national and global public goods. Held et al. (1999: 1–10) distinguish between three different theoretical understandings of the globalization process or waves of globalization theory provided by so-called hyperglobalists, sceptics and transformationalists. These three understandings cannot be unequivocally linked to the main theories of International Relations (Held et al. 1999: 2). While, for instance, the arguments of neoliberal as well as of new Marxist scholars can be subsumed within the so-called hyperglobalists, the assumptions and conclusions of 'conventional' and critical voices in International Relations theory appear not to differ that much within the sceptics of the contemporary globalization. (→ *Theory Concept: Marxism and Critical Theory; Theory Concept: Liberalism and Neoliberalism.*)

Coming back to the three theoretical understandings of globalization, hyperglobalist authors such as Kenichi Ohmae (1996) argue that globalization is a linear and progressive but primary economic process. Induced by the ongoing transnational integration of markets and societies, states face a decreasing acting capacity in addition to a global shift in authority towards non-state actors, such as non-governmental organizations or transnational corporations. This is considered a positive development by neoliberal authors as it is supposed to result in overcoming the 'traditional' nation-state and thus to lead to a multi-dimensional and complex, but also more democratic and efficient, system of (→) global governance. In a negative new Marxist interpretation, contemporary globalization demonstrates the final triumph of capitalism and market rationality over social demands – a development described by Marx and Engels in their *Communist Manifesto* more than a hundred years ago. In light of this, scholars in the Marxist tradition frequently claim that he was the first major theorist of globalization. New Marxist scholars fear the ongoing creation of political institutions according to economic demands, and the political consequences of the deepening gap between the 'haves' and 'have-nots' of economic interdependency and the global competition of growth rates and open markets.

Second, from a sceptical perspective, the entire discussion about the scope and the density of the contemporary globalization process is deceptive. Authors such as Paul Hirst and Grahame Thompson (1996) and realist Robert Gilpin (→ *Theory Concept: Realism and Neorealism*) describe globalization as a strictly economic process that has continuously repeated itself throughout history and is controlled by states as the central actors in world politics. Instead of perceiving globalization as a contemporary phenomenon, sceptical scholars point to its comparability in terms of quantity and quality to the economic interdependency at the end of the nineteenth century. Additionally, they highlight the remaining importance of states, especially of the USA, in establishing the present global economic order. Gilpin, for example, argues in favour of strong political regulations to correct market failures and especially control financial flows, thus keeping the process of globalization under political control. In a nutshell, sceptical authors consider the current debate about the decline of state authority and capability as well as the rise of private authority to be a 'myth', which is based on faulty empirical assumptions (Hirst and Thompson 1996: 2–3).

The third, transformationalist, understanding considers globalization as an essentially open-ended and highly differentiated process and thus places itself in between these two diametrical positions (Held and McGrew 2007; Scholte 2005). Here, contemporary globalization is perceived as a challenge to statehood, as it erodes the relations between (→) sovereignty, (→) territoriality and political (→) power. Additionally, non-state actors are granted increasing importance including the potential to contribute to and influence global political processes. While the transformation of world politics induced by globalization is assumed to be open-ended, i.e. it can lead into different directions, transformationalists emphasize that it cannot be characterized *per se* as negative or positive with regard to its effects on state authority, legitimacy and power. Instead, transformationalist authors pragmatically argue for creating new, innovative and functional solutions to global problems.

The differentiation of globalization theory into these three understandings has been contested by Luke Martell, mainly on the grounds that there is no proper third understanding. Instead, 'third-wave authors come to conclusions that try to defend globalization yet include qualifications that in practice reaffirm sceptical claims' (Martell 2007: 175). Revising globalization literature, Martell demonstrates that transformationalists overstate their differences from sceptics. In fact, the two understandings have more in common than they would have it – both understandings, for example, assume that the state remains an autonomous and powerful enough actor to determine global politics. Additionally, most of the assumed differences between these two understandings can be traced back to a transformationalist misunderstanding of the sceptical position. Martell concludes in unison with Colin Hay and David Marsh (2000), who themselves aimed to elaborate a view of globalization moving beyond the second wave, that the debate about globalization has moved 'toward a third wave but has not gotten there yet' (Martell 2007: 193).

4. EMPIRICAL PROBLEMS

Empirical research on the scope and the density of the contemporary globalization process is commonly conducted in three key dimensions of globalization: the political, the economic and the environmental (Held and McGrew 2002: 2).

The empirical assessment of the economic dimension of globalization is disputed among two sets of authors: those who see contemporary economic globalization as historically unique and constantly increasing, and the others who deny this observation by comparing the present status of the world economy to historical situations. Authors within the first group declare that 'international trade has grown to unprecedented levels' (Held and McGrew 2002: 2). On the contrary, authors such as Gilpin claim that contemporary economic globalization is neither historically unique nor unlimited: 'considered in relation to the size of national economies and of the international economy, trade, investment, and financial flows were greater in the late 1800s than they are at the end of the 1900s' (Gilpin 2000: 294–6). Notwithstanding their differences, both positions agree on two empirical observations: first, the levels of international trade differ greatly in the various regions of the world and, second, the gains of globalization are distributed highly unevenly both between and within countries as well as being restricted to specific economic sectors. For instance, the exchange process of economy and technology and the degree of economic interconnectedness concentrate highly within the western, high-income countries, plus economically strong Asian countries such as China and Japan. At the same time, even within these countries, globalization 'produces' clear winners and losers. The increasing power of global finance is widely held to be the key governance challenge (Held and McGrew 2002: 2–4; Gilpin 2000: 295).

Economic globalization is directly linked to its environmental consequences. Until the early to mid-twentieth century most environmental damage was concentrated in particular regions, resulting from prior increasing capacities of industrial, resource-intensive production (Held and McGrew 2002: 4–6). The industrialization of many southern countries as well as global population growth intensified the consequences of environmental pollution. The public visibility of detrimental environmental effects increased through both scientific research and organized environmental movements. It became obvious that environmental pollution does not stop at state borders and that environmental degradation in distant parts of the world can have massive consequences on the international community. As a direct reaction, new global institutions, regimes and networks have emerged in order to tackle environmental problems and share the costs of globalization between all members of the international community (→ *Global Governance*). The crucial questions, however, remain open: how can these environmental consequences be regulated? How can the costs of globalization be reduced while at the same time allowing southern countries and emerging global economies to industrialize and develop their economies in their own right?

The political dimension of globalization is characterized by an ongoing debate about the consequences of globalization on states' capacity to fulfil central governance functions. Traditionally, the main task of a political system is to identify promising solutions for existing problems, to translate these solutions into rules of conduct and to ensure their compliance. Mainstream literature argues that although the (→) sovereignty of states is weakened by the increasing influence of non-state actors and the appearance of transnational problems, states remain the most important political agents. Their power is not necessarily diminishing but has to be reconstituted and adapted to the new challenges. Despite the ongoing transformations, states are considered the most important organizational form of political community and, as such, still have the autonomy and capacity to react and to determine the world system's future (Held and McGrew 2002: 5–8; Martell 2007: 189).

5. CORE READING

Baylis, John, Steve Smith and Patricia Owens (eds) (2008) *The Globalization of World Politics* (Oxford: Oxford University Press). Provides an introduction to the principal theoretical debates on world politics as well as a comprehensive overview of the current issues discussed.

Held, David, A. McGrew, D. Goldblatt and J. Perraton (1999) *Global Transformations: Politics, Economics and Culture* (Cambridge: Polity

globalization

83

Press). Provides the reader with a range of conceptual as well as empirical perspectives on the ongoing global transformation processes.

Scholte, Jan Aart (2005) *Globalization: A Critical Introduction* (Basingstoke: Palgrave Macmillan, 2nd edn). A widely cited and coherent view of contemporary globalization.

6. USEFUL WEBSITES

http://qed.princeton.edu/main/MG. The Mapping Globalization Project of Princeton University designed as an empirical resource centre for globalization data.

http://www.globalresearch.ca/index.php. The Centre for Research on Globalization offers a critical look on contemporary global events.

http://www.journoz.com/global/index.html. Offers link lists to a range of key organizations for globalization as well as to watchdog sites of globalization's critics.

Hegemony

1. CORE QUESTIONS ADDRESSED

- What distinguishes hegemony from other forms of power?
- What is the difference between a realist and a critical definition of hegemony?
- Why does hegemony facilitate cooperation?

2. DEFINITIONS

In everyday parlance, the term hegemony often simply characterizes the relationship between a great power and the states that it dominates. A hegemon then becomes a state that is able to dictate the behaviour of other states. Yet the Hellenic origins of 'hegemony' indicate that more is at stake here – in Greek, it stands for 'leadership'. A leader however does not simply get his will through the application of brute force. Indeed, leadership implies duties for the leader and a sense of responsibility.

In International Relations, there are two broad definitions of hegemony. A first one comes out of (neo)realist thinking and is close to the everyday understanding of the term. (→ *Theory Concept: Realism and Neo-realism.*) A hegemon is a state that dominates politics in a particular region and can impose actions on other states because it commands the material resources, both economically and militarily, to do so. Among the economic resources, Keohane (1984: 32) lists four as particularly important: control over raw materials, capital, markets and 'competitive advantages in the production of highly valued goods'. The consequent interactions between the states that are part of this domination amount to a regional international system under the control of the hegemon (Gilpin 1981: 29), or what Buzan and Wæver (2003) call a 'regional security complex'.

Traditional Marxist definitions of hegemony are similar to the neo-realist one. (→ *Theory Concept: Marxism and Critical Theory.*) In his seminal article on 'three instances of hegemony', for instance, Wallerstein (1984: 38) defines hegemony as 'the situation in which the ongoing rivalry between the so-called "great powers" is so unbalanced that . . . one power can largely impose its rules and its wishes'. For Wallerstein, too, the economic basis is crucial for such hegemonic power – he stresses superiority in 'agro-industrial production, commerce, and finance' (Wallerstein 1984: 39).

In contrast to these purely materialist definitions, understandings of hegemony that draw on the Italian philosopher Antonio Gramsci's work include a cultural dimension. For Gramsci, a core aspect of hegemony was the support that a leadership system can draw on. In his analysis of the failure of revolutions in the bourgeois state, Gramsci noted that the bourgeoisie maintained its power without resorting to direct physical means – the state apparatus performed this function but was separate from the bourgeoisie, who, however, dominated the culture and self-understanding of the state so that they not only could take a back seat in the actual running of the state, but also found that their basic norms and values enjoyed the support of the public at large. Gramsci's notion of hegemony was introduced into International Relations by Robert Cox (1983, 1987). In a crucial article published in 1983, Cox (1983: 171) identifies the main characteristics of hegemony: first, the hegemon must support an order that other states 'find compatible with their interests'; second, hegemony must be founded on a 'mode of production of global extent' that in turn forges links between civil societies and thus contributes to the spread of a particular type of societal organization and culture. International organizations play an important role in stabilizing such hegemony in that they 'embody the rules which facilitate the expansion of a hegemonic world order', serve as ideological agents that legitimize this order, 'co-opt the elites from peripheral countries' and 'absorb counter-hegemonic ideas' (Cox 1983: 172).

Ernesto Laclau and Chantal Mouffe (1985: 138–9), drawing on Gramsci, give the concept of hegemony a discursive twist. Hegemony now becomes a discourse that draws together a set of meaning-producing practices ('articulations') and thereby provides a particular order. While Gramsci still wanted to maintain the concept of classes, Laclau and Mouffe, under the impression of an increasing variety of social movements, give up this notion. They also stress that even the negation of a hegemonic order may reinforce the order because it accepts the latter's core terms. As a consequence, the formulation of counter-hegemonic ideas becomes more problematic than it initially seems, as such ideas presuppose the redefinition of fundamental terms on which societal understanding builds. While the work of Laclau and Mouffe has had a significant impact on political science through what is sometimes referred to as the 'Essex School' of discourse theory, its impact on the analysis of international relations has so far been limited, with a concentration on the analysis of European integration, where governance structures are further developed than elsewhere (see e.g. Howarth and Torfing 2005).

3. THEORETICAL PERSPECTIVES

As already indicated, the different definitions of hegemony are tied to different theoretical perspectives. For the neorealist, hegemony provides the main possibility of cooperation in an otherwise anarchical and war-prone international system. Neorealists have therefore developed what is usually referred to as the hegemonic stability theory: for an international system to be stable, it needs a hegemon that provides leadership in setting up institutions and imposing norms, and has the capabilities to enforce the rules that are based on these norms (e.g. Gilpin 1981). Hegemony from this perspective is a good thing: it provides a degree of order and stability, even if that order will involve the threat of force.

Such hegemony however will always be a temporary phase. The power of the hegemon is likely to decline over time as its sphere of influence increases beyond the manageable and rising powers start to balance rather than bandwagon (→ Balance of Power). For the neorealist, cooperation will end as the hegemon declines and can no longer enforce its rules. Here, neoliberals (→ Theory Concept· Liberalism and Neoliberalism), who accept the idea that hegemons tend to be beneficial to international cooperation, part ways with neorealists and argue that cooperation in (→) international regimes can persist beyond hegemonic decline because the states involved will have seen its benefits (e.g. Keohane 1984).

For Gramscian Critical Theorists, hegemony is much more problematic as it imposes a particular world order (and, particularly in the Laclau/Mouffean version, a particular way of seeing the world) and marginalizes alternatives that may be more peaceful and just. This is particularly true for the capitalist hegemony, which is seen as an exploitative system. Yet because of its complex web of domination, it is not sufficient to balance a specific state, say the United States, in the system, as realists may suggest. Rather, resistance would have to take place through long and difficult struggles among social forces on the domestic and transnational levels to start establishing a counter-hegemony.

This already indicates that Critical Theory's negative understanding of hegemony is strongly linked to a critique of the capitalist system, and therefore also to a particular contemporary configuration. Strictly speaking, hegemony is not *per se* only bad, but at least ambiguous. On the one hand, it always marginalizes alternatives; on the other hand, it provides some basic meaning to social life that is necessary to build social and political orders. The aim for Cox (1987), for instance, is therefore to work towards an alternative hegemonic order – one in which there is less exploitation and more freedom.

4. EMPIRICAL PROBLEMS

The empirical issues covered in most Critical Theory works on hegemony therefore cover the historic contextualization of the rise of the modern capitalist state system and the role of the United States as the western hegemon after the Second World War and then on a global scale after the end of the Cold War. The current status of the US, however, is disputed, in particular regarding the extent to which the forces of production can be allocated to a specific territory in the context of globalization, or whether hegemony and (→) empires need to be reconceptualized as non-territorial entities. As part of this focus, a core problem also concerns the resistance to (→) globalization as a form of counter-hegemony.

For the neorealist, the more pertinent question is whether it is possible to prolong hegemony so as to ensure a longer period of cooperation (see Doran 1971). Otherwise, neorealists as well as world systems theorists writing from a structuralist perspective have worked on the cycles of the rise and fall of hegemons in a historical perspective. Neoliberals, in contrast, and as outlined above, are more interested in the possibilities of extended cooperation beyond the decline of the hegemon and therefore in analysing the norms and rules installed during hegemony and their prospects. Intriguingly when it comes to the US, empirical analyses have tended to exaggerate the decline of the hegemon. A good deal of the neoliberal literature on (→) international regimes is a consequence of a perceived deterioration of the US position in the international system as a consequence of the Oil Shock and the ensuing economic crisis in the 1970s. Barely two decades later, such analyses seemed curiously anachronistic, to say the least.

5. CORE READING

Cox, Robert W. (1987) *Production, Power and World Order: Social Forces and the Making of History* (New York: Columbia University Press). Still a core reference point of neo-Gramscian work in International Relations, with hegemony as a core analytical concept.

Gilpin, Robert (1981) *War and Change in World Politics* (Cambridge: Cambridge University Press). One of the first elaborate statements of hegemonic stability theory in International Relations from a neorealist point of view.

Keohane, Robert O. (1984) *After Hegemony: Cooperation and Discord in the World Political Economy* (Princeton: Princeton University Press). The initial neoliberal 'counterpart' to hegemonic stability theory.

6. USEFUL WEBSITES

http://www.theory-talks.org/2010/03/theory-talk-37.html. Interview in the 'Theory Talks' series with Robert W. Cox on world orders, historical change and theory in international relations.

http://www.ianangus.ca/cp1.htm. Transcript of an interview by Ian Angus with Ernesto Laclau and Chantal Mouffe in the 'Conflicting Publics' series run by the Institute for the Humanities at Simon Fraser University in cooperation with the Knowledge Network.

http://www.english.emory.edu/Bahri/hegemony.html. Offers an overview of Gramsci's concept of hegemony, and links to other websites on his works as well as websites related in theme and topic.

Human Rights

1. CORE QUESTIONS ADDRESSED

- What are the rights owned by any individual human being?
- How are these rights guaranteed?
- What role do human rights play in international relations?

2. DEFINITIONS

A traditional liberal definition sees human rights as rights that apply to all human beings independent of their nationality, ethnicity, religion or other individual characteristics. They therefore are presumed to have universal applicability, although, as we will see below, this universality is also often challenged. There are several subcategories of rights, and there have been many theoretical and political disputes over which rights to include in the list of universally valid human rights.

One distinction differentiates between negative and positive rights. Negative rights protect the individual against infringements of their rights, especially by political authorities. Article 4 of the Universal Declaration of Human Rights, for instance, outlaws torture and 'cruel, inhuman or degrading treatment or punishment'. Positive rights, by contrast, entitle individuals to specific forms of assistance. One example is the right to education codified in Article 26 of the Universal Declaration. In this case, it is not state action that infringes on human rights; instead, state action may be needed to provide the structure and assistance required for the individual to obtain the right.

A second distinction categorizes human rights according to the aspect of human life they cover. This is reflected in two International Covenants on human rights that translate the rights laid out in the Universal Declaration into concrete measures to be taken by the signatory states. The first one on Civil and Political Rights deals with the first 21 articles of the Universal Declaration and issues such as the right to freedom of peaceful assembly (Art. 20), the right to freedom of opinion and expression (Art. 19) or the already mentioned right to the freedom from torture. It therefore refers mostly to negative rights. The second International Covenant on Economic, Social and Cultural Rights focuses on the remaining nine articles of the Universal Declaration and mostly positive rights. The Covenant, in Article 7(a) for instance, recognizes the right to 'remuneration which provides all workers, as a minimum, with . . . a decent living for themselves and their families', or in Article 9 the 'right of everyone to social security'.

Finally, one can distinguish between individual, group and collective rights. Most of the rights mentioned above refer to the individual as a participant in societal life and are thus predominantly individual rights. Sometimes such rights are invoked on behalf of a particular group that feels it is discriminated against, for instance an ethnic or religious minority. In these cases the literature sometimes refers to group rights (e.g. Sanders 1991). Collective rights, in contrast, are held by the group as such and cannot be reduced to the rights of individuals. Collective rights are often cultural rights such as the right of linguistic minorities to recognition of their language as an official state language or the right of religious communities to opt out of some state legislation (see Sanders 1991: 378–80). On this basis, one can distinguish between the individual's right to speak in a language of their choice, the right of the individuals within a specific group to speak in their mother tongue (group right), and the right of members of that group to have access to official forms in their own language (collective right).

3. THEORETICAL PERSPECTIVES

While few people if anyone will contest the existence of human rights, their exact meaning and content is a lot more contested, which has led to some fierce theoretical and political debates. One of them is the question of the foundation of human rights. This is not solely a philosophical debate, but has far-reaching consequences for the validity and applicability of human rights. Traditionally most widespread has been a natural law perspective, which holds that there is a state of nature (whether given by God or not) in which all human beings enjoy unalienable rights (see Vincent 1987). Yet such a state of nature is a fictive construct and as such contested. Defenders of human rights who accept that there is no such foundation see human rights as social constructs (→ *Theory Concept: Social Constructivism*) rooted in human experience and moral visions (see e.g. Donnelly 2003: 15–1). As in a social contract, they are what humans agree upon. This makes them part of a political project and subject to relativist claims. Thus, other authors have given up the idea of universally valid human rights and see the need for equivalent rights to emerge from the culture in which people live (see the discussion in Brown 1999). Many have struggled with the recognition that a fictive state of nature is a problematic assumption on the one hand and the desire to maintain human rights on the other, and many different positions have therefore emerged. A prominent one is that of 'pragmatic liberals' who propose that there are universal human rights but that these need to be adapted to local circumstances (e.g. Forsythe 2006: 6). From the opposite angle, there have been attempts to construct a universal framework of rights through a dialogue between religions and cultures (e.g. An-na'im 1992).

A second theoretical debate that has tremendous political consequences is over which rights are to be included in the concept of human rights. A restrictive liberal view of human rights focuses on civil and political rights. A more expansive view includes economic, social and cultural rights. Again, there are attempts to combine both categories of rights, for instance in the work of Craig Scott (1999), who argues that the two need to be seen as interdependent. Likewise, it is contested whether collective rights should be considered human rights. Those in favour of collective rights argue that the preservation of a variety of cultures is a basic human need. Further, some individual rights such as the right to free speech may be difficult to enjoy without collective rights because they rely on the protection of different cultures, religions and languages, none of which can be left simply to the rights of individuals (Sanders 1991). On the other side, those arguing against collective rights propose that they are not irreducible to individual rights, and that their objectives can also be achieved through individual rights (Donnelly 2003: 204).

4. EMPIRICAL PROBLEMS

The above theoretical debates have not been taking place outside a political context in which debates over human rights have often gone along with the grand politics of international relations. During the Cold War, for instance, the debate was in particular between those, predominantly western, states that argued for the primacy of civil and political rights. They saw these as basic rights to guarantee the liberty of human beings, and were reluctant to agree to what they saw as wide-ranging economic and cultural rights that may provide grounds for demands for interference into the market, although this did not mean that the guarantee of such rights was completely ruled out in particular in western welfare states (Whelan and Donnelly 2007). On the other side, many socialist states argued that individual rights are useless in the absence of the economic means to pursue them and therefore championed economic and social rights. While the end of the Cold War has taken some of the heat off these debates, they are by no means settled and continue to play a role even within western states, such as in the criticism in the United Kingdom of the European Union Charter of Fundamental Rights as interfering with the freedom of business. In the meantime, some countries in the 'third world' have started to push so-called 'third generation rights', which include collective rights, as a means to resist the impact of liberal, western-dominated globalization.

Historically, scholars have noted the evolution of the human rights regime in both an extension of human rights and in their increasing codification. While the history of human rights can be traced back to antiquity, their modern relevance in international politics took off with the Universal Declaration of Human Rights, adopted by the United Nations General Assembly in 1948. The Declaration has been followed by a number of further agreements addressing specific human rights such as the Convention on Elimination of All Forms of Racial Discrimination (1969) or the Convention on the Rights of the Child (1989), as well as the two Covenants mentioned above. Yet human rights are also codified in regional treaties and proclamations, including the European Convention on Human Rights (1950) or the already mentioned EU Charter (2000).

Among the recurring problems related to human rights is their status, monitoring and the sanctioning of violations ($\rightarrow$ *International Law*). At the heart of this is the conflict between an ($\rightarrow$) international society organized in sovereign states and the universal applicability of rights pertaining to the individual. The controversial discussions about the International Criminal Court have clarified that there remain strong objections to notions of a judiciary on the international level that would deal with individuals even within the narrow confines of war crimes, genocide and crimes against humanity. More effective judiciaries with a broader remit exist on the regional level, particularly in the form of the European Court of Human Rights. Other human rights organizations on the level of the United Nations, such as the Human Rights Council, established in 2006, also suffer from the sovereignty/human rights dilemma and are often subject to severe political disputes about the membership of their committees.

While this entry has focused on the normative controversies about human rights, many studies in International Relations have also analysed the mechanisms of the spread of human rights. A standard reference point in this respect is the work of Risse, Ropp and Sikkink (1999) who, arguing from a social constructivist perspective, have put forward the idea of a 'spiral model' of human rights impact. In this model, rulers often see human rights conditions in agreements with other countries as unimportant and thus agree to them in order to achieve their interests. This however empowers human rights activists who can point to these conditions in order to legitimize their claims, supported by transnational networks of non-governmental organizations. When this leads to a regime change, a new generation of politicians may be socialized in accepting human rights as the standard, thus completing the 'spiral'.

5. CORE READING

Dunne, Tim and Nicholas J. Wheeler (eds) (1999) *Human Rights in Global Politics* (Cambridge: Cambridge University Press). An excellent collection of articles addressing the role of human rights in international relations.

Risse, Thomas, Stephen C. Ropp. and Kathryn Sikkink (eds) (1999) *The Power of Human Rights: International Norms and Domestic Change* (Cambridge: Cambridge University Press). An influential work that tries to demonstrate the impact of human rights from a social constructivist perspective, developing a 'spiral model' to illustrate the mechanisms though which human rights may lead to regime change.

Vincent, R. J. (1987) *Human Rights and International Relations* (Cambridge: Cambridge University Press). An excellent treatment of the role of human rights in international relations from an English School perspective.

6. USEFUL WEBSITES

http://www.un.org/en/rights/index.shtml. Central UN portal with links to other UN sites, including the High Commissioner for Human Rights, the Human Rights Council and the Universal Declaration of Human Rights.

www.hrw.org. Website of Human Rights Watch, one of the main NGOs dealing with human rights violations.

www.amnesty.org. Website of Amnesty International, another major human rights NGO.

www.cartercenter.org. Website of the Carter Center, founded by former US president Jimmy Carter, at Emory University, US.

human rights

www.liberty-human-rights.org.uk. Website of Liberty, a major UK-based human rights, NGO.

www.echr.coe.int. Website of the European Court of Human Rights, with links to the European Convention of Human Rights and other relevant legal texts.

Humanitarian Intervention

1. CORE QUESTIONS ADDRESSED

- What are the problems in defining humanitarian intervention?
- When can humanitarian intervention be considered as just?
- Do humanitarian interventions work?

2. DEFINITIONS

The idea of humanitarian intervention, which originates in the 'just-war' tradition (→ *International Ethics*), is almost as old as the modern state system. Humanitarian intervention is understood as 'the use of military force on the territory of a state without its consent with the goal of protecting innocent victims of large-scale atrocities' (Thakur 2007: 388). In contrast to (→) peacekeeping, humanitarian intervention has thus been called 'an uninvited breach of sovereignty' (Bell 2007). It became a topic of increased significance in international public law and international relations thinking after the Second World War, triggered by mass atrocities and the genocide of the European Jews. The years of the Cold War saw a number of controversial military actions that may be labelled humanitarian intervention, such as Vietnam's 1978 intervention in Cambodia to end the genocidal Khmer Rouge regime. Yet, these were met with strong global opposition and condemnation. Humanitarian intervention took on a more concrete form throughout the 1990s in the context of debates on the nature of (→) sovereignty,

Humanitarian intervention is a sensitive concept as it embodies conflicts between several core principles of (→) international society. States as the addressees of humanitarian intervention find themselves in a dilemma situation: 'Intervention by force may be the only means of enforcing global humanitarian norms, but this fundamentally challenges the established principles of non-intervention and non-use of force' (Wheeler 2000: 1).

When trying to apply the concept of humanitarian intervention in practice, discussion focuses mostly on what exactly constitutes 'large-scale atrocities'. Two documents of international public law with very different legal status offer rival definitions: the 1948 *Convention on the Prevention and Punishment of the Crime of Genocide* and the 2001 *Responsibility to Protect*. The 1948 convention is legally binding to those states party to it and provides a relatively clear understanding of what constitutes genocide (Article III). Yet its provisions concerning humanitarian intervention remain elusive: 'any Contracting Party may call upon the competent organs of the United Nations to take such action under the Charter of the United Nations as they consider appropriate for the prevention and suppression of acts of genocide or any of the other acts enumerated in article III' (United Nations 1948). More precise wording toward the so-called 'just cause threshold' is given in the Report of the International Commission on Intervention and State Sovereignty (ICISS 2001). Here, the grave violations of human rights are connected to large-scale loss of life and large-scale ethnic cleansing. While the general principle of the *responsibility to protect* gained acceptance in the international community, even its status as customary law, implying tacit state consent, remains contested (→ *Sovereignty*, → *International Law*) – a crucial deficit seeing that the agents of humanitarian intervention are states.

3. THEORETICAL PERSPECTIVES

Theoretical considerations regarding humanitarian intervention centre around a dual question: if or when is humanitarian intervention just, and second, how far have states accepted humanitarian intervention as a norm of international society? International Relations' discussion on the subject is based on English School (→ *International Society*) and constructivist thought (→ *Theory Concept: Social Constructivism*), which assumes that 'states form a society of states constituted by the rules of sovereignty, non-intervention and the non-use of force' (Wheeler 2000: 6). International relations are thus presumed to take place within a profoundly social context that is marked by shared legal and moral obligations.

Two strands within the English School relate to the practice of humanitarian intervention, and they reach divided outcomes: pluralism and solidarism. Pluralism purports that only minimal agreement on the basic rules of co-existence, mainly non-intervention and sovereignty, is possible within international society. Because humanitarian intervention violates these basic rules and therefore contains the possibility of abuse by the strong, pluralists reject its practice as detrimental to the orderly structure of a peaceful interstate co-existence. In contrast, solidarism perceives of humanitarian intervention to alleviate extreme cases of human suffering as a duty of international society. Acting on it can strengthen the legitimacy of international society. In his famous contribution to the debate, Nicholas Wheeler, a solidarist, rejects the pluralist claim of humanitarian intervention undermining international order and instead conveys that 'there is often a compatibility between protecting the national interest, promoting international order, and enforcing human rights' (2000: 309). Solidarists thus assume that states benefit from promoting and enforcing human rights because this would make the world more just and as a consequence more orderly. Based on the 'just-war tradition', Wheeler further suggests four key criteria to be met if an intervention is to be both legitimate and humanitarian: there has to a 'supreme humanitarian emergency'; all peaceful means of solving the crisis have been attempted; the use of force has to be in proportion to the harm done; and there has to be strong expectation that intervention will lead to a favourable humanitarian outcome (2000: 33–7).

Constructivist authors have focused on the evolution and content of a norm of humanitarian intervention by examining state practice. Norms and rules are thought to work in a dual way by both constraining and enabling actors. Changes in norms and the normative context thus directly impact on state interests and state interaction patterns (Finnemore 1996). Changes in state practice towards humanitarian intervention thus become understandable by changes in the normative context (Wheeler 2004a). One of these changes concerns heightened expectations for government performance including less international tolerance for state-sponsored internal violence and repression (Finnemore 2003). Discursive state practice plays an important role in this regard as states verbally endorse rules and norms to legitimate their behaviour. Verbal adherence to norms through justifications changes the normative context and is thought to contribute just as much to defining what is legitimate behaviour as state action. Martha Finnemore also addresses the selectivity of intervention practice: simply put, while there is a developing norm towards humanitarian intervention, it does not exist in a vacuum (2003). Rather, it is part of a web of norms, a larger normative system that contains controversies and contradictions.

4. EMPIRICAL PROBLEMS

The theoretical contradictions and the empirical problems of humanitarian intervention are inextricably linked, especially in relation to the most crucial empirical question: when is it right to intervene and when is it right not to intervene?

The international legal basis of humanitarian intervention is elusive. First, there is no multilateral convention explicitly authorizing states to intervene in other states for humanitarian purposes. The Charter of the United Nations contains contradictory legal provisions that may point to intervention's legality in certain circumstances. As the Security Council is delineated to be the primary responsible for the maintenance of international peace and security (Article 24.1), it is capable of authorizing agents even to the point of taking military measures, should the Council deem an act to threaten international peace and security (Chapter VII, UN Charter). At the same time, the Security Council provisions stand in direct legal tension with those concerning the non-use of force (Article 2.4) and non-intervention (Article 2.7). The UN Charter further commits states to protect fundamental human rights – indeed, Article 1.3 mentions the promotion and encouragement of human rights as one of the United Nations' main purposes. Customary international law witnessed a number of cases of *multilateral* humanitarian intervention throughout the 1990s: 1991 Somalia, 1992 Bosnia and Herzegovina, 1999 Kosovo and 1999 East Timor. Scholars have also pointed to instances of humanitarian intervention in state practice, i.e. a customary right to humanitarian intervention that preceded the UN Charter, such as the British, French and Russian intervention in Greece (1827).

Yet, the two criteria a rule requires to reach customary law status, i.e. consistent state practice and a sense of legal obligation, are not met ($\rightarrow$ *International Law*). State behaviour on intervention has in no way been consistent since the 1990s: the international community still fails to treat like cases of severe human rights violations alike, as its passivity in the face of the humanitarian catastrophe in Darfur illustrates. The authorization of intervention by the UN Security Council crystallized out of state practice as a necessary provision. Yet again, state practice is not consistent in this regard as there have been cases of unauthorized intervention, such as the intervention of NATO forces in Kosovo. The legal boundaries of humanitarian intervention are thus ambiguous, to say the least. This is particularly problematic as the current selectivity of response contains the possibility of abuse: humanitarianism may serve as a welcome rhetorical cover for the implementation of geopolitics and the realization of powerful economic interests. The ICISS's 'just-cause thresholds' were specifically targeted at solving this problem. As it would be very difficult to meet these principles in cases where there was no compelling humanitarian rationale to act, the likelihood of abusing humanitarian justifications would be decreased. Yet, as has been said, these provisions have not been accepted.

A second set of analyses turn around the questions whether humanitarian interventions actually work or delay or even exacerbate the problems they seek to resolve. The outcomes are differentiated into short-term effects, i.e. immediate alleviation of human suffering, and long-term effects, i.e. conflict resolution and the reconstruction of societies and polities following intervention. The number of lives saved by a humanitarian intervention is frequently used to determine its success as it represents something of a 'lowest common denominator', especially in the short term. Taylor Seybolt argues that 'a [humanitarian] intervention is most likely to save lives when it (a) addresses the cause of suffering – whether privation, violence or both; (b) focuses on the appropriate actor – whether the victims, the perpetrators or both; and (c) uses the strategies demanded by the type of intervention pursued' (2007: 43). The mid-1990s intervention in Bosnia and Herzegovina thus clearly addressed the wrong causes as it focused on the delivery of food and medical assistance without providing any protection to the displaced or encircled population vulnerable to attack – leading to the international response being accused of 'handing out sandwiches at the gates of Auschwitz'.

While there are possibilities for short-term positive outcomes, fragmented empirical evidence suggests that the brief intervention of military personnel does little in terms of building long-term peace. Alongside its recommendations on intervention, the International Commission on Intervention and State Sovereignty (ICISS) insists that the military part is only one of three consecutive international responsibilities. The other two relate to long-term commitments to build the political, social-economic and legal conditions necessary for the promotion and safeguarding of human rights. Indeed, most of the countries in which relatively recent interventions took place, notably Kosovo and East Timor, remain subject to considerable international influence. Long-term measures are thus frequently considered separately to questions of humanitarian intervention, as the resolution of the root conflict and the building of peace require decisively more time (→ *Conflict Resolution*).

5. CORE READING

Finnemore, Martha (1996) 'Constructing Norms of Humanitarian Intervention', in Peter J. Katzenstein (ed.), *The Culture of National Security: Norms and Identity in World Politics* (New York: Columbia University Press), 153–87. A constructivist account on the historical and current evolution of the norm for humanitarian intervention.

Seybolt, Taylor B. (2007) *Humanitarian Military Intervention: The Conditions for Success and Failure* (Oxford: Oxford University Press). Develops a framework to judge the effects of interventions and uses this on the prominent interventions of the 1990s.

Wheeler, Nicholas J. (2000) *Saving Strangers: Humanitarian Intervention in International Society* (Oxford: Oxford University Press). Builds up a theoretical argument for humanitarian intervention and comprehensively evaluates state practice using post-1945 case studies.

6. USEFUL WEBSITES

http://www.iciss.ca/. Website of the International Commission on Intervention and State Sovereignty, offering research material and various resources published on humanitarian intervention.

http://www.globalpolicy.org/qhumanitarianq-intervention.html. Section with articles, speeches and reports on humanitarian intervention and the responsibility to protect, launched by the Global Policy Forum, which monitors the work of the United Nations.

http://www.responsibilitytoprotect.org/. The International Coalition for the Responsibility to Protect.

http://globalr2p.org/. Global Centre for the Responsibility to Protect.

http://www.un.org/preventgenocide/rwanda/about.shtml. 'Lessons from Rwanda' is a United Nations information and educational outreach programme on the prevention of genocide.

Ideas and Norms

1. CORE QUESTIONS ADDRESSED

- What is the difference between ideas and norms?
- How do ideas and norms relate to interests in international politics?
- Do ideas and norms matter at all?

2. DEFINITIONS

With the rise of various forms of constructivism (→ *Theory Concept: Social Constructivism*) in International Relations since the 1980s, there has emerged a new interest in the contribution of non-material, 'ideational' factors to policy-making. In contrast to rationalism, such approaches argue that interests cannot serve as the only explanation of action; that actors often do not act rationally according to 'objective' cost–benefit calculations; and that subjective preference orders are decisive but do themselves require an explanation. All of these arguments point to the relevance of ideas and norms. However, there are substantial differences in the conceptualization of 'ideational' factors.

In a classic definition, Judith Goldstein and Robert O. Keohane (1993: 3) define ideas as 'beliefs held by individuals'. They thus focus on the individual character of ideas. Indeed, framed in such a way, ideas belong to the sphere of cognition, or mental processes inside an actor's head. As such, the definition proposed by Goldstein and Keohane brings their work into the tradition of cognitive approaches in (→) foreign policy analysis. Even their subdivision of beliefs into worldviews and principled and causal beliefs shares resemblances with the attempts by cognitive approaches to differentiate between different forms of beliefs or cognitive concepts. Thus, worldviews are very basic beliefs that make sense of the world; principled beliefs provide normative assumptions and guidance; whereas causal beliefs supply a set of cause–effect assumptions (Goldstein and Keohane 1993: 8–11).

In contrast to ideas, norms do not operate on the level of individuals but require intersubjectivity and are therefore social phenomena. Norms in this sense are statements that guide behaviour. In order to become a norm, such statements need to be generally accepted by a society, although acceptance in this context does not mean that norms are not violated. Indeed, it is often in the context of violation that the existence of norms becomes visible, for instance because those who violate norms feel a necessity to justify their norm violation at length, or because the other members of a society condemn the norm violation and respond with sanctions. Thus, while on the one hand the validity of norms require 'rule-consistent behaviour' and the acceptance of their 'prescriptive status' (Risse and Sikkink 1999: 31–3), the general validity of a norm is not undermined by individual violations as long as these violations are the exception, and as long as those who violate the norm are actually aware of the existence of the norm and the violating character of their action. Furthermore, because of the societal quality of norms, their meaning often tends to be contested (Wiener 2007, 2008) so that norms may exist and prescribe behaviour although individuals may draw different inferences from them.

Various attempts have been made at further subdividing the category of norms. One common distinction is between regulative and constitutive norms, in the sense that regulative norms primarily prescribe behaviour, whereas constitutive norms also assign identities. Yet as Alexander Wendt (1999: 165–6) has pointed out, norms often have both a regulative and a constitutive effect.

Norms also need to be distinguished from institutions, yet especially in constructivist work, this is often not easy. As constructivists tend to use a broad sociological definition of institutions as patterns of behaviour, yet informal norms can only be seen through such patterns of behaviour, institutions and norms blend into each other. Thus, (→) 'sovereignty' is sometimes treated as a norm (e.g. Reus-Smit 2001: 526), sometimes as an institution of (→) international society (e.g. Sørensen 1999). A common answer to this problem is to define institutions as sets of norms and more specific rules that are derived from these norms (e.g. Simmons and Martin 2002: 194).

3. THEORETICAL PERSPECTIVES

Ideas and norms are often seen as constructivist concepts, but this is an oversimplification. The notion of ideas as beliefs, for instance, is easily compatible with a rationalist perspective (Laffey and Weldes 1997: 195–9). Thus, ideas can inform subject preferences, they can constitute the 'boundedness' of rationality, they can simply be 'hooks' (Goldstein and Keohane 1993: 4) to legitimize interests, or they can serve as 'pivotal mechanisms for coordinating expectations and behaviour' (Garrett and Weingast 1993: 178). As a result, in none of these instances do ideas challenge the basic underlying model of rationality. However, in contrast to constructivism, rationalism depicts ideas and beliefs as factors translatable into interests, i.e. into cost–benefit calculations, thus neglecting the fact that these factors might have an intrinsic value for individuals.

To the extent that behaviour follows norms in the sense that it is considered appropriate to behave in a certain way, and without engaging in cost–benefit calculations on the basis for instance of reputational gains or damages, the concept of norms provides for an alternative, non-rationalist logic of action, which James March and Johan Olsen (1989) famously labelled the 'logic of appropriateness'. Likewise, actors can engage in a 'logic of arguing' in which they utilize norms, yet again without seeking to maximize their gains (Risse 2000). Yet, norms are also sometimes used merely as an 'addendum' to rationalist approaches, where they are seen as an explanation of interests that then in turn explain behaviour (see Finnemore 1996).

A fundamental division between different treatments of norms lies in the question of whether norms are a powerful factor in their own right, or whether norms are simply rhetoric to conceal interests. In this context, Frank Schimmelfennig (2001: 48) has coined the term 'rhetorical action', which he defines as 'the strategic use of norm-based arguments', for instance to improve one's reputation. Such action, Schimmelfennig shows, can however lead to other actors basing their own claims on the norms used initially only in a strategic fashion, in which case the actor engaged in the rhetorical action finds it difficult to deny such claims without jeopardizing the reputational gains that he wanted to achieve. Schimmelfennig explains the enlargement of the European Union through this mechanism.

One of the difficulties in this debate is the question of whether 'ideational' and 'material' factors can indeed be separated, both ontologically and methodologically. Discursive approaches (→ Discourse, → Theory Concept: Postmodernism and Poststructuralism) tend to propose a dissolution of the ideational/material dichotomy and argue that discourses combine the ideational and the material, not least because we cannot grasp the material without a discursive context that ascribes meaning to the 'hard facts' (Hansen 2006: 17–18; Laffey and Weldes 1997: 199–201). In contrast, Goldstein and Keohane (1993: 26) explicitly set out to determine the contribution that ideas as opposed to interests make to the explanation of variation in foreign policy behaviour.

4. EMPIRICAL PROBLEMS

The concepts of ideas and norms have been applied in most fields of international relations. Among the more prominent areas of application are (→) human rights and European integration (→ *Regional Integration*). In relation to human rights, Martha Finnemore and Kathryn Sikkink (1998: 896) have developed the 'norm life cycle', starting with 'norm emergence', followed by 'norm cascade' and completed with norm 'internalization'. They also emphasized the role of 'norm entrepreneurs', especially during the stage of norm emergence. This model has informed a greater study on the domestic impact of human rights norms (Risse, Ropp and Sikkink 1999) as well as many other works on international norms. In relation to European integration, one of the core questions has been about the contribution of ideas (e.g. Garrett and Weingast 1993) and norms (e.g. Checkel 1999) to the integration process. Since 2002, when Ian Manners (2002) suggested it, the concept of the EU as a 'normative power' that is both constituted by norms and sees itself as pursuing these norms in international relations, has created a considerable debate.

Let us end this entry on a methodological note. It is notoriously difficult to trace the impact of norms and ideas, especially within a positivist, causal framework. A correlation between a specific idea and a policy is not as such evidence for a causal link, although it should be noted that the same can be said for correlations between interests and policies, which often only work on the basis of rationalist ontological assumptions. Albert S. Yee has provided an excellent treatment of this problem. Yee (1996) claims none the less that causal analysis is possible but requires the development of 'causal stories' (Yee 1996: 85), much in the same way as causal mechanisms need to be found that link particular interests and policies.

5. CORE READING

Finnemore, Martha and Kathryn Sikkink (1998) 'International Norm Dynamics and Political Change', *International Organization* 52 (4), 887–917. A highly influential article that provides a theoretical framework for the analysis of the role of norms in international relations, including the concepts of 'norm life cycle' and 'norm entrepreneurs'.

Laffey, Mark and Jutta Weldes (1997) 'Beyond Belief: Ideas and Symbolic Technologies in the Study of International Relations', *European Journal of International Relations* 3 (2), 193–237. An in-depth critique of mainstream conceptualizations of ideas and norms, emphasizing their social and constitutive character.

Wiener, Antje (2008) *The Invisible Constitution of Politics: Contested Norms and International Encounters* (Cambridge: Cambridge University Press). An investigation into the different ways in which norms function in international relations, developing the notion of 'contested norms' and linking norms to different logics of action.

6. USEFUL WEBSITES

http://www.international.ucla.edu/burkle/podcasts/article.asp?parentid=112623. Lecture by Robert O. Keohane on 'Social Norms and International Relations'.

http://www.normativeorders.net/en/research/areas. The 'normative orders' cluster of excellence at the Goethe University Frankfurt and its research areas on meanings of normativity and transnational justice, democracy and peace.

http://www.jilir.org/. The *Journal of International Law and International Relations* with a special issue on 'Contested Norms in International Law and International Relations'.

http://www.watsoninstitute.org/project_detail.cfm?id=103. Research project on international norms and sanctions by the Watson Institute for International Relations at Brown Unversity.

International Ethics

1. CORE QUESTIONS ADDRESSED

- To what extent is it possible to speak of an 'international ethics'?
- What are the possible foundations of such an ethics?
- What is the difference between global and international ethics?

2. DEFINITIONS

Ethics, Mark Amstutz notes, is 'the application of the appropriate moral norms to private and public affairs' (2005: 9). International ethics is thus concerned with the application of moral norms to international relations. Its prime question is how states ought to behave towards each other. In contrast to (→) international law, international ethics is not primarily concerned with the codification of rules or the development of judicial control of such rules. Yet there is a clear linkage between the two in that international law concretizes and formalizes the norms of international ethics.

Some scholars prefer to use the term 'global ethics' instead of 'international ethics'. In a narrow sense, global ethics exceeds the (→) international society. Thus, global ethics tackles problem of world society as a whole. It therefore is wider in scope both in terms of issue areas and addressees, which can now include individuals and various social groups as well as states. In practice, international and global ethics are often used interchangeably (see e.g. Booth et al. 2000). This is in part at least a consequence of (→) globalization and the increasing use of forms of (→) global governance, which transform the role of states in tackling cross-border issues.

3. THEORETICAL PERSPECTIVES

For some, ethical considerations do not matter in international politics. For a neorealist, for instance, there is no scope for ethics in the analysis of international politics as it is the structure of the system that determines behaviour. (→ *Theory Concept: Realism and Neorealism.*) In a classic reading of Machiavelli, moral considerations always have to be subjugated to interest (Forde 1992: 65). Yet this is not the only interpretation of realism, and the classical, pre-neorealist writers of the twentieth century have displayed a much more attentive attitude to the question of values and norms in international politics (Ashley 1984; Donnelly 1992: 94–9, 2008; Murray 1996). Apart from anything else, the ethics of realism stems from a commitment to safeguard the community of the nation. Classical realism therefore takes a classic communitarian position.

Indeed, one would have to have a highly impoverished notion of statehood and the international system to argue that questions of ethics do not matter. The debates about constructivist and critical approaches in International Relations since the mid-1980s have also re-opened the space for the probing further into the role of norms in international politics, and have revived the field of international ethics. (→ *Theory Concept: Social Constructivism.*) There are two core debates within international ethics, one concerning the general foundations of ethics, the other one debating the main referent point of ethics on an international or global scale.

international ethics

The first of these concerns the question of whether normative reasoning should take the form of *consequentialist* or *deontological* reasoning (Shapcott 2008: 194). Consequentalist ethics sets certain goals as the standards to be attained, and sees any means to achieve those standards as justifiable. In contrast, deontological ethics focuses on rules of behaviour, and therefore questions the justifiability of means independent of their goals. This is a debate particularly relevant, for instance, in the question of the legitimacy of war: one may see war as justified on the basis of changes that the resort to military action is hoped to bring about, or one may see war in principle as inappropriate behaviour unless there are specific rules accepted by all that allow military means in exceptional cases (Fixdal and Smith 1998: 287). That such exceptional cases exist is a sign that in practice, the two forms of ethics are often intertwined (Walzer 2004).

The second debate in international ethics, and by far the most prominent one, is that between *cosmopolitanism* and *communitarianism* (e.g. O'Neill 2000). Cosmopolitanists consider the world as a whole. Their main reference point for ethical judgements is humanity. Communitarianists, in contrast, place value in the existence of a plurality of communities, each with their own identity and prevailing norms. This debate pervades a great number of issues on the agenda of international politics, most prominently on (→) human rights (Dunne and Wheeler 1999) and the possibilities of humanitarian intervention (Bellamy 2002: 475–9). However, framing cosmopolitanism and communitarianism in a dichotomy is misplaced, as many arguments, voiced for instance by so-called solidarists in the English School of International Relations (→ *International Society*), will respect some degree of difference while acknowledging the existence of a single human race and globe (see also Brown 2002; Cochran 1999; Shapcott 2001).

It should come as no surprise that theoretical approaches focusing on critical or normative theorizing are more open to questions of international ethics than explanatory approaches. Thus, international ethics has played a particularly important role in Critical Theory, poststructuralism and feminism, although with great variation. (→ *Theory Concepts: Marxism and Critical Theory; Postmodernism and Poststructuralism; and Feminism and Gender.*) While Critical Theorists, for instance, see the construction of alternative political horizons based on strong principles as part of a defensible international ethics, poststructuralists, arguing in defence of multiple perspectives on politics, are much more critical of putting forward such horizons or pursuing a set principle (Campbell 1993; George 1994).

4. EMPIRICAL PROBLEMS

We have already mentioned some of the empirical problems that international ethics has addressed above. One of the main issues, however, that international ethics has been concerned with is the problem of just war (e.g. Walzer 2006). The engagement of thinking about the justification of war started from Christian principles but is now a broader enterprise. Theorists working in this tradition distinguish the right to war (*ius ad bellum* in Latin) and the right in war (*ius in bello*). While *ius in bello* focuses on issues concerning for instance the proportionality of means and the protection of non-combatant civilians, *ius ad bello* provides guidelines for when a war may be justified. In a classic, pluralist international society, the main justification for war consist of the defence of a state's territorial integrity. Even so, war must be a measure of last resort and be guided by the intention to resort to peace. With the end of the Cold War, the question of war in the name of (→) humanitarian intervention has increasingly become topical again in international politics, although this is far from a novel debate, as the question of how to respond to the genocidal threat of Nazi Germany shows. The terrorist attacks of 11 September 2001 have also raised new questions about when war may be just, against whom and in which form (Bethke Elshtain 2004).

Another core question of international ethics concerns the problem of global social equality, or what is called distributive justice. The philosopher John Rawls has been particularly influential in this debate. On the one hand, his ideas of creating equal opportunities for those with similar talents, outlined in his *Theory of Justice* (Rawls 1971), have been widely applied beyond the nation-state to make claims about equality on a global level in a cosmopolitan fashion (e.g. Beitz 1979). On the other hand, Rawls (1999) himself differentiates between different kinds of states according to how well they are 'ordered' in the sense of the degree to which they follow liberal principles, and therefore seems to apply cosmopolitan principles to international relations only within liberal borders. This is of course a much more complex debate than we can summarize here, but it should be clear from the above that the basic problems of the tensions between an international society organized in states, and a world society with the human being at the centre, run through this debate as much as they do through many other concepts that we cover in this book.

5. CORE READING

Booth, Ken, Tim Dunne and Michael Cox (2001) *How Might We Live? Global Ethics in the New Century* (Cambridge: Cambridge University Press). Book version of a special issue of the *Review of International Studies*, presenting the state of the art in international ethics.

Nardin, Terry and David R. Maple (eds) (1993) *Traditions of International Ethics* (Cambridge: Cambridge University Press). A selection of essays exploring the different approaches to international ethics.

Rawls, John (1999) *The Law of Peoples* (Cambrigde, MA: Harvard University Press). The classic liberal reference point for international ethics.

6. USEFUL WEBSITES

http://www.cceia.org/index.html. Website of the Carnegie Council for Ethics in International Affairs, one of the main organizations promoting international ethics, and editor of the journal *Ethics and International Affairs*.

http://www.globalethics.bham.ac.uk/. Home of the Centre for Global Ethics at the University of Birmingham, with links to further websites, research projects and the *Journal of Global Ethics*.

http://www.philosophytalk.org/pastShows/JohnRawls.html. Radio show on John Rawls with Stanford Professor Joshua Cohen on Philosophytalk.

International Law

1. CORE QUESTIONS ADDRESSED

- What are the sources of international law?
- What is the legalization of world politics?
- Why is the status of customary international law problematic?

2. DEFINITIONS

International law is a set of rules, norms and principles to regulate state conduct and guide state interaction by setting standards of what is and what is not permissible (Barash and Webel 2009: 340). International law may also regulate the conduct of international organizations, such as the United Nations. Developments of international law especially in the last century have also increasingly made individuals referents of international rules (→ *Human Rights*). While international law thus originally only applied to states, and the nation-state continues to be its main subject, it gradually evolved into regulating the conduct of a variety of other actors.

The rules, norms and principles of international law derive from four main sources as stated in Article 38 of the Statute of the International Court of Justice (ICJ): international conventions, customary international law, general principles of law, and 'teachings of the most highly qualified publicists of the various nations' (United Nations 1945). International conventions and customary international law are considered the primary sources as they are expressions of actual and tacit state consent to certain conduct – a crucial qualification in the system of consent-based sense of legal obligation that is international law.

International conventions are explicit, written agreements between two (bilateral) or more (multilateral) states. Conventions are legally binding to all state parties and states accede by ratification. Usually, a minimum number of ratifications is set for a treaty to enter into force – only when this number has been reached is the treaty legally binding to all state parties.

The second source of international law is customary law which, in contrast to conventions, is non-written. In order to be considered as customary law, a certain rule has to meet two criteria which have been confirmed by several ICJ judgements. First, it has to be reflected in consistent state practice adhered to over a period of time, and second, states need to act in this consistent way out of a sense of legal obligation – so-called *opinio juris*. Customary international law contains norms of different status. The most cogent are termed peremptory norms or *jus cogens*. A peremptory norm is defined as one 'accepted and recognised by the international community of states as a whole as a norm from which no derogation is permitted' (Vienna Convention on the Law of Treaties 1969: Article 53). The prohibition of maritime piracy, slavery, torture, mass atrocities and wars of aggression are generally presumed to have *jus cogens* status (Goldstone and Smith 2009: 22). Each of these crimes has been codified in the international legal canon through conventions or treaties – yet codification does not necessarily equal an end to their debate. What elements precisely constitute a war of aggression, for example, have yet to be defined. While states thus agreed on what constitutes a peremptory norm, there is no agreement on how this status can be reached.

The third source of international law, general principles of law, refers to basic, underpinning legal principles instead of specific rules of conduct. One such principle is so-called *pacta sunt servanda*, indicating that once a state acceded to a treaty, this treaty must be observed. Following the increasing legalization of international relations throughout the last 60 years, this third source has lost most of its importance.

The fourth and final source, the 'teachings of the most highly qualified publicists', is a subsidiary means for determining the rules of international law more precisely. While, for example, case law from international courts such as the ICJ, the International Court for the Former Yugoslavia (ICTY) or the International Criminal Court (ICC) is not a source of law in itself, it plays a decisive role in determining the scope of most given international norms as even international conventions and treaties leave considerable room for interpretation.

3. THEORETICAL PERSPECTIVES

Initial theoretical debate on international law is associated with thinkers such as Hugo Grotius of the natural law tradition in sixteenth- and seventeenth-century Europe. International law was conceived as an extension of natural law, 'a set of divinely ordained principles of state conduct' (Reus-Smit 2008: 282). In his work *On the Law of War and Peace* (1625), Grotius developed the notion of a fundamental, natural law stemming from the fact that all human beings are members of the same community (2001). Natural law as a philosophical approach provided initial respect for the concept of international justice.

Theorists of International Relations and international law have long thought of the disciplines as categorically distinct and occasionally even rivalling entities (Armstrong et al. 2007: 69). When realism replaced liberalism (→ *Theory Concepts: Realism and Neorealism; Liberalism and Neoliberalism*) as the theoretical mainstream of International Relations in the 1930s and 1940s, international law received little attention from IR theorists as it was widely considered an epiphenomenon to the international struggle for power of self-interested nation-states (Byers 2008: 613). Indeed, the interwar liberal notion of 'peace through law' was realism's primary grounds for rejecting liberalism as utopian. E. H. Carr, for example, considers international law to be the law of 'an undeveloped and not fully integrated community' lacking the three crucial parts of a developed legal system: a judicature, an executive and a legislature (Carr 1946: 170). If they consider it at all, realists perceive of international law as a tool of the powerful or a matter of 'low' politics violated with impunity.

In contrast to realists, liberals, particularly after the end of the Cold War, have openly called for bridging the perceived disciplinary divide between International Relations and international law. Remaining more 'conservative', neoliberals perceive of the role of international law as functional, as a regulatory institution in state conduct. Neoliberal regime theory (→ *International Regimes*) is a good example for the logic of this approach: international law is categorized as an intervening variable between state interests and policy outcomes without having an impact on interests in its own right. So-called new liberal authors such as Anne-Marie Slaughter and Andrew Moravcsik go a lot further in putting domestic preference formation into the foreground of their analyses. Slaughter considers the state and state preferences as derived from individuals and private groups and their transnational linkages. She proposes a three-tiered conception of international law: (1) the voluntary law of individuals and groups in transnational society; (2) the law of transnational governmental institutions; and (3) the law of interstate relations (Slaughter 1995). New liberalism thereby reflects the empirical trend towards the expansion of actors subject to international law. New liberal scholarship has been particularly engaged in the study of legalization, i.e. a particular form of institutionalization of sets of rules, norms and decision-making processes (Goldstein et al. 2000: 2). Scholars have tried to analyse these phenomena in putting forward three main dimensions to evaluate degrees of legalization: (1) obligation, i.e. if states or other actors are bound by a rule; (2) precision, i.e. does the rule unambiguously define the conduct they require, authorize or prescribe; and (3) delegation, i.e. have third parties been granted the authority to implement, interpret and apply rules (Abbott et al. 2000). Conceptualized as a continuum, legalization may be 'hard' (when all three dimensions or at least obligation and delegation are high), 'soft' or absent (Abbott et al. 2000: 18).

Constructivist scholars of International Relations have also integrated the study of international law by focusing on the constitutive qualities of international rules, norms and principles. Instead of portraying international law as merely a functional constraint to state behaviour, constructivists focus on how the ideational structure that is international

international law

law impacts on actors' identities, interests and behaviour through discourse and socialization (Finnemore 1996).

4. EMPIRICAL PROBLEMS

Empirical reasoning has disproved the realist perspective on several accounts: scholars point to instances when powerful states did show deference to international law all the while it appeared to be in contrast to their interests (Franck 1990: 3–4), and frequently went to considerable lengths in order for their actions to remain within international legal boundaries (Akehurst 1995; Wheeler 2004b). Realists further struggle to provide explanations for the post-Second World War growth of a complex international legal order. Advances in public international law have been twofold: it has expanded and differentiated in terms of both its content and its subjects. First, the United Nations was explicitly charged with the responsibility of codifying and progressively developing international law – signifying an at least symbolical commitment of the community of states to further international legal progress. Second, a number of legal or quasi-legal institutions began to play an increasing role in world politics. In its most extreme form, this refers to the integration process of Europe, whose Courts (the European Union's European Court of Justice and the Council of Europe's European Court of Human Rights) are able to issue binding decisions for its member states. On the global level, institutions such as the World Trade Organization established formal dispute settlement mechanisms for its members. International criminal jurisdiction solidified with the formation of international criminal tribunals after the Second World War, following the violent conflicts in Rwanda and the former Yugoslavia in the 1990s, and finally culminated with the permanent instatement of the International Criminal Court (ICC) in 2002.

This development of international criminal jurisdiction is connected to the increased inclusion of the individual as a subject of international law. Following the atrocities of the Second World War, states' legal commitment to the human rights of the individual grew and became codified in a number of international conventions. Again, the European Human Rights Court is most advanced as it even allows complaints to be issued by individual applicants. The war crimes tribunals of the 1990s and the standing ICC were a crucial innovation as they included the capacity of punishing individual violators. Thus, they were the first human rights and international legal institutions with real teeth.

Despite its considerable progress, international law remains faced with two substantial problems: its limited enforcement capacities and its ambiguity. First, while states' verbal commitments as concerns human rights are far-reaching, the numerous conventions at the international level do not include effective enforcement mechanisms beyond treaty verification provisions and the possibility of sanctions by the UN Security Council. International law's primary subjects, the nation-states, continue to be reluctant to consent to an authority superseding their (→) sovereignty. While the international judiciary has been decidedly strengthened by the ICC, the lack of an executive authority to enforce its decisions remains.

Second, as the bulk of international law is customary, its ambiguity, elusiveness and contested nature remain a major detriment. A study published by the International Committee of the Red Cross identified 161 rules as customary law (Henckaerts 2005: 175). The study controversially stated that non-international conflicts are customarily included under the protections afforded in the Geneva conventions which were explicitly designed for international conflicts (Goldstone and Smith 2009: 24). Controversies like these stem from the fact that states by and large recognize the above definition of customary law but there is no consensus on how long a practice must be displayed for it to be considered 'consistent' nor are there means to determine whether such a practice is undertaken because of supposed legal obligations (Goldstone and Smith 2009: 24). Scholars have pointed to General Assembly resolutions as sources of customary law: while they are not binding, the fact that they are usually adopted by all member states of the UN in consensus lends them as evidence of what states consider customary and thus attributes them with legal significance (Detter 1994; Falk 1970).

5. CORE READING

Akehurst, Michael (1995) *A Modern Introduction to International Law* (London: Routledge, 6th edn). Classic and very readable introductory textbook to the study of international law.

Armstrong, David, Theo Farrell and Hélène Lambert (2007) *International Law and International Relations* (Cambridge: Cambridge University Press). An interdisciplinary introduction to the historical, theoretical and empirical relationships of International Relations and international law.

Reus-Smit, Christian (2003) *The Politics of International Law* (Cambridge: Cambridge University Press). A collection of constructivist works on the subject of international law.

6. USEFUL WEBSITES

http://www.un.org/en/law/. The international law page of the United Nations website offers links to related UN bodies, thematic areas, UN offices and news.

http://www.asil.org/. The American Society for International Law website contains various publications, including analyses of current affairs, and a guide to internet resources.

http://www.ili.org/. A not-for-profit organization that conducts scholarly research, and practical legal training and publishing on different aspects of international law.

International Regimes

1. CORE QUESTIONS ADDRESSED

- What are the reasons for the emergence and persistence of international regimes?
- How do international regimes facilitate international cooperation?
- What is the difference between international regimes and international organizations?

2. DEFINITIONS

In everyday life most people associate the notion of regimes with the negative image of authoritarian states. But, while in Comparative Politics the term regime serves to characterize the type of governance present within a political system, for instance democratic or totalitarian regimes, the concept of international regimes in International Relations is different. Here, it describes a specific international institution, facilitating cooperation among actors despite the anarchical state of the international system. The most prominent examples of international regimes are the Nuclear Non-Proliferation Regime, created to inhibit the spread of nuclear weapons; the Climate Change Regime, which aims to stop climate change by reducing the greenhouse gases to a particular, non-dangerous level in the global climate system; as well as the (→) Human Rights Regime, seeking to establish and protect human rights worldwide.

A 'consensus definition' by Stephen Krasner defines regimes as 'sets of implicit or explicit principles, norms, rules, and decision-making procedures around which actors' expectations converge in a given area of international relations' (Krasner 1983: 2). According to Krasner's definition, international regimes display the following characteristics: they are created to tackle specific international problems, such as global environmental or health issues. International regimes are composed of principles and norms. As Krasner further elaborates, principles can be thought of as beliefs of fact or causalities in regard to a particular issue, whereas norms translate social behaviour into rights and obligations. Furthermore, international regimes are composed of rules and procedures, which not only have to be consistent with the principles and norms, but also convert the regime's principles and norms into specific instructions for action. Following this logic, Krasner concludes that a change in the norms and principles of a regime equals a change in the regime itself, while a change of the procedures and rules is a change within the regime (Krasner 1983: 3–4).

As already mentioned, international regimes fall into the broader concept of international institutions. Conceptualized as 'sets of rules meant to govern international behavior' (Simmons and Martin 2002: 194), international institutions can be divided into international organizations and international regimes. The most basic differences between an international organization and an international regime consist in the capacity of international organizations to function as an actor in international politics and to transcend the boundaries of issue areas, in contrast to international regimes, which always relate to specific issue areas and do not function as actors (Hasenclever et al. 2002: 11). With regard to international regimes this distinction is most visible in the fact that they do not have an administration or an office.

Krasner's definition has been criticized on various grounds, for example for not being precise enough, since the distinction between norms and rules is difficult to identify empirically. On a more fundamental level, other scholars, such as social constructivists (→ *Theory Concept: Social Constructivism*) argued that international regimes should be conceptualized in behavioural or intersubjective terms rather than being reduced to functional logics. Oran Young, for instance, argues in favour of a behavioural approach to the identification of international regimes, stating that it is not that important which norms and rules a regime rests upon, but rather if the regime is effective, i.e. if there is an effect of the regime's norms and rules on the behaviour of the actors addressed (Young 1989: 134). Consequently, Young defines international regimes as 'practices consisting of recognized roles linked together by clusters of rules or conventions governing relations among the occupants of these roles' (Young 1989: 12). Constructivist approaches to international regimes have in turn not put much emphasis on the compliance factor of international regimes but instead highlighted the role of intersubjective meaning and shared understanding. In this vein, Friedrich Kratochwil and John Ruggie stated that the common definition of international regimes puts an 'emphasis on convergent expectations as the constitutive basis of regimes' and thus gives them 'an inescapable intersubjective quality. It follows that we know regimes by their principled and shared understandings of desirable and acceptable forms of social behaviour' (Kratochwil and Ruggie 1986: 764).

So while rational approaches tend to identify international regimes only by the functions they perform, definitions offered by social constructivist approaches to international regimes usually include aspects of the constitutive effects of international regimes on the identity of the members of the regime.

3. THEORETICAL PERSPECTIVES

Interest-based or neoliberal (→ *Theory Concept: Liberalism and Neoliberalism*) theories have become the mainstream approach to analyse international regimes. To provide a broad overview of these rationalist theories, the most widely discussed and thus most influential functional theory of international regimes, by Robert Keohane, is presented in the following. In *After Hegemony* Keohane seeks to explain the reasons for the function, emergence and persistence of regimes as a form of international cooperation. He starts with the precondition of the existence of a particular situation: states, active in a specific issue area of international politics, share common interests which can only be realized through cooperation (Keohane 1984: 6). But, despite these common interests, it cannot be taken for granted that their existence will automatically lead to cooperation since a particular constraint hinders cooperation attempts: uncertainty about the compliance with terms of cooperation already agreed upon by other states. To illustrate this problematic situation, called 'problem of collective action', Keohane points to rational-choice theory, particularly the single-play, two-person Prisoners's Dilemma (→ *Game Theory*). He demonstrates that 'barriers to information and communication in world politics can impede co-operation and create discord even when common interests exist' (see Keohane 1984: 69).

Yet if players engage in repeated interaction, the probability for co-operation increases (Keohane 1984: 75–8). As both players realize that betraying a cooperation partner will reduce the possibility of future cooperation agreements and might further lead to a bad reputation within the international system, both have a strong incentive for playing fair. However, this 'shadow of the future' (Axelrod 1984) is not enough, according to Keohane: international cooperation is only likely if the cooperation is institutionalized through an international regime, since international regimes do have specific advantages, such as the reduction of transactional costs and the provision of information about the other actors within a regime. By offering a negotiation framework with well-defined parameters of cooperation, international regimes can reduce transaction costs that originate in the efforts of establishing and main-taining international negotiations. Furthermore, international regimes reduce the incentives of misbehaviour by stating and implementing specific control mechanisms while producing incentives to play fair and thus reducing the aforementioned uncertainty. In addition, institutional-ized cooperation in international regimes creates possibilities for pack-age deals within a particular issue of international politics (Keohane 1984: 89–109).

In summary, Keohane states that the main reason for the emergence of international regimes is their function, i.e. their capacity to facilitate cooperation (thus this is often called the 'functional' approach to inter-national regimes). Depending on the degree of interdependence within a specific issue area of international politics, states as rational actors calculate the possibilities of gaining better outcomes through institu-tionalized cooperation.

Keohane's approach towards the understanding of international regimes has been widely debated and has influenced subsequent perspectives in the theory of international regimes. Although Keohane writes his theory of international regimes as a result of the failing of (→) neorealism to explain the persistence of international regimes, he admits that hegemony facilitates their establishment. According to neorealists such as Stephen Krasner (1976) or Charles Kindleberger (1976), the emergence and function of international regimes can be explained by the distribution of power within the specific issue area of international politics. From this theoretical perspective an international regime emerges once a powerful state is willing and has the resources to establish the institution and guarantee the implementation of its rules. Consequently, as soon as the power of the (→) hegemon declines, the international regime ceases to exist.

Furthermore, Keohane's attempt to illustrate problems of international cooperation using game theory has been further developed by Arthur Stein (1983) and Duncan Snidal (1986), focusing not only on the Prisoner's Dilemma as the basic problematic situation in world politics. The authors add different problem constellations, which increase or decrease the probability for cooperation, depending on the interests of states within a particular issue area of world politics and potential benefits of double-crossing the other player in the game.

The theory of international regimes postulated by neoliberals has been criticized by neorealists such as Joseph Grieco (1988) or Stephan Krasner (1991), arguing that these institutional and functional explanations for cooperation underestimate the consequences of anarchy. Grieco, for instance, highlights one particular constraint: he states that within anarchical structures the major problem for cooperation is not only uncertainty, but the unequal distribution of gains. Within an anarchical self-help system, states are not only concerned about their own absolute gains: they always have to have an eye on the gains of the others. Given that today's cooperation partner might be the future adversary, states are seen to prevent increasing relative power capabilities of other states. And since they cannot afford relative losses, stable cooperation within international regimes is not likely.

The main social constructivist criticism on neoliberal theories of international regimes centres on the assumption of states as rational actors with constant interests in question. According to Alexander Wendt (1992, 1999) international regimes do not only reflect the interests of states, they are able to influence and even change these interests and the underlying identities. This theoretical view highlights the interpretation of international regimes as social institutions, enabling debates and communication. States not only pursue their rational interest, but sometimes might need an institutionalized norm-based communication process to identify what their particular interests concerned are. International regimes provide a normative structure which influences state behaviour and ultimately influences state identity: 'Even if egoistic reasons were its starting point, the process of cooperating tends to redefine those reasons by reconstituting identities and interests in terms of new intersubjective understandings and commitments' (Wendt 1992: 417). In this logic, not only do international regimes reflect the rational interests of states, but the principles and norms of international regimes become constitutive for the state's interests and identities (see for instance Müller 1993).

4. EMPIRICAL PROBLEMS

As already mentioned, the concept of international regimes has been applied to a variety of institutions, such as the human rights regime (Donnelly 1986), or the General Agreement on Tariffs and Trade (GATT) (Finlayson and Zacher 1985). The most prominent example during the initial research phase on international regimes was the Nuclear Non-Proliferation Regime, which we therefore use as an illustration: after the beginning of the nuclear age, marked by the powerful demonstration of nuclear weapons' destruction capacity during the Second World War, the international community realized that a spread of nuclear weapons would pose a major threat to international security. The international non-proliferation regime was established in order to prevent the proliferation of nuclear weapons through a complex network of national and international institutions and, in addition, limit the number of nuclear powers to the five then in existence. The core element of the regime is the Nuclear Non-Proliferation Treaty (NPT), which entered into force in 1970, and consists of a preamble and 11 articles. The treaty proscribes the proliferation of nuclear weapons and calls on the existing nuclear powers to dismantle their nuclear capacities while highlighting the right to peaceful-usage nuclear technology (Goldblat 1985: 3). According to Müller, who applied Krasner's functional theoretical conceptualizations to the Nuclear Non-Proliferation Regime, the regime rests upon four principles, such as the belief that proliferation increases the likelihood of war, and the belief that a peaceful use of nuclear technologies is compatible with the aim of non-proliferation of nuclear weapons. Furthermore, Müller identifies several norms of the regime which are closely related to the aforementioned principles, such as the obligations that non-nuclear states shall not seek to acquire nuclear weapons and that nuclear states should respectively not assist non-nuclear states in any efforts to acquire these weapons. Moreover, these norms are translated into specific rules, such as the proscription for any nuclear-weapon(s) state to transfer nuclear weapons to any recipient, and can be differentiated into three categories: rules concerning export of nuclear technologies, rules related to the norm of cooperation, and rules with regard to the norm to safeguard, regulating the civilian use of nuclear technologies (Müller 1998: 282–90). In addition to these principles, norms and rules, the regime consists of several *decision-making procedures*, such as the procedures for the establishment of safeguard agreements between non-nuclear-weapon states, parties to the treaty and the International Atomic Energy Agency (IAEA), created on the one hand to inhibit the use of nuclear capacities for military purposes, while on the other hand safeguarding the possibilities of non-nuclear states for economic development by the peaceful use of nuclear technologies (Goldblat 1985: 3–16).

Although the concept of international regimes is still applied today, the mainstream focus of liberal IR research has shifted away from the establishment of international regimes as specific forms of international institutions and has instead become involved with the analysis of prospects to tackle problems of (→) global governance. After the end of the Cold War and against the background of the contemporary globalization process the majority of liberal scholars started to refer more frequently to the broader concept of global governance despite the fact that both concepts rest upon the same liberal theoretical foundations.

5. CORE READING

Krasner, Stephen D. (ed.) (1983) *International Regimes* (Ithaca, NY: Cornell University Press). Introduces conceptualization and theoretical approaches towards the study of international regimes.

Keohane, Robert O. (1984) *After Hegemony* (Princeton, NJ: Princeton University Press). Explains how international cooperation is possible without the support of a hegemonic power by the establishment of international institutions.

Hasenclever, Andreas, Peter Mayer and Volker Rittberger (1997) *Theories of International Regimes* (Cambridge: Cambridge University Press). Examines three different theoretical approaches to international regimes.

6. USEFUL WEBSITES

http://www.un.org/Depts/dda/WMD/treaty/. Official UN website about the Nuclear Non-Proliferation Treaty.
http://unfccc.int/2860.php. Official website of the United Nations Framework Convention on Climate Change.

International Society

1. CORE QUESTIONS ADDRESSED

- What is the difference between an international society and an international system?
- How has international society evolved, and what are its present challenges?
- How does international society relate to world society?

2. DEFINITIONS

The concept of international society is one of the core contributions of the so-called 'English School' of International Relations to the study of international politics. Hedley Bull, one of the most important scholars working from within this school, defined international society as 'a group of states, conscious of certain common interests and common values' that 'conceive themselves to be bound by a common set of rules in their relations with one another, and share in the working of common institutions' (Bull 1977: 13). The society is therefore 'international' in that its constitutive units are states: it operates between ('inter') nation-states. This makes the use of the term society unusual, as we would normally expect individuals to be what a society is made up of. Bull's argument however is that states have built relations with each other that do have distinctively societal characteristics: they have common interests, common values, and share common institutions. In particular, the international society as embodied in the United Nations after the Second World War has operated on the basis of two interrelated core norms: (→) sovereignty and non-intervention. These characteristics set the international society apart from a mere system. The units that are part of a system do relate to each other, but they are not conscious of these relationships, there is no reflection on shared interests and values, and there is no commitment to common norms and institutions.

The concept of an international society also needs to be set apart from the concept of a world society (Buzan 2004). While the constitutive units of an international society are states, those of world society are individuals; world society therefore refers to the idea that we witness the emergence of societal links between individuals that transcend the nation-state, including global norms (such as (→) human rights) that refer to the individual human being directly, rather than, as has been the case in international society, through the state. Groups of individuals, such as non-governmental organizations or multinational companies, are therefore part of world society, whereas groups of states, such as alliances or intergovernmental organizations, are part of international society.

3. THEORETICAL PERSPECTIVES

The 'English School' grew out of the regular meetings of the 'British Committee for the Theory of International Politics' after the Second World War, which was centred around the University of Cambridge and the London School of Economics and Political Science, thus the label 'English' despite the fact that most of the participants were not English at all (Bull, for instance, was Australian). Proponents of this school follow Martin Wight's argument that international politics is not simply realist or liberal in nature (→ Theory Concepts: Realism and Neorealism; Liberalism and Neoliberalism), but that there are always three traditions at play: realism in the tradition of Hobbes; revolutionism in the tradition of Kant (usually, and in the present book as well, labelled as 'liberalism', although Wight (1977, 1991) wanted to emphasize the revolutionary changes that liberalism involves for the state system); and rationalism in the tradition of the seventeenth-century international lawyer Hugo Grotius (→ International Law). The latter tradition of rationalism is the one that emphasizes most the core characteristics of international society, especially the common legal framework within which states operate. So while the English School argues there are always three traditions at play, its proponents also often have a normative commitment to the further development of the international society and therefore to strengthening the rationalist strand of international politics.

The emphasis on norms and institutions brings the English School in close proximity to social constructivism (Dunne 1995, 1998) (➔ *Theory Concept: Social Constructivism*). Both share, for instance, an emphasis on socialization – the process through which states adopt the identity, norms and institutions of international society. In contrast, such a socialization process is absent from the conceptual toolkit of neorealism, for which international relations remains an international system but not a society. Socialization is also a rather problematic concept within neoliberalism. While neoliberalism emphasizes the role of common institutions and therefore a particular element of international society, the bulk of neoliberal work focuses on the interests that states have in participating in such institutions and the benefits that signing up to common norms and principles brings with it, rather than on the constitutive aspects of such norms. However, as with the relationship between neoliberalism and social constructivism, and as in the discussion of (➔) international regimes, the dividing line between neoliberalism and the English School when it comes to international society is not clear-cut, and some authors have emphasized their similarities (e.g. Buzan 1995).

4. EMPIRICAL PROBLEMS

Most of the debates within the English School focus on the exact nature of international society, and its relationship with world society. One core theme is the evolution of international society, which emerged with the rise of the modern territorial state (➔ *Territoriality and Borders*) in Europe. Often, the Peace of Westphalia – ending the Thirty Years' War in 1648 and establishing the principle of rule over a specific territory (rather than, for instance, on the basis of personal allegiance) – is seen as an important threshold in this process, but it is important to bear in mind that it took several hundred years before the state system, without which there cannot be an international society, was established on a global level. On the one hand, entities such as the Holy Roman Empire did not operate fully according to the principle of exclusive territoriality until the early nineteenth century; on the other hand, the domination of the world by (➔) empires meant that the notion of an international society until the twentieth century had been by and large restricted to Europe (Watson 1992). It was only after the advent of nationalism and the formation of nation-states, and after decolonization, that one could speak of a truly global international society (Bull and Watson 1984).

There is then the question of what the core principles of this international society are. We have already mentioned sovereignty and non-intervention above, but these are clearly very rudimentary norms. The English School has generally been divided between so-called pluralists, emphasizing the need for safeguards to the existence of individual states to guarantee the pluralist nature of international society, and so-called solidarists, arguing for normative commitments of states to each other beyond merely respecting each others' existence (Wheeler 1992; Buzan 2004). Since the end of the Cold War, the question of (→) humanitarian intervention has become a core issue of this debate (Wheeler 2000). Pluralists tend to be sceptical towards intervention unless it is in response to an already existing violation of sovereignty, such as when Iraq invaded Kuwait in 1991. Solidarists, in contrast, advocate intervention if there are overriding humanitarian concerns, such as mass starvation caused by civil war, as in the case of the long-running dispute in Sudan.

The pluralism/solidarism debate is closely related to the question of how world society interacts with international society (Buzan 2004). Arguably, if world society does not exist, there is no ground on which another norm may override the principle of sovereignty and non-intervention. If however there is a societal element that binds people together across state borders, then there may be a responsibility we bear towards others that transcends state borders. From a pluralist point of view, such an understanding of world society has the potential to undermine the order provided by international society: if the principle of sovereignty is no longer absolute, the core of the existence of states may soon be called into question by reference to all sorts of universal principles. This is why pluralists continue to advocate the guarantee of (→) human rights through the state system rather than through the possibility of direct appeal to a world human rights court. Solidarists on the other hand point out that an international society can only be built when there are some common norms that people share. They see human rights therefore not necessarily as a threat to the order of international society, but as potentially enhancing and deepening international society.

Clearly, these disputes have become more pertinent with the transformations often associated with the term (→) globalization, with the further development of international jurisprudence (including the International Criminal Court, where individuals can be tried independent of their nationality), and with the intensification of (→) regional integration processes, particularly in the European Union (Diez and Whitman 2002). There is therefore the question of whether the era of the classic international society–based on the predominance of territorial states and the norms of sovereignty and non-intervention – is already coming to an end. However, even if this is the case, it is not clear what will replace it. One feature of the emerging world order seems to be the co-existence of regional international societies with a rather more dense institutional and normative framework than we are used to from the classic international society. Another feature is likely to be the increased importance of world society actors as diverse as non-governmental organizations, multinational companies and (→) terrorist groups.

5. CORE READING

Bull, Hedley (1977) *The Anarchical Society: A Study of Order in World Politics* (Basingstoke: Macmillan). The classic statement of a pluralist conception of international society by one of the most important thinkers of the English School.

Buzan, Barry (2004) *From International to World Society? English School Theory and the Social Structure of Globalisation* (Cambridge: Cambridge University Press). An up-to-date assessment of the value of the English School for the analysis of international relations, with a focus on the relationship between international and world society.

Dunne, Tim (1998) *Inventing International Society: A History of the English School* (Basingstoke: Palgrave). An excellent history of the English School, linking the English School to more recent strands of theorizing such as social constructivism.

6. USEFUL WEBSITES

http://www.polis.leeds.ac.uk/research/international-relations-security/english-school/. Website initiated by Barry Buzan, Richard Little and Ole Wæver to strengthen ties within the English School community, including a detailed bibliography and working groups.

http://www.theory-talks.org/search?x=0&y=0&q=hedley+bull. Interview with Barry Buzan on 'International Society, Securitisation, and an English School Map of the World'.

http://www.e-ir.info/?p=3070. 'English School and Constructivism: A Model of Co-operation Rather Than Synthesis' on the website e-International Relations, which is a hub of information and analysis.

1. CORE QUESTIONS ADDRESSED

- What are the levels of analysis in International Relations?
- To what extent do levels of analysis matter for our analyses?
- What are the problems with the neorealist conception of the system level?

2. DEFINITIONS

The idea of different levels of analysis in International Relations was originally brought into the discipline by Kenneth Waltz, but its most famous statement remains David Singer's 1961 article 'The Levels-of-Analysis Problem in International Relations' (Singer 1961). Singer considers a level of analysis to be an 'orientation' (Singer 1961: 82) with which analysts approach a problem, in which they can always look 'upon the components or upon the system' (Singer 1961: 77). In International Relations, the components are usually considered to be states, and the system the international system. Singer essentially argues that research in International Relations, at least at the time when he wrote his piece, tends to conflate these levels and therefore produce muddled results. In Singer's view, a scientific analysis of international relations needs to be aware of the level on which it operates, as both a focus on the state, for instance in explaining foreign policy through domestic factors, and a focus on the system, for instance in explaining the stability of international politics through the polarity of the system, put their own emphasis on specific aspects in describing, explaining and making predictions about an issue. They also have their advantages and disadvantages. Thus, in Singer's view, research on the systemic level provides 'a more comprehensive and total picture', whereas research on the national level gives us 'richer detail, greater depth, and more intensive portrayal' (Singer 1961: 89). Above all, however, Singer argues that research on different levels also wants to explain different puzzles, or at least different aspects of a puzzle, and thus cannot easily be integrated (Singer 1961: 91).

3. THEORETICAL PERSPECTIVES

The levels-of-analysis problem is tied to a scientific conceptualization of International Relations, which since the late 1950s increasingly phrased analyses in terms of causal explanations which required the definition of variables, the gathering of data and the testing of hypotheses (see Buzan 1995: 199). In this context, the question of whether one can explain systemic phenomena with subsystemic variables became a major issue. More than any other theory, it was neorealism (→ *Theory Concept: Realism and Neorealism*) that brought this issue to the fore. Already in 1959, Waltz had argued that war had been explained by reference to individual characteristics of human beings (the classical realist argument), by reference to the character of a state (→ *Democratic Peace*) or by reference to the structure of the system (Waltz 1959). Just like Singer two years later, Waltz thought that it is important to be aware of the levels at which an analysis operates, and he also thought it difficult to move between levels. Thus, he insists that one cannot explain a specific foreign policy, in this case the decision to attack another state, by reference to the structure of the state system. To explain war, therefore, it will always be necessary to make references to the individual and state levels, or in Waltz's terminology, the 'first and second image' (Waltz 1959: 232). However, Waltz also suggests that the systemic level of analysis, or what he calls the 'third image', is none the less highly important and in some ways prior to the other two, as it provides the framework in which states have to act (Waltz 1959: 238). These initial thoughts became the cornerstones of Waltz's *Theory of International Politics*, in which he transforms realism into a systemic theory (Waltz 1979). Waltz can call his book, perhaps slightly arrogantly, *Theory of International Politics* because he wants to focus on the international level and explain systemic outcomes by systemic factors (1979: 78).

Other theoretical approaches, unsurprisingly, have taken issue with Waltz to various degrees. Neoliberalism (→ *Theory Concept: Liberalism and Neoliberalism*) has tended to take the move to the systemic level on board, but differed in its conceptualization of the system, which is in the view of Keohane and Nye (1989) characterized by complex interdependence rather than polarity. Generally speaking, many critics of Waltz have pointed to the lack of a conceptualization of meaningful interaction in neorealism (see Buzan 1995 for a summary). Such interaction cannot simply be relegated to the unit level, and it changes the entire picture of a system, as interaction brings with it the possibility of change (Ruggie 1983).

With the rise of social constructivism (→ *Theory Concept: Social Constructivism*), the levels-of-analysis debate has gained importance again since the late 1980s, although with a twist. Firstly, quite a few constructivists have pointed to the effects of systemic factors, such as the human rights discourse, on state behaviour (e.g. Risse et al. 1999b). Moving in the opposite direction, the emergence of new international institutions such as the International Criminal Court has given rise to the study of systemic effects of state behaviour (e.g. Deitelhoff 2009). As it is, both of these approaches take their lead from the importance of interaction. Thus, Alexander Wendt (1999: 147) considers unit-level approaches to include only those studies that exclusively focus on domestic explanations of foreign policy, which he calls 'atomist'. Instead, he works with what he calls micro- and macrostructure, where microstructure comprises interaction between units, and macrostructure the core norms of the system. In such an understanding, both 'levels' are interlinked and constitute each other.

4. EMPIRICAL PROBLEMS

A core site of contention in relation to the levels-of-analysis debate has been the explanation of foreign policy. This is partly a consequence of using neorealism as a systemic theory, against Waltz's own insistence, in such an endeavour. Most analysts have agreed however that one has to amend neorealism in order to make it useful in this sense, and include arguments about state response to systemic pressures (see e.g. Baumann et al. 2001).

The levels-of-analysis problem also plays a role in the debate about (→) democratic peace, as the latter can be located on the state level (democratic states do not go to war), the interaction level (democracies do not go to war with each other), and the systemic level (international systems dominated by democracies are more peaceful than others) (Gleditsch and Hegre 1997).

5. CORE READING

Buzan, Barry (1995) 'The Level of Analysis Problem in International Relations Reconsidered', in Ken Booth and Steve Smith (eds), *International*

Relations Theory Today (Oxford: Polity), 198–216. An excellent discussion of the concept from a position sympathetic yet critical towards neorealism.

Singer, J. David (1961) 'The Levels-of-Analysis Problem in International Relations', *World Politics* 14 (1), 77–92. The classic exposition of levels of analysis in IR.

Waltz, Kenneth N. (1959) *Man, the State and War: A Theoretical Analysis* (New York: Columbia University Press). Waltz's highly influential first work, based on his 1954 doctoral thesis, that introduced the idea of different levels of analysis for the first time in IR in a consistent way – still a classic worth reading.

6. USEFUL WEBSITES

http://globetrotter.berkeley.edu/people3/Waltz/waltz-con0.html. In the series 'Conversations with History', Waltz among other things describes his understanding of the levels-of-analysis problem developed in *Man, the State and War.*

http://sitemaker.umich.edu/jdsinger/home. Homepage of David Singer includes his bibliography and syllabi of past courses.

Theory Concept:
Liberalism and
Neoliberalism

1. CORE QUESTIONS ADDRESSED

- Which of the diverse approaches under the umbrella-term liberalism are applied to the study of International Relations?
- How does liberalism explain international cooperation?
- In what ways does neoliberalism connect to international regimes and game theory?

2. OVERVIEW AND BACKGROUND

Liberalism is one of the central approaches towards the understanding of world politics and is commonly referred to as the theoretical 'opponent' of realism (→ *Theory Concept: Realism and Neorealism*). It entered academic International Relations in the period after the First World War, but rests upon a tradition of thought that includes Immanuel Kant and Hugo Grotius. Today's usage of the term liberalism includes a variety of different theoretical approaches not always directly related to world politics, which sometimes makes it difficult to differentiate for students of International Relations. In this overview, liberalism refers both to the theoretical approaches of classical liberalism, also called idealism, as well as neoliberalism, or neoliberal institutionalism, which was long the mainstream theoretical approach towards understanding international institutions.

Liberalism in International Relations is not to be confused with liberal economic approaches, such as Milton Friedman's monetarism, which argues for attributing priority to capitalism and free trade and explicitly rejects political interference into markets and economies. In addition, liberalism in International Relations is to be distinguished from the theoretical approach towards international relations elaborated by Andrew Moravcsik in the 1990s, which the author also termed 'new liberalism', largely because of its focus on the bargaining process between domestic interest groups in the formulation of foreign policy preferences. Moravcsik's considerations refer to the importance of domestic variables, such as winning coalitions, for the creation of national preferences which are translated into foreign policy actions. Moreover, there is a further liberal approach, also referred to as liberal peace or the (→) democratic peace thesis, arguing that a state's political system is key in explaining a state's foreign policy

Classical liberalism

As already mentioned, classical liberalism was introduced to the study of world politics in the first half of the twentieth century, in particular as a theoretical answer to the historical events of that time. In order to investigate prospects for peace and identify the causes of war, liberal scholars as well as politicians, including US president Woodrow Wilson, concluded that exaggerated nationalism not only had led the European states into an imperialistic rivalry for colonies, but also resulted in aggressive competition for (→) power and influence. In order to prevent the recurrence of war, liberals emphasized that the options for political actions of nation-states must and can be constrained through international law and the establishment of international institutions. The establishment of international institutions would increase the interdependence among states, allowing for a peaceful settlement of disputes through negotiation or mediation, and hence reducing the probability of war. To this end, Wilson induced the establishment of the League of Nations during his presidency of the United States – somewhat ironically, an institution the United States would never become a member of. The ideas of classical liberalism bear close connection to theoretical concepts introduced by Hugo Grotius (1583–1645), who highlighted the possibilities and emphasized the importance of the enforcement of (→) international law, and the work of Immanuel Kant (1724–1804), who stated that democracies are less war prone than other types of political systems and that they should establish a league of republican states in order to pursue their common interests and ensure lasting peace (→ *Democratic Peace*).

In the history of academic International Relations, classical liberalism is also referred to as idealism, highlighting that this theoretical approach rests upon normative premises: although liberals accept that different societies might have different values and norms, they nevertheless believe in peace as the one common interest of all societies. Owing to this belief in men and society, idealists have been severely criticized by realism, in particular after the failure of the League of Nations and the outbreak of the Second World War. Liberals, such as David Mitrany, reacted to these critiques and political events by focusing on functional instead of normative approaches towards the establishment of international institutions (→ *Functionalism*).

Neoliberalism

Neoliberalism, also called rationalist institutionalism, emerged as a response to the increase in number and variety of international institutions in the 1970s, which challenged the neorealist hypothesis of cooperation among states as being very unlikely under the condition of anarchy. According to Robert O. Keohane, who defined international institutions as 'persistent and connected sets of rules (formal and informal) that prescribe behavioural roles, constrain activity and shape expectations' (1989: 3), the existing variety of international institutions, including international organizations such as the United Nations, as well as (→) international regimes such as the Nuclear Non-Proliferation Treaty (NPT), indicated that realist considerations about the consequences of anarchy might be wrong. In contrast to classical liberalism, neoliberalism accepts realist assumptions of the international system's anarchical nature as well as the premise of states as single and rational actors in world politics. But, in contrast to realists, neoliberals drew different conclusions: while realists emphasize that international cooperation under the condition of anarchy is only possible with the protective support of a hegemon to guarantee the enforcement of rules and norms, neoliberals argue that the potential for international cooperation is greater than realism assumes (Keohane 1989: 1–16). This potential for international cooperation originates in the fact that states in the international system are connected through a variety of social and economic transactions, a condition described by Keohane and Joseph Nye in *Power and Interdependence* as mutual interdependence: 'Interdependence in world politics refers to situations characterized by reciprocal effects among countries or among actors in different countries' (Keohane and Nye 1977: 7). According to Keohane and Nye, mutual interdependence challenges the premise of states as autonomous actors in world politics and reduces the importance of military capacities and power politics since it forces states to react to external demands and, in consequence, increases the incentives for cooperation, in particular in the economic sector. A restriction in trade, for instance, would produce detrimental and costly effects for nation-states. As a result, the pursuit of international cooperation becomes a rational strategy for states, in particular in order to avoid or reduce costs.

Neoliberalism further disagrees with realism on the assumption that states focus on relative gains. Instead, neoliberals argue that, under the condition of interdependence, states pursue absolute gains and are interested in cooperation since they share common interests (→ *International Regimes*). But, according to Robert O. Keohane, these shared interests do not automatically translate into cooperation: under the state of anarchy, the fundamental constraint to interstate cooperation is the lack of authority to enforce rules and the fear of states of being double-crossed by their partners causing so-called problems of collective action (→ *Game Theory*). At this point, international institutions, such as international regimes or international organizations, can facilitate cooperation by establishing an organizational framework characterized by rules of procedure and mechanisms of collective sanctions (Keohane 1988:

380–6). According to Keohane, 'in order to cooperate in world politics on more than a sporadic basis, human beings have to use institutions' (Keohane 1988: 386).

3. METHODOLOGIES

While classical or idealistic liberalism seeks to overcome the war-prone condition of anarchy through the establishment of international institutions underlined by the belief in human reason and morality, neoliberalism, just like its opponent realism, is based on rationalist premises. Neoliberalism accepts the concept of self-interested actors (*homo oeconomicus*) and assumes that by understanding their preferences and motivations, even complex political outcomes can be explained (*logic of consequentiality*). As a result of these premises, neoliberalism relies exceedingly upon game theoretical scenarios such as the Prisoner's Dilemma which provide a useful tool for explaining actors' choices in International Relations. The rationalist approach is flexible enough to allow for variations in preferences: not only can preferences differ substantially with regard to the contents, but states' preferences can also differ with regard to time perspectives. But, as Lisa Martin (2007) has argued, rationalism does not tell us what state preferences exactly are. Although in theory a cost–benefit calculation should enable the scholars to identify the preferences of an actor, this approach has in practice proven to oversimplify the complex situation of decision-making. Here, social constructivism (→ *Theory Concept: Social Constructivism*) has pointed to the importance of role-playing and social or moral considerations, rather than simple cost–benefit calculations, throughout the decision-making process (Martin 2007: 112; Keohane 1988: 381).

4. EMPIRICAL APPLICATIONS

As already mentioned, the theoretical approach of neoliberalism has been developed in order to answer the question of how to explain the emergence and spread of international institutions under the condition of anarchy in the 1970s, as well as the likelihood of cooperation in general. In consequence, empirical applications focus mostly on specific institutions, such as (→) international regimes and the preceding negotiation processes. Presupposing that there is always a need for international institutions whenever cross-border relations lead to interactions which states view as undesirable in light of their own interests, neoliberalism has been applied to illustrate negotiation or decision-making processes, such as the negotiation of the General Agreement on Tariffs and Trade (GATT) or the Nuclear Non-Proliferation Treaty (NPT). Furthermore, game theoretical approaches illustrated the initiation and maintenance of arms races between superpowers by depicting this problematic situation as a classical collaborative problem.

5. CENTRAL CRITICISMS

The neoliberal premise of cooperation as more likely under the condition of interdependence has been severely criticized by neorealists, arguing that neoliberals underestimate the importance of power in world politics. Particularly in the issue domain of security, but also more generally whenever a problematic situation relates to coordination problems, the importance of relative gains for the survival and the rank of a particular nation-state should be considered carefully (see for instance Grieco 1988).

From a social constructivist point of view, social behaviour and complex decision-making processes cannot adequately be comprehended by only referring to rationalistic premises or self-interested individual calculations. According to Wendt, these approaches overestimate human ability for rationality while at the same time underestimating the consequences of social environments and communicative processes (Wendt 1992).

According to Andrew Moravcsik (1997), neoliberalism does not take into account the importance of domestic political processes for the creation of preferences towards foreign policy. He argues that neoliberalism further underestimates the importance of private actors in world politics in general.

Critical Theory (→ *Theory Concept: Marxism and Critical Theory*) accuses neoliberalism of simply reproducing existing patterns of exploitation and injustice, by accepting realist premises about the consequences of anarchy and the importance of power politics, without critically reflecting their origin and outcomes.

6. CORE READING

Axelrod, Robert (1984) *The Evolution of Cooperation* (New York: Basic Books). Basic considerations about the prospects for cooperation in world politics.

Keohane, Robert O. (1983) *After Hegemony: Cooperation and Discord in the World Political Economy* (Princeton, NJ: Princeton University

Press). Underlines the mechanisms for how international cooperation is possible without hegemonic support.

Keohane, Robert O. and Joseph Nye (1977) *Power and Interdependence: World Politics in Transition* (Boston, MA: Little-Brown). An introduction to the main theoretical considerations about the consequences of interdependence.

7. USEFUL WEBSITES

http://plato.stanford.edu/entries/liberalism/. Detailed account of liberalism as a philosophical tradition of thought by the *Stanford Encyclopedia of Philosophy*.
http://www.youtube.com/watch?v=5foxGFXNI-s. As part of UC Berkeley's series 'Conversations with History', Robert O. Keohane talks about liberal IR theory and international institutions.

Theory Concept: Marxism and Critical Theory

1. CORE QUESTIONS ADDRESSED

- What are the fundamental assumptions of Marxism?
- What are the main differences between conventional theory and Critical Theory?
- Why does Marxism continue to be relevant for the study of international relations?

2. OVERVIEW AND BACKGROUND

Marxism entered the field of International Relations in the late 1960s with the structuralist works of dependency and world systems theory authors such as Fernando Henrique Cardoso and Immanuel Wallerstein.

Today, it constitutes one of its main theoretical approaches, a development which was halted neither by the end of the Cold War nor the fact that Marx's writings do not directly relate to the international realm (Hobden and Jones 2008: 146). While not theories of International Relations as such, theories of imperialism (→ *Empire*) share a number of fundamental Marxist assumptions. In contrast to International Relations theories such as realism (→ *Theory Concept: Realism and Neorealism*), there is no single Marxist perspective on world politics. Instead, there is a variety of theoretical strands with different connections to 'orthodox' Marxism. New Marxism bases its theoretical foundations directly on Marx while his work is only a first base for authors in Critical Theory, occasionally referred to as post-Marxists, who frequently have a strong connection to poststructuralism (→ *Theory Concept: Postmodernism and Poststructuralism*). The relation of Critical Theory to Marxism is best characterized by the Frankfurt School's self-presented intellectual challenge to preserve the 'spirit' but not the 'letter' of 'classical' Marxism (Friedman 1981: 35–6). What all Marxist perspectives have in common is, first, a desire to subject 'conventional' International Relations to critical questioning and examination and, second, therein identify possibilities for social transformation.

It is further necessary to separate the everyday understanding of critical from the specific purpose of Critical Theory. Robert Cox puts forward a number of basic premises for Critical Theory which all refer to the researcher's awareness of a 'framework for action' within which all action, also that of the theorists, takes place (1981: 135). Critical theorists seek to understand the dynamics and changes this framework undergoes over time.

There are five basic 'classical' Marxist assumptions that are necessary to understand the reasoning of the different strands. First, the global capitalist system underlies and therefore influences the entirety of world politics. Marxism is interested in exposing this underlying structure and analysing it in open view. Second, the global capitalist system seeks to perpetuate itself, thereby keeping the current power structure in place. In essence, this means that the prosperity of the powerful structurally depends on the destitution of the powerless – and the powerful have no intention of changing this. Third, history is conceived of as materialist. Every historical change is a product or rather a reflection of economic developments within a society. Fourth, the central dynamic within economic development and thus the force of history itself is the tension between the means of production, i.e. the physical, non-human assets used in production, and the relations of production, i.e. the socio-economic relationships or roles of people towards production such as the capitalist or the wage worker. Together, they form the economic base of society. This economic *base* is supposed to dictate all other human social, political and cultural activities, which Marx calls the social and political *superstructure*. Politics thus mirrors economic patterns of power and control. For critical theorists, the connection is not quite so rigid: while the character of the capitalist economic system is generally exploitative, the social and political systems have certain degrees of autonomy that may open up possibilities of change for the exploited. The economic system is thus perceived as a constraint to human agency and not as making it impossible. Fifth, social life is further essentially shaped by recurring class struggle between the bourgeoisie, which owns the means of production, and the proletariat, which owns only its own labour power. As capitalism is by its very nature expansionist, this fault-line between proletariat and bourgeoisie replicates itself throughout the world. Social life in capitalism is thus shaped by a relationship of inequality and *exploitation* between the social classes. While the bourgeoisie has an inherent interest in maintaining the status quo, the proletariat struggles to change it. This is also termed dialectical materialism. Scholars in Critical Theory again expand on this by complementing class struggle with a number of further categories that may lead to social inequality and exclusion such as gender or ethnic origin – the effect of a struggle of social groups remains largely the same.

As these assumptions serve to show, Marx's writing does not easily fit into separate social sciences such as political science or economics; rather, like many of his contemporaries, he thought of the social world as a whole that can only be understood in its totality, without separating 'out' vital parts. This line of thought is discernable in the writings of scholars in the Marxist tradition, especially with regard to those concerned with international political economy.

Critical Theory

Aside from Marx, Critical Theory in International Relations is most directly inspired by the Frankfurt School of the 1920s and 1930s, including theorists such as Theodor Adorno, Herbert Marcuse and Max Horkheimer, Italian communist Antonio Gramsci and writers in the Frankfurt tradition such as Jürgen Habermas. The Frankfurt School theorists expanded on Marxist insights into the workings of capitalism by integrating thoughts on the downsides of modernity, mainly how an instrumental rationality driven by 'means–ends' calculations began to pervade all aspects of social life and therefore 'commodified' it. The combination of this phenomenon with the influence of mass culture and media has, following Marcuse's argument, absorbed the working class of European societies which subsequently ceased to be a threat to the existing system structure. People were essentially indoctrinated to accept their situation instead of understanding the true nature of their exploitation.

This line of thought is comparable to Gramsci, who answered his key question of why it has proven so difficult to promote and stage a revolution in western Europe, with the ability of ruling hegemonic groups to legitimize their rule by ideologically convincing the public of its justice (→ Hegemony). The way out of this situation of domination thus does not only concern winning the control over the material structures, but, perhaps more importantly, the development of an alternative set of counter-hegemonic concepts and values in order to successfully change the dominant ideology. While Gramsci thus focused on explaining the mechanisms of bourgeois rule within western nation-states, critical theorists in IR extended this analysis to transnational power relations and developed a critique of global capitalism. This goes hand-in-hand with substantial criticism of 'conventional' IR theories such as realism, liberal institutionalism and even world systems theory (→ Dependency) as regards their static nature, their focus on nation-states as the sole actors and their ensuing inability to explain change. In contrast to Critical Theory, these 'problem-solving theories', as Cox calls them, are not only unable to analyse structural change, but also contribute to perpetuating the current power structures with all their injustices. The existing power structures are sustained through (→) hegemony which emerges from concrete historical structures on three levels of action: first, social forces, i.e. the totality of social relations in their material, institutional and discursive forms; second, forms of state; and third, world orders (Cox 1981: 138). The relationship of these three levels is not linear but dialectical, which means that each of these levels can be a starting point for analysing historical processes, and thus a cause in their own right. This stands in direct connection to Cox's criticism of neorealism as it puts states' power relations into a broader perspective: 'state power ceases to be the sole explanatory factor and becomes part of what is to be explained' (Cox 1986: 223). However, it also breaks with 'classical' Marxist assumptions, as forms of state and world orders are not solely determined by the dominant social classes. Instead, through analysing a historical structure, i.e. a specific constellation of social forces, state and world order, Cox seeks to reconstruct hegemonic structures and thereby reveal the social and international interrelation of production, power and rule.

The crucial elements of this Gramscian analysis thus concern the origins, development and possible transformation of global hegemonic structures (Linklater 2009; Gill 1993b). In this regard, Stephen Gill put emphasis on the maintenance of hegemony through both the cooperation of powerful elites in the centre and the periphery (→ *Dependency*) and the international economic and political institutions of (→) global governance. Gill terms the latter assumption 'disciplinary neoliberalism' to indicate the way global governance institutions urge national governments to adopt their hegemonic, neoliberal conceptions of the state, society and the world market (1995, 2003). Both Gill and Cox, in Gramscian tradition, further contain premises on how 'counter-hegemony' can challenge these dominant political structures.

The theoretical works of Jürgen Habermas proved an important addition to Critical Theory in International Relations – especially in regard to their provision of alternatives to the aforementioned process of 'commodification'. Habermasian concepts, such as communicative action (→ *Discourse*), introduced the importance of language and communication into Critical Theory and provided ways of settling arising conflicts by consensus rather than the exercise of (→) power. Andrew Linklater draws on Habermas in extending his contribution to the global as opposed to merely the domestic realm, arguing for a theory of world politics that would be 'committed to the emancipation of the species' (1990: 8). Linklater's work is therefore centred on developing an advanced understanding of human community subdivided into three dimensions that would contribute to eliminating any constraints on human beings' potential and freedom. The first dimension relates to a normatively based philosophical critique of the state as a form of political organization that deliberately promotes exclusion by creating artificial boundaries between 'citizens' and 'non-citizens' (Linklater 1982). Linklater's second dimension to community includes a sociological analysis, or rather historical reconstruction, of the development of the modern state system, the 'bounded communities', to identify its inherent problems, mainly its totalistic nature (Linklater 1998). Finally, the third, praxeological dimension is concerned with identifying possibilities of reconstructing community and international relations to their full emancipatory and cosmopolitan potential (1998). One of these possibilities lies in expanding the moral boundaries of political community, leaving the borders of the sovereign nation-state behind. Linklater's thought on these three dimensions has been taken up and expanded on by other critical theorists.

New Marxism

Marxism in its classical form, especially with regard to historical materialism, returned to International Relations from the early 1990s onwards. In the spirit of the fourth debate, authors such as Justin Rosenberg and Benno Teschke use a critique of realist works as a stepping stone. Rosenberg focuses on demonstrating that geopolitical systems, for example the classical Greek *polis* or the modern system of sovereign states, cannot be understood in isolation from the different modes of production and reproduction and wider social structures they are part of, in contrast to what realist authors had been doing for the past decades. The key to explaining International Relations is thus sought to lie in subjecting geopolitical systems to succinct historical-materialist analyses of their societies – in other words, denaturalizing them and allowing room for historical contrast (Linklater 2009: 129). Teschke's work follows similar paths. He denaturalizes the defining moment of the modern system of sovereign states, thereby rejecting the 'simplifying notion of the Westphalian era' (2003). His study of social property relations concludes that the appearance of the first capitalist state in the transition from the early modern to the modern system is more important for understanding today's international relations than the heralded Peace of Westphalia.

3. METHODOLOGIES

In contrast to rationalist approaches, Marxism and especially Critical Theory display a normative aim with regard to doing research. Both theory and theorist are part of the processes and events it or they analyse – it is thus neither possible nor even desirable for the researcher to remain neutral with regard to their subject. Following Cox, 'theory is always *for* someone, and *for* some purpose' (1981: 128). For him, any kind of theory is contingent on a certain space and time, as is all knowledge. Knowledge can therefore never be objective. All theories contain ideas and values present in the mind of the researcher – who has to become aware of this as it, if remaining unconsciously done, impacts on the quality of their theory. As values enter every kind of research, the question as to what values should govern analysis becomes central. Cox distinguishes between conventional problem-solving theories of international relations, such as realism and neoliberal institutionalism (→ *Theory Concept: Liberalism and Neoliberalism*), which disregard their own contingency, and Critical Theory. Conventional theories portray the current parameters of the global order as 'normal' or seek to find ways of making the current system run more 'smoothly', and thereby reinforce ruling (→) hegemony, i.e. the status quo. Critical Theory, in contrast, challenges the current order by critically reflecting on it. This also refers to reflection on theory itself. By 'denaturalizing' or defamiliarizing traditional theoretical ways of thought in this way, Critical Theory seeks to expose the dogmatism inherent to mainstream International Relations (Fierke 1998: 13).

Any kind of theory is supposed to have an inherently practical purpose and serve the cause of emancipation. Increased awareness and a better understanding of the researcher's subject, e.g. social processes, should thus be helpful in identifying ways of working towards their change. Marx formulated this point in his early theses on Feuerbach: 'the philosophers have only interpreted the world, in various ways; the point is to change it' (1977a: 100). In contrast to poststructuralism, which is often accused of relativism, both Marxists and critical theorists thus believe in the possibility of true consciousness: while problem-solving theories prevent people from recognizing and realizing their 'real' interest, this is precisely what theorists in the critical tradition seek to bring out through their normative modes of inquiry. The emancipation aspired to by critical theorists would serve to improve human existence and remove constraints to human freedom by putting an end to socially produced injustices and exploitation.

Habermas adds another cultural and ethical dimension to the emancipatory project. Criticizing Marxist overestimation of the role of 'labour' and instead putting more explanatory emphasis on the moral and cultural spheres, Habermas concludes that emancipation cannot be complete by challenging material inequalities alone. Instead, complete emancipation can only be achieved through the democratization of institutions on all levels, leading to people's full representation in all decision-making processes that may affect them (Habermas 1979).

While the normative objective of emancipation is pervasive, the means of achieving it are somewhat limited. In *The Eighteenth Brumaire of Louis Bonaparte* (1852) Marx famously stated that 'Men make their own history, but they do not make it as they please'; instead human beings make history under historically transmitted circumstances (1977b: 300). Human action, while possible and meaningful, is therefore structurally constrained and, up to a certain degree, structurally conditioned. This Marxist tendency towards attributing explanatory primacy to structures, or structuralism, is found in most Marxist and critical perspectives. At the same time, these structures are not natural or given, but historically made. Through human action it is thus also possible to change them, and both Marxism and Critical Theory seek to think in the direction of alternative structures, reverting back to emancipation.

4. EMPIRICAL APPLICATIONS

Following the theoretical 'bashing' of neorealism that was the starting point of Marxist perspectives on International Relations, authors in the tradition were mostly concerned with issues from international political economy. Frequently, Marxist studies make a point to present rival and alternative explanations to the ones outlined by liberals within the same area. This especially applies to economic (→) globalization, which Marxism has been hailed to have anticipated in writings such as the *Communist Manifesto*: 'The bourgeoisie has through its exploitation of the world market given a cosmopolitan character to production and consumption in every country' (Marx and Engels 1977: 160). Specific phenomena of globalization such as the growth of integrated transnational production patterns and the resulting creation of a 'transnational business class' beyond national boundaries have supplied manifold explanatory opportunities for Marxist International Relations (Teschke 2009: 181). Studies have analysed the shifting role of nation-states in these developments, who are responsive to transnational business class interests and act as 'transmission belts' (Cox 1992; Van der Pijl 1998).

(→) Global governance has also been analysed from a Marxist perspective, perceiving of the major governance institutions such as the World Bank and the International Monetary Fund as arenas used for the dispersion of ideological discourse by the USA and leading capitalist powers (Callinicos 2002: 263). Theorists such as Cox and Rupert also provided analyses of hegemonic power, mainly with respect to the United States of America, but also with regard to the ruling, hegemonic idea of free trade. Free trade is the very essence of a hegemonic idea – the claim that the free trade system benefits everybody has become so widely accepted that it has attained commonsense status.

New Marxists have further debated how to include Trotsky's notion of 'uneven and combined development' into the analysis of international relations. While authors such as Rosenberg view the process of 'uneven and combined development' as a transhistoric general abstraction, i.e. an overall dynamic of human history, others argue for it to be historically rooted in the relations and processes of a capitalist mode of production (Rosenberg 2006; Ashman 2009: 29). It should be noted that Marxism as a viable perspective towards analysing international relations is some-what geographically restricted: while it constitutes a proper theoretical alternative to other International Relations approaches in Europe and mainly Great Britain, its application is virtually non-existent in the American mainstream of the discipline.

In contrast, applications of Critical Theory to particular topics of International Relations have particularly mushroomed in the years since 2000 on a global scale, partly through the great interest taken in apply-ing the works of Habermas to the field (Devetak 2009: 15). Three Habermasian contributions have encouraged particularly fruitful ana-lytical and empirical results: his distinction between different types of interests (i.e. instrumental, technical, critical and cognitive) and the concepts of discursive ethics and communicative action (Diez and Steans 2005: 131). Critical insights have found application to questions as diverse as security, humanitarian intervention, European integration and the 'war on terror' (Wyn Jones 1999; Hopgood 2000).

5. CENTRAL CRITICISMS

Most of the critique targeted at 'classical' Marxism is fundamental in that it refers to its explanatory reliance on economics and class relations and the resulting neglect of the importance of issues such as nationalism, diplomacy, international law or the organizing principle of world poli-tics. This critique of economic reductionism has resurfaced with regard to all Marxist perspectives applied to International Relations and has gathered some force in the years following 9/11. Interestingly, Critical Theory as well as feminist contributions have continued to fill signifi-cant lacunae of Marxist perspectives, such as the constructions of iden-tity and difference.

Some critical theorists, particularly from a feminist position, and post-structuralist writers have questioned the emancipatory project. While

Marx was overtly critical of the social structures of his time, his works nevertheless share his period's Enlightenment. The universalism derived from Enlightenment ideas, also in the form of universal emancipation, thus runs the risk of ignoring certain marginalized groups, subjecting them to 'universal' values while repressing legitimate differences. Critical theorists with a stronger background in poststructuralism were thus apprehensive of the idea of universal emancipation as it could perpetuate the relations of power and domination it sought to eliminate. Theorists such as Linklater and Shapcott make amends in this regard by promoting 'thin cosmopolitanism' that encourages universal values without moral hierarchy, thereby doing justice to difference (Linklater 1998; Shapcott 2001).

6. CORE READING

Cox, Robert W. (1981) 'Social Forces, States and World Orders: Beyond International Relations Theory', *Millennium: Journal of International Studies* 10 (2), 126–55. Seminal article that criticizes conventional IR theories and instead suggests a dialectical understanding of international processes.

Gill, Stephen (ed.) (1993) *Gramsci, Historical Materialism and International Relations* (Cambridge: Cambridge University Press). Collects articles of the most important scholars of Gramsci in the context of IR.

Linklater, Andrew (1998) *The Transformation of Political Community: Ethical Foundations of the Post-Westphalian Era* (Cambridge: Polity Press). Critical international political theory account on what constitutes political communities in the globalization era.

7. USEFUL WEBSITES

http://www.marxists.org. Useful internet archive comprising sections on key Marxist authors, an encyclopaedia and many literary sources.

http://www.victoryiscertain.com/gramsci. A collection of writings and resources by and about Gramsci.

http://www.monthlyreview.org. Independent, openly socialist journal offering free access and publishing authors from academia and journalism.

Migration

1. CORE QUESTIONS ADDRESSED

- What are the different types of migration?
- How can migration be conceptualized theoretically?
- How is international migration related to world politics and what are the institutions regulating international migration on the global scale?

2. DEFINITIONS

Migration generally refers to the movement of people that is not merely temporary. If such movement takes place across state boundaries, we refer to it as international migration. In contrast, movement of people within the territory of a state is usually referred to as intrastate or internal migration. Migration across long distances can have various reasons and is not a recent phenomenon, although the political organization of the world into territorial states has altered the possibilities for migration. In fact, massive flows of migrants have accompanied human existence since its very beginning – among the most well-documented migration periods is the so-called 'migration of nations' from 300 to 700 AD in Europe, which involved diverse ethnic tribes such as the Slavs and the Goths.

The literature on migration commonly draws a distinction between voluntary and involuntary, or forced, migration. Voluntary migration often takes place for economic reasons, whereas forced migration tends to occur as a consequence of war, natural disasters or political, ethnic or religious persecution (Bali 2005: 173–4). However, this distinction is problematic as it is not always possible to clearly determine whether people migrate out of their own volition or out of coercion (Betts 2009: 4). Within the International Relations literature the most prominent discussion about the causes and consequences of international migration has been led with regard to a specific type of forced migrants – refugees. The term 'refugee' refers to people who 'owing to a well-founded fear of persecution . . . find themselves outside their country of origin, and are unable or unwilling to avail themselves of the protection of that country' (Article 1a of the 1951 Convention of the Status of Refugees).

3. THEORETICAL PERSPECTIVES

Although international migration is a phenomenon that has been present throughout human history, a coherent theoretical framework is still missing, probably due to its considerable variety. A fruitful attempt towards summarizing existing theoretical approaches towards international migration has been made by Massey et al. (1993) who differentiated approaches operating at different levels of analysis, starting with different theoretical assumptions and focusing on different objectives. Neoclassical economists, such as Arthur W. Lewis (1954), explain international (labour) migration in the context of macro-level economic development. In this logic, migration is caused by uneven economic growth rates between geographic regions, resulting in differences in market wages and thus inducing a movement of unskilled labour from low-wage countries into countries characterized by high market wage. In the neoclassical variation on the micro-level, international migration is conceptualized as the outcome of a rational cost–benefit calculation of individuals, calculating the prospective outcomes of movement against the expected costs (e.g. Todaro 1989). An additional theoretical approach towards the understanding of international migration has been made by the new economics of international migration, placing the cost–benefit analysis for movement into families or households as 'culturally defined units of production and consumption' while at the same time taking additional types of markets into account for the analysis (Massey et al. 1993: 439).

In response to these rationalist approaches, representatives of the so-called dual labour market theory as well as of world systems theory (→ *Dependency*) rejected the importance of rationalist individual decision-making and highlighted structural or macro-level approaches instead. Dual labour market theorists, such as Michael Piore (1979), stated for instance that immigrant labour is an intrinsic, structural demand of modern industrialized societies. In this manner, world systems theorists, following Immanuel Wallerstein (1979), related international migration to the structure of the capitalistic world market, where the consequence of the capitalist need for increasing growth rates and profits results in an ongoing exploitation of the periphery of the world by an ever-increasing demand for resources as well as for labour (Massey et al. 1993: 432–48).

The Copenhagen School (→ *Security*) highlighted the problematic relationship between security and migration. Conceptualizing 'societal security' as jeopardized by immaterial external threats to values and identities, in particular towards cultural identity, immigrating minorities can easily be perceived as threatening the integration and identity of a formerly 'well-defined' social group through 'importing' different cultural habits and languages. Ole Wæver elaborates on how the issue of immigration has been discursively cast as a security problem in the European Union by understanding migration as a threat towards 'traditional' European cultural values thus legitimating extraordinary measures and policies (Wæver 1993). Jef Huysmans continued this analysis in examining attempts to link migration to negatively connotated concepts such as terrorism and crime in order to influence European decision-making procedures in favour of stricter regulation policies (2002). However, he has also warned that linking security and migration analytically may reinforce such linkages politically.

An attempt to understand the relationship between forced migration, sovereignty and the state system through the perspectives of conventional IR theories has further been made by Alexander Betts (2009). Betts elaborates on how IR theories can be used as a tool for understanding how the important categories of migration, such as forced migration and internally displaced persons, are deeply related to the state system and the underlying conceptualization of a specific 'state–citizen–territory relationship' (Betts 2009: 58). Furthermore, Betts tries to illustrate how the attempts to institutionalize international regimes governing migration and refugee issues can be explained using 'classical' approaches to IR such as neoliberalism (→ *Theory Concept: Liberalism and Neoliberalism*).

A critical feminist perspective (→ *Theory Concept: Feminism and Gender*) on the theoretical conceptualization of migration emphasizes the blindness of conventional migration theories towards the gender dimension of international migration. Navnita Chadha Behera, for instance, argues that classical economic approaches simply regard migrants as 'non-gendered beings, or . . . assume that both men and women were subject to the same motivations to migrate' (2006: 27). These concepts tend to underestimate the possible consequences of specific gender constellations within the countries of origin which might either constrain or induce the need or want for migration. In order to understand the consequences of migration, special attention should be paid to the change of gender relations during the migration process, as for example changes in the role models of Muslim women and men migrating into western societies. By introducing the category of gender into the studies of the motivation and origins of migration, feminist approaches account for the subjective as well as for the structural and historical circumstances leading to the decision for migration (Behera 2006: 27–31).

4. EMPIRICAL PROBLEMS

As already mentioned, the assumed motivations and causes of migration differ widely but they are nevertheless always related directly or indirectly to world politics. As Betts argues, one would paint an imperfect picture of the causes of international migration, in particular forced migration, by just analysing trends within the countries of origin. Developments inducing migration, such as high rates of unemployment or political instability, are usually somehow related to a broader regional or international framework or problem. Taking the case of Sierra Leone as an example, the outbreak of a civil war, leading to internal displacement as well as to a flight into the neighbouring countries, was heavily related to the countries' richness in natural resources, in particular diamonds, and therefore indirectly related to the global political economy and the increase in demand for exploitation of natural resources. On the macro-level, key explanatory variables for the displacement of people can be identified in the global political economy, geopolitics or the international system (Betts 2009: 11–12). In addition, the consequences of international migration confront international institutions, governments and societies with a wide range of dilemmas and problems, including the control and regulation of migration as well as the increasing demand for the protection of ethnic minorities within the host states (Bali 2005: 174).

According to the Global Commission on International Migration the number of migrants increased from 82 million to 200 million between 1970 and 2005. Yet, despite its increasing scale, in comparison to other issues of world politics, international migration remains comparatively unregulated, owing to the fact that states insist on their sovereign right to decide who is allowed to enter their territory under which conditions. The only widely accepted regulated issue is a state's option to respond to refugees, an issue area in which an international regime has been established based on the Universal Declaration on Human Rights (1948) and the Convention Relating to the Status of Refugees (1951) (Bali 2005: 174; Betts 2008: 2; GCIM 2005). The fundamental principle of this convention is the norm of so-called *non-refoulement*, stipulating that no person should be sent back into a territory where they face a fear of persecution. This principle is supervised by a special agency within the United Nations System established in 1950: the Office of the United Nations High Commissioner for Refugees (UNHCR) (Betts 2009: 6).

5. CORE READING

Bali, Sita (2005) 'Migration and Refugees', in Brian White, Richard Little and Michael Smith (eds), *Issues in World Politics* (Basingstoke: Macmillan, 3rd edn). Provides a brief overview of empirical facts and current developments in the field.

Betts, Alexander (2009) *Forced Migration and Global Politics* (Oxford: Wiley-Blackwell). Analyses the emergence of a complex global refugee regime through the perspective of major IR theories.

Massey, Douglas S., et al. (1993) 'Theories of International Migration: A Review and Appraisal', *Population and Development Review* 19 (3), 431–66. Widely cited article summarizing the principal classical theoretical approaches towards international migration.

6. USEFUL WEBSITES

http://www.iom.int/jahia/jsp/index.jsp. Homepage of the International Organization for Migration (IOM), which also publishes the journal *International Migration*.

http://www.un.org/esa/population/migration. Collection of UN documents, publications, presentations, data and statements about international migration.

http://www.unhcr.org/cgi-bin/texis/vtx/home. Homepage of the United Nations High Commissioner for Refugees, the UN Refugee Agency.

http://www.gcim.org/en/. Homepage of the Global Commission on International Migration working on a framework for the formulation of a coherent, comprehensive and global response to the issue of international migration.

http://www.cmsny.org/. The New York-based Center for Migration Studies, a non-profit organization dedicated to research and publishing the peer-reviewed journal *International Migration Review.*

migration

Nationalism and Ethnicity

1. CORE QUESTIONS ADDRESSED

• What are the different forms of imagining a political community?
• How is nationalism linked to the development of the international society?
• What are the normative dilemmas of thinking in terms of national and ethnic groups?

2. DEFINITIONS

Nationalism and ethnicity are two concepts that are crucial for determining the basic group identities that are relevant to international relations and indeed to political order in more general terms. Unfortunately, both terms are notoriously difficult to pin down. Broadly speaking, ethnicity refers to the attachment to a particular group that shares a common culture and heritage. It is important to emphasize that ethnicity is therefore not a natural given, but that it is a social construction (Horowitz 1985: 53). In other words, belonging to an ethnic group does not presuppose common ancestry, even if this is sometimes invoked by those who see themselves as leader of such a group; it simply requires a belief in the existence of common bonds. Ethnicity is therefore a broad category that includes a variety of groups such as tribes, nations and races (ibid.).

In contrast to ethnicity, nationalism is not a characteristic but a political ideology that seeks to grant a particular group of people (the nation) a particular territory (the state) (Breuilly 1982: 3; Gellner 1983: 1; Hobsbawm 1990: 9). The word 'nation' in itself derives from the Latin *natio*, which comes close to what we would now call an 'ethnic group'. Used in that sense, we find references to nations in sacred texts such as the Old Testament as well as mediaeval writings. As a politically relevant concept, the nation only comes into being in modern times. Above all, it presupposes the possibility to communicate common myths and symbols across a large distance and to a mass of people, which historically only became viable with the invention of print and was then coupled with a series of other technological and economic developments that enabled not only the advent of the modern territorial state (→ *Territoriality and Borders*) but also the imagination of the nation (Anderson 1991: 43).

In this sense, then, nationalism arose in the eighteenth and nineteenth centuries within two distinct but related movements: on the one hand, the attempt to strip absolutist rulers from their power and locate (→) sovereignty in the hands of the people (viz.: the nation), with the French revolution of 1789 as the symbolic focal point; on the other hand, the attempt to unite nations that had previously been split into a number of smaller states with a common culture, epitomized in the German and Italian national movements. In the cultural sense, nation and state in the German usage are not identical (the German nation, based on a concept of citizenship by blood bondage, or in legal terms the *ius sanguinis*, may thus exceed the state), but in its definition, the German nation, too, cannot be decoupled from this form of political nationalism that ultimately defines the nation through the notion of self-government. Indeed, as John Breuilly (1982: 77) notes, the fact that German nationalism was not successful in creating a German state in the nineteenth century is partly due to the limited penetration of political communication in a largely agrarian society with strong regional identities linked to the multiplicity of political territories at the time.

3. THEORETICAL PERSPECTIVES

In very crude terms, there are two theoretical perspectives in the literature on nationalism that differ primarily in their ontological treatment of the nation, at least as far as its cultural understanding is concerned. On the one extreme, so-called 'primordialists' accept the notion of the ancient origins of nation and therefore come close to sympathizing with the romantic nationalist movements of the nineteenth century. This has however become a very rare position in International Relations and the social sciences in general (Smith 1998: 145). Perhaps one of those who come closest is Conor Cruise O'Brien (1993), who, while seeing nationalism as an 'intellectual position' (p. 143), at the same time considers this position to be prominent from ancient times, rather than being a distinctly modern phenomenon. Likewise, Hugh Seton-Watson (1977: 17), while distinguishing the 'modern nation' from the 'mediaeval *natio*', none the less emphasizes the links between the two. On the other end of the spectrum, a constructivist position (→ *Theory Concept: Social Constructivism*) emphasizes the 'invention' (Hobsbawm and Ranger 1992) of traditions in the process of 'imagining' the nation (Anderson 1991). A middle position recognizes the constructed nature of nations and their modern character as a political concept, but emphasizes the linkages between the modern imagination of nations and the myths and symbols that existed before (Smith 1986). Following in the footsteps of the French revolutionary movement, civic conceptions of the nation meanwhile do not emphasize common myths as much as the bonds created by common citizenship and membership in a political system (Brubaker 1992), although even such conceptions are often not devoid of references to a common culture and heritage (see Silverman 1992).

In terms of international relations, nationalism is important because it establishes the nation-state that is the ideal-typical unit of the international system. For realists (→ *Theory Concept: Realism and Neorealism*), the nation typically merges with the state, so that Hans Morgenthau's classic, for instance, bore the title 'Politics among Nations', and not 'Politics among States' (Morgenthau 1961). It is therefore the interests of nations that are pursued by statesmen on the international level. This stands in contrast to the neorealist reformulation, in which states become formally like units in a system in which concepts such as the nation nearly disappear from view in any meaningful way. Liberalism (→ *Theory Concept: Liberalism and Neoliberalism*) tends to be much more critical of the 'nation': classical liberals warned against war-prone nationalistic tendencies; neoliberals emphasized transnational interaction and interdependencies. It goes without saying that constructivism, let alone the various strands of Critical Theory (→ *Theory Concept: Marxism and Critical Theory*), are likewise wary of nationalism and see national identities as constructs that are, at least in part, formed through the interaction with others (Campbell 1998: 68–72; Wendt 1999: 326–35).

4. EMPIRICAL PROBLEMS

From a historical point of view, one of the crucial empirical questions that arises from nationalism is its influence on the formation of the (→) international society. Scholars working in the tradition of the English School of IR have traced the emergence of the international society through the rise of nationalism and the break-up of (→) empires, and the subsequent process of decolonization, in which elites took on board the nationalist ideas they had encountered during their studies in the imperial centres (e.g. Mayall 1990). In this sense, nationalism has an emancipatory effect on international relations, establishing the concept of self-determination in international law.

Yet at the same time, nationalism poses two immediate problems. Firstly, nationalism may lead to war. Some of the discussion in this respect concerns the issue of whether nationalism, as an ideology, is inherently expansive and therefore whether there is always a 'struggle for power on the international scene' (Morgenthau 1961: 103); or whether there is a 'good' and a 'bad' nationalism, or in the words of John Herz (1950: 160), whether there is a 'peaceful', 'idealist' nationalism that needs to be distinguished from an 'aggressive', 'expansionist', so-called 'integral' nationalism – what Edward Hallett Carr (1946: 21) considered to be an 'inflation' of nationalism.

Secondly, questions have emerged about the future role of nationalism. To the extent that state power is undermined by (→) globalization or other forces, the modern conception of the nation as tied to the state becomes increasingly problematic. As a consequence, ethnicity as a broader concept has come to prominence again, from the rise of ethnic tensions within central and eastern European states after the end of the Cold War to the significance of tribal leaders in Afghanistan or parts of Africa.

5. CORE READING

Anderson, Benedict (1991) *Imagined Communities: Reflections on the Origin and Spread of Nationalism* (London: Verso, 2nd edn). An absolute classic that not only coined the term 'imagined community' but also locates the construction of national identity in a postcolonial setting.

Horowitz, Donald L. (1985) *Ethnic Groups in Conflict* (Berkely, CA: University of California Press). Remains the major treatment of the role of ethnicity in conflict, seen from a rationalist perspective, but based on an immense historical knowledge from many different conflict sites.

Mayall, James (1990) *Nationalism and International Society* (Cambridge: Cambridge University Press). Traces the importance of nationalism in the development of the international society from an English School perspective.

6. USEFUL WEBSITES

http://www.lse.ac.uk/collections/ASEN/. Homepage of the Association for the Study of Ethnicity and Nationalism founded by research students and academics from the

London School of Economics and Political Science, also publishing the journal *Studies in Ethnicity and Nationalism*.

http://www.tandf.co.uk/journals/cnap. Home of *Nationalities Paper*, a leading journal on nationalism, ethnicity, ethnic conflict and national identity.

http://www.surrey.ac.uk/Arts/CRONEM/. The University of Surrey's multidisciplinary research centre in the field of nationalism, ethnicity and multiculturalism.

www.ecmi.de. Webpage of the European Centre for Minority Studies that sponsors policy-relevant research on the question of how ethnic and national minorities can live peacefully together with the majorities in a society.

·················· Peace and War ··················

1. CORE QUESTIONS ADDRESSED

- What is the difference between negative and positive peace?
- What is the 'new war' thesis?
- Why do quantitative conflict datasets reach different conclusions?

2. DEFINITIONS

To define peace, scholars have used three conceptual pairs: narrow and wide, positive and negative, and peace as state and peace as process. First, in everyday usage, peace and war are simply understood as opposites to one another – a notion reflected in the 'traditional' definition of peace as the absence of warlike conflict and violence or the threat thereof. This is exemplified by Raymond Aron's well-known definition of peace as a condition of 'more or less lasting suspension of rivalry between political units' (1966: 151). Scholars following this definition see war as defined by the use of physical violence between such political units, and in particular states. As peace research progressed, this understanding began to be termed the narrow definition of peace precisely because it merely focused on physical violence. Johan Galtung suggested a wider definition of peace as 'the absence of structural violence', i.e. the absence of systematic ways in which a state prevents individuals from reaching their full potential (1969). Examples of structural violence include hunger, institutionalized racism or sexism, and political repression. Violence may thus not only be observable in bodily harm or inflicted pain but may be subtly built into the very structure of social, cultural, and economic institutions, denying people important rights. Scholars have debated the broad scope of structural violence, questioning whether it is analytically useful to include phenomena such as social inequality and restricted access to education, jobs and medical care.

Thought on structural violence is connected to the second conceptual pair added to the definition of peace: positive and negative peace. The previous absence of direct violence is termed negative peace while positive peace denotes a social condition in which 'exploitation is minimized or eliminated and in which there is neither overt violence nor structural violence' (Barash and Webel 2002: 7). A strong notion of justice is therefore an inherent part of positive peace. Critical and feminist (→ *Theory Concept: Feminism and Gender*) scholars have drawn attention to the negative impact a narrow or negative definition of peace can have on efforts to further it. If peace is not conceptualized in a positive way, 'strategies to end war may freeze status quo inequalities that represent violence in their own right' (Sylvester 1980: 307).

Finally, scholars have defined peace as either a state to be reached, for example with a peace contract, or an ongoing process. Understanding peace as a process acknowledges that peaceful relations in society need to be worked on continuously. Peace can therefore never be finally 'completed' (Boulding 2000).

Akin to peace, there are narrow and wide definitions of war, and definitions have been subject to substantial change, particularly since the 1990s. In the Westphalian system, wars were defined as fought between states; they included a formal declaration of war, the movement of troops, and a clear division between combatants and non-combatants; and they ended with an interstate truce or contract of peace. All these elements are part of Karl von Clausewitz's understanding of war as 'an act of violence intended to compel our opponent to fulfil our will' and famously considered 'war as the continuation of politics by other means' (1982: 119). Definitions of war usually include quantitative elements. Scholars such as J. David Singer and Melvin Small, for instance, sought to define wars and differentiate them from violent conflicts by the number of deaths occurred. In their Correlates of War project, Singer and Small (1972) set a number of 1,000 combat-related casualties per year as the minimum threshold qualifying a war.

These conceptualizations are particularly relevant following the changing nature of warfare from the end of the Second World War onwards. Authors such as Mary Kaldor have argued that interstate wars have declined substantially in numbers relative to civil wars, signalling 'the end of old-fashioned war between states' (Kaldor 1999: 16). This is captured in the 'new wars' thesis. In contrast to 'old' interstate wars, 'new' wars are supposed to have changed on at least five accounts: first, they are predominantly intrastate in nature; second, they involve new kinds of actors such as private military companies; third, they are fought because of ethnic, religious or identity politics rather than territorial aggrandizement; fourth, combatants employ a more brutal mode of warfare targeting civilians and resulting in higher loss of life; and fifth, they are financed by a globalized war economy that makes war an end in itself (Kaldor 1999; Münkler 2005; Van Crefeld 1991). The 'new war' thesis was widely acknowledged to offer an important contribution to understanding post-Cold-War conflicts such as in Sudan or in the Democratic Republic of Congo. All the while, critics have made the observation that not all that is claimed to be 'new' about 'new wars' in fact is. Practically all of the 'new' factors have been present in warfare for the previous 100 years to varying degrees – what has changed are their respective degrees and above all their conscious integration into political analysis (E. Newman 2004: 179).

3. THEORETICAL PERSPECTIVES

The study of the causes of war and the conditions of peace has long been a central preoccupation of International Relations. Consequently, the discipline has produced a wide variety of studies on the subject which are strongly influenced by the theorists' choice of specific definitions of peace and war. There is a decidedly practical emphasis as theoretical results find their translation to real-life suggestions, which have been subject to change with changing understandings of peace and war. While (→) peacekeeping, for example, rests on a negative concept of peace, emphasis on peacebuilding and good governance in post-conflict societies clearly derives from positive peace.

Generally, International Relations has witnessed a move from the exclusive focus on the causes of war to a focus on its termination and the conditions for peace in the late 1960s with the works of Johan Galtung. Scholars of the causes of war continue to use the (→) levels-of-analysis framework attributing the causal impact to either individuals, societal or systematic factors, or the interplay of the three of them (Waltz 1959). On the individual level, cognitive theories seek to uncover psychological explanations for the choices leaders make to escalate or de-escalate violent conflicts (Farnham 1990; Hermann 1980). On the societal level, authors from, for example, a Critical Theory perspective (→ *Theory Concept: Marxism and Critical Theory*) consider the nature of capitalist society to be the root cause of violent conflict, because of its inherent extreme inequality and because it reproduces enemy images in order to distract from said inequalities (Senghaas 1972). Liberal accounts on (→) democratic peace also fall in this category (Doyle 1997). Finally, explanations on the systemic level derive from the structure of the international system and its changes. Studies on this level had long dominated the study of war, especially the realist tradition (→ *Theory Concept: Realism and Neorealism*), building its explanations on the struggle for power under anarchy, (→) the balance of power and (→) the security dilemma (Waltz 1959; Fearon 1995).

Peace research has been primarily concerned with identifying the conditions enabling lasting peace, which can again be differentiated into societal conditions and systemic conditions. Dieter Senghaas' civilizatory hexagon exemplarily combines six societal conditions for a positive peace as a process: first, the efficient monopoly over the use of force; second, effective control by an independent legal system; third, interdependence of social groups; fourth, democratic participation; fifth, social justice; and finally, sixth, a political culture of constructive and peaceful conflict transformation (1995).

4. EMPIRICAL PROBLEMS

Empirical evidence from quantitative research on wars by and large confirms the thesis on the changing nature of warfare (Schlichte 2002; Human Security Centre 2005). The number of wars waged per year has risen since the end of the Second World War, reaching its climax in the early 1990s, and has since been decreasing. More than 90 per cent of the wars since 1945 have taken place in less or least developed countries and are intrastate wars, while the share of interstate wars has decreased decisively. Intrastate wars have proven hard to regulate and are less frequently terminated by third parties, particularly international organizations.

While the relevant data sets more or less all share these observations, there are immense differences in the collected data owing to the operationalization of war used by the data sets. The Correlates of War project, originating in 1972, as mentioned above, uses 1,000 casualities per year as a threshold to qualify a war. Other data sets, such as the Uppsala Conflict Data Project, have tried to capture the 'new war' phenomenon quantitatively by significantly lowering the minimum threshold of armed conflict to 25 annual battle deaths (Gleditsch et al. 2002). The Conflict Data Project further distinguishes between different-intensity conflicts, i.e. minor armed conflicts (a minimum of 1,000 casualties throughout the entire conflict), intermediate armed conflicts (more than 1,000 casualties throughout the entire conflict) and highest-intensity-level conflicts (more than 1,000 casualties per year) (Wallensteen and Sollenberg 1999; Gleditsch et al. 2002). Based on these differences in statistical measurement, the data sets come to very different conclusions of what actually constitutes a war or an armed conflict – the Cyprus conflict would thus, for example 'qualify' as a conflict for the Conflict Data Project but not for the Correlates of War. Provocatively put, 'the world of war is what researchers make of it' (Eberwein and Chojnacki 2001: 29).

Another problem of peace research lies in the demanding definition of what constitutes peace and the substantial disagreement regarding the goals and means needed to foster peace (→ *Conflict Resolution*). Its self-assigned practical approach makes peace researchers' disagreement an even more decisive detriment. Also, while combating structural violence is certainly more crucial in achieving lasting peace, its identification poses empirical problems. In contrast to direct violence which is fast, visible and immediately dramatic, structural violence often is less visible and works with a much slower, though potentially more destructive pace to impoverish human lives (Barash and Webel 2002: 8).

5. CORE READING

Galtung, Johan (1969) 'Violence, Peace, and Peace Research', *Journal of Peace Research* 6 (3), 167–91. Influential conceptual article from one of the main figures in peace research.

Gleditsch, Nils Petter, Peter Wallensteen, Mikael Eriksson, Margareta Sollenberg and Håvard Strand (2002) 'Armed Conflict 1945–2001: A New Dataset', *Journal of Peace Research* 39 (5), 615–37. Presents the new data set of the Conflict Data Project, which has become a major data source, for instance for publications such as the Human Security Report.

Kaldor, Mary (1999) *New and Old Wars: Organized Violence in a Global Era* (Stanford, CA. Stanford University Press) Introduces the 'new wars' thesis in its most comprehensive and empirically detailed form.

6. USEFUL WEBSITES

http://www.prio.no/CSCW/Datasets/Armed-Conflict. The Uppsala data set of violent conflicts from 1945 onwards; contains data on inter- and intrastate wars as well as geographical and resource datasets.

http://www.sipri.org/. The Stockholm International Peace Research Institute is an institute dedicated to research regarding conflict, armaments, arms control and disarmament, providing data, analysis and recommendations on its website.

http://www.peaceresearchfoundation.org/default.asp?str_string=Home~Current%20 News~none. Foundation concerned with the creation and application of a body of knowledge concerning the subject of peace; website includes a useful link list.

Peacekeeping

1. CORE QUESTIONS ADDRESSED

• How has peacekeeping evolved since its inception after the Second World War?
• When are peacekeeping missions likely to be effective?
• What are the problems inherent to peacekeeping missions?

2. DEFINITIONS

Peacekeeping is a tool of conflict management (→ *Conflict Resolution*), involving the deployment of soldiers in impartial, non-offensive military roles to the field. This deployment is coordinated by international organizations and occurs with the consent of all conflict parties concerned. The UN defines it as a 'technique designed to preserve peace where fighting has been halted and to assist in implementing established peace agreements' (United Nations 2008: 15).

While peacekeeping is not provided for directly in the UN charter of 1945, its legal basis lies within both the provisions for the peaceful settlement of disputes of Chapter VI and the military enforcement provisions to counter breaches of peace of Chapter VII. Consequently, peacekeeping mandates operate in a 'grey zone', especially as peacekeeping missions have evolved over time from the mere monitoring of ceasefires to the stronger enforcement missions of the 1990s. This duality of peacekeeping is illustrated by it sometimes being referred to as 'Chapter VI and a half'. Peacekeeping missions are commonly differentiated as belonging to three distinct generations that follow each other chronologically: first-generation or traditional peacekeeping, second-generation or multidimensional/complex peacekeeping and third-generation or robust peacekeeping.

Peacekeeping is an ambiguous concept, frequently used interchangeably with the terms 'peace enforcement', 'peacemaking' and 'peacebuilding'. To differentiate the term briefly, peacekeeping and peace enforcement differ mostly on two accounts: first, peacekeepers are supposed to use military force only in self-defence and as a last resort, and second, peacekeepers are deployed with states' consent. As noted before, however, this distinction was increasingly blurred by both peacekeeping mandates and empirical realities. As a consequence, traces of peace enforcement are frequently integrated into third-generation peacekeeping missions. Peacemaking refers to bringing hostile parties to agreement by way of the peaceful means of dispute settlement, such as mediation, enquiry and negotiation, provided for in Chapter VI of the UN Charter (Boutros-Ghali 1992). In contrast to traditional peacekeeping, peacebuilding indicates not only safeguarding the cessation of hostilities between warring factions but also the 'creation of a new environment' thereby preventing the recurrence of conflict (Boutros-Ghali 1992). Peacebuilding is seen to address the 'root causes' of conflict, promoting not merely conflict management but (→) conflict resolution. Elements of peacebuilding found their way into the peacekeeping missions of the second generation, and its assumptions are now very much part of the peacekeeping consensus.

First-generation peacekeeping was used during the Cold War to provide impartial stabilization of an achieved truce in interstate conflicts until a final peace agreement could be reached. Peacekeepers essentially provided a buffer zone between hostile factions and were thus either unarmed or only lightly armed. Both second- and third-generation peacekeeping are the products of the successes of the traditional peacekeeping missions as well as the challenges posed by the international environment following the end of the Cold War, such as violent civil conflicts and complex humanitarian emergencies, for example in Somalia and Mozambique.

Second-generation peacekeeping missions are commonly termed 'complex' or multidimensional because their mandates involved not only military but also civilian tasks such as peacebuilding, e.g. rebuilding and training police, and providing an interim civil administration and humanitarian assistance. The introduction of peacebuilding tasks is the crucial innovation in second-generation peacekeeping as it signified the realization that 'formal agreement ending a civil war is meaningless unless coupled with long-term programs to heal the wounded society' (Weinberger 2002: 248). The new task list necessitated the involvement of civilian actors beyond the military personnel, including UN agencies such as UNHCR, UNICEF and UNDP, thus considerably increasing the size of the mission presence in the field.

The key differences between second- and third-generation peace-keeping lie in two points: (i) third-generation missions do not necessarily require consent from all parties involved and (ii), the third generation's mandate is 'robust' when it comes to using force in order to protect civilians or refugees. This robust mandate makes third-generation missions more costly and (even) more dependent on leadership by major military powers as it requires decidedly more logistical expertise, personnel and heavy equipment. While the new mandates are blurring the line between peacekeeping and peace enforcement, the peacekeepers deployed on them frequently neither had the force size nor the equipment to carry out the enforcement part of the mission. Third-generation peacekeeping has thus provoked by far the most criticism among the different peacekeeping generations.

3. THEORETICAL PERSPECTIVES

While peacekeeping is essentially a practical concept, it has become subject to theoretical evaluation as it evolved and its importance as a mode of (→) security governance grew. There are two issues of specific theoretical importance: the relation of peacekeeping to a particular notion of conflict management (→ *Conflict Resolution*) and questions of peacekeeping's effectiveness.

A first point of substantial theoretical relevance is the close connection between peacekeeping, particularly of the second and third generations, and the liberal democratic peace thesis (→ *Theory Concept: Liberalism and Neoliberalism*). As illiberal governance and violent conflict within states are increasingly viewed as just as much a threat to international peace and security as conflict between states, creating liberal

peacekeeping

democratic societies and polities as a core feature of peace- or state-building is supposed to secure future international order. This logic has been subject to criticism by authors from Critical Theory and feminist backgrounds. (→ *Theory Concepts: Marxism and Critical Theory; Feminism and Gender.*) To Oliver Richmond (2005), liberal peace is a hegemonic discourse propagated by well-intentioned, mainly western actors that unconsciously levels contested und unstable elements of the peace concept. Richmond identifies four strands within liberal peace that are in tension with each other: first, victor's peace emphasizing the importance of military strength; second, constitutional peace, which focuses on the importance of democracy, trade and cosmopolitanism in fostering peace; third, institutional peace, which perceives of political entities as bound within international normative and legal frameworks that regulate their behaviour; and fourth, civil peace focusing on citizens, political participation and human rights as prerequisites for stable peace. 'Selling' the idea of liberal peace as universal despite these conceptual tensions has detrimental effects. Richmond argues that the idea of liberal peace enshrined in peacekeeping 'dehumanizes' the entire peace concept in perceiving it as a methodological governance problem to be solved by the international community. Affected communities are thereby conceptually denied the opportunity to take on political responsibility for their own societies. The current peacekeeping logic, and especially enforcement missions, are thereby seen to uphold a division of labour that favours powerful states in their efforts to control or isolate 'unruly parts of the world' and it thereby sustains a particular world order (Pugh 2004: 39).

Clearly, this stands in contrast to the liberal peace strand of civilian peace with its emancipatory purposes. Richmond (2005) therefore strongly encourages explicit reflection on different types of peace that are sought to be created by different forms of peacekeeping. Further criticism on peacekeeping's notion of conflict management comes from feminist scholars: while missions since the mid-1990s have included sizeable civilian components, feminists point to their continuous reliance on soldiers, i.e. 'people skilled in the arts of violence' (Whitworth 2004: 12). Sandra Whitworth examines the crucial question of whether soldiers do actually always make the best peacekeepers, countering that 'often, it is the nonwarrior qualities of soldiering that leave an impact on local people's security' (2004: 18–19).

Providing answers to questions about if and when peacekeeping missions are effective is a second theoretical focal point closely examined by a variety of mostly statistical studies. Barbara Walter's 'credible commitment theory' is concerned with the effectiveness of peacekeepers' presence (2002). In her analysis, the 'real' hurdle towards solving conflicts lies not in resolving the underlying issues behind conflict breakout but rather in designing credible guarantees on the terms of a peace agreement. Here, third-party assistance in the form of security guarantees and power-sharing agreements becomes crucial: Walter's data set of civil wars fought between 1940 and 1992 indicates that conflicts were rarely resolved without third-party intervention. Michael Doyle and Nicholas Sambanis support this finding, yet distinguish between different peacekeeping generations: second-generation multidimensional peacekeeping missions significantly increase the likelihood of successful peacebuilding, while they conclude that traditional peacekeeping has practically no effect on the chances of achieving lasting peace (2000: 798). Responding to these mixed results, scholars argue that one should not 'compare apples and oranges'; in other words, they suggest that different types of missions should be evaluated with different criteria. While traditional missions may be solely assessed by their ability to halt fighting, criteria to evaluate second- and third-generation missions should be more mixed and demanding (Diehl 2008).

4. EMPIRICAL PROBLEMS

Much has changed since the 1948 deployment of unarmed military observers as the first UN peacekeeping force – the UN Truce Supervision Organization – to the Middle East to monitor a truce between Israel and its Arab neighbours. On a basic level, since the permanent UN military forces envisioned by the UN Charter (Articles 43–5) were never created, peacekeeping operations were dependent on the political will and the *ad-hoc* military troop contributions of member states. Frequently, this resulted and continues to result in lengthy and frequently unsuccessful negotiation processes between the Department of Peacekeeping Operations (DPKO) and UN member states in order to recruit the contingent size designated in the respective resolution. As the mandates grew qualitatively and quantitatively more demanding and involved a higher risk of casualties, states became even more reluctant to allow their troops to participate. The multinational composition of peacekeepers is another problematic factor as personnel differ widely in terms of their training, their expertise and even their equipment – not to mention the communication difficulties associated with language differences. Looking at the record, some country's units have proven more effective than others, making them more desirable for future missions. Yet while the DPKO is charged with determining the exact force requirements, it has limited control over what country's troops and therefore peacekeepers it gets. Consequently, even if deployed in their mandated size, peacekeeping troops operate from a less than ideal starting point.

Problems of peacekeeping intensified with the growing mission demands of second- and third-generation peacekeeping associated with the changing modes of warfare in the last decades (→ *Peace and War*). In the post-Cold-War world, missions such as the United Nations Protection Force (UNPROFOR) in Croatia and Bosnia and Herzegovina were frequently deployed to where there was no peace to keep. Mandated with ensuring the demilitarization of designated areas and monitoring 'safe areas' – a task it was neither equipped nor prepared for – UNPROFOR was caught between remaining impartial towards conflicting parties and protecting civilians in besieged Sarajevo and other cities (Power 2008).

The presence of UN peacekeepers under robust mandates raised protection expectations among the civilian population that the mission was unable or, in some cases, reluctant to keep. This often resulted in catastrophic consequences as the case of the 1995 Srebrenica massacre of more than 7,000 Bosnian Muslim men who were supposed to be under UN protection illustrates. The state of neither being prepared nor equipped for the tasks it was supposed to perform in second- and third-generation peacekeeping became a feature of practically all peacekeeping missions since the early 1990s.

As UN peacekeeping missions grew in complexity, so did their side-effects: not only did they frequently not produce their intended results, but also they generated unintended consequences, i.e. negative economic, social and political effects (Aoi et al. 2007: 7). Unintended consequences are manifold; the following three examples should only serve as an illustration. The most drastic are human rights violations, such as sexual exploitation and abuse, committed by peacekeepers for example in the Democratic Republic of the Congo. The severe negative impact of these events went far beyond the mission to the UN itself, as UN personnel were in fact violating the same people's human rights they were deployed to protect. Further unintended consequences were brought about by the high demands and connected strength of the mandates UN peacekeepers were charged to fulfil, such as the comprehensive set of peace and state-building tasks that compromised the United

Nations Transitional Administration in East Timor (UNTAET). Although this is frequently credited as a success story, the UN was criticized for establishing an international protectorate in East Timor, with all the diminished accountability this entails. The UN Security Council chose to put in place a UN transitional administrator 'empowered to exercise all legislative and executive authority, including the administration of justice', i.e. near-absolute powers, instead of integrating East Timorese self-governance in the resolution (UN Security Council, S/RES/1272 1999). The field presence of sizeable UN missions may also lead to economic distortions such as the creation of dual public sector economies – literature indicates that multidimensional missions are particularly susceptible on this account (Diehl 2008). As unintended consequences of peacekeeping missions have long been ignored, concerted research on first understanding and subsequently preventing, containing and managing them has only just begun. It certainly opens up wide-ranging questions on the legitimacy of peacekeeping actions.

5. CORE READING

Aoi, Chiyuki, Cedric de Coning and Ramesh Thakur (eds) (2007), *Unintended Consequences of Peacekeeping Operations* (Tokyo: United Nations University Press). Collection of studies that analytically addresses the issue of unintended consequences of peacekeeping for the first time.

Diehl, Paul F. (2008) *Peace Operations* (Cambridge: Polity Press). Comprehensive yet brief overview on the history, organization and challenges of peacekeeping.

Doyle, Michael and Nicholas Sambanis (2006) *Making War and Building Peace: United Nations Peacekeeping Operations* (Princeton, NJ: Princeton University Press). Combines quantitative and qualitative analysis of peacekeeping's failures and successes with special attention to civil wars.

6. USEFUL WEBSITES

http://www.un.org/en/peacekeeping. Central UN website on UN peacekeeping operations including manifold resources on past and current operations as well as the development and normative background to peacekeeping.

http://www.ipacademy.org/programs/coping-with-crisis/details/11/30.html. Provides information about the publications and work of the International Peace Academy, this section focusing on peace implementation and peacebuilding.

http://www.watsoninstitute.org/project_detail.cfm?id=92. Watson Institute at Brown University resource page including several research tools (e.g. a searchable database with over 2,000 entries on peace operations).

http://www.peacekeepingbestpractices.unlb.org/. Peacekeeping Research Hub including numerous resources both by practitioners and academics.

Theory Concept: Postmodernism and Poststructuralism

1. CORE QUESTIONS ADDRESSED

- What is the difference between postmodernism and poststructuralism?
- To what extent is postmodernism/poststructuralism a critical theory?
- What are the basic challenges of postmodernism/poststructuralism to International Relations?

2. OVERVIEW AND BACKGROUND

Postmodernism has become a central approach in IR as well as in social sciences more generally. It was initially associated with architecture, art, literature and music, and then found its way into the humanities and social sciences. Its effects upon IR were first felt as part of the 'third debate' (Lapid 1989) during the 1980s, when the discipline was opening up to self-reflection, and are now central to many of the debates within the discipline. This is no doubt in large part due to a certain radical chic, but it is also because the depth of postmodernism's challenge has forced its critics to engage with it. The quality of this engagement has varied, meaning that as well as being highly contested, understandings of post-modernism can often be caricatured and/or quite confused.

Postmodernism, at its boldest, is a radical critique of all claims to truth and the existence of an objective reality. Postmodernism is a rejection of the totalizing claims of modernity, that is, the attempts to understand life as coherent and as such knowable through grand theories, such as (→) liberalism, (→) realism and (→) Marxism (see the relevant *Theory Concepts*) (George 1994). Instead of such totalizing attempts to understand society, postmodernism encourages a radical reflexivity; that is, one must continually question the basis of all claims to knowledge, not dissimilar to the small child flummoxing their parent with a series of 'why?'s. It is guided by a political and ethical conviction that the world is inherently plural and different, but that this difference is suppressed by totalizing visions (→ *International Ethics*) (Campbell 1993, 1998; Connolly 1991). The aim should therefore be to denaturalize all those things that are taken for granted, and highlight their arbitrariness.

There is a central place for the role of language in the processes of reality-making and the critique of these processes (Shapiro 1984). Postmodernism argues that the fabric of the world (ontology) is discursive (→ *Discourse*). That is, life is constituted, or made, through language and other representational practices. Postmodernist authors also suggest that because the world is discursive, and not purely material, life is much more plural, contingent, and ambivalent than we might think. This is not only something to be understood, but also to be celebrated and encouraged, which helps to explain why postmodernists reject all totalizing claims.

Poststructuralism is a particular style of analysis within postmodern thought more generally, and one of the most important and influential. Poststructuralism emerged from France during the 1960s and 1970s in the field of linguistics. It developed as a critique of structuralism and is therefore best understood in relation to structuralism. Structuralism itself emerged as a critique of approaches that sought to explain the world at the level of individuals. Structuralism instead suggested that there were deeper structures that are far more important in explaining society. Structuralism was key to developments in linguistics, primarily the work of Ferdinand de Saussure, but was also influential in Marxism (Louis Althusser), and anthropology (Claude Lévi-Strauss). Saussure argued that it was possible to scientifically study the underlying structure of language (*la langue*) to understand where everyday meaning comes from. The structure is made up of a system of signs, where signs are the relationship between words and meanings. He highlighted the crucial distinction between the object (the signified) and the sound or image used to convey that meaning (the signifier). In contrast to previous theories of meaning, which had focused upon the essential and intrinsic links between the signified and signifier, Saussure showed that links were no more than arbitrary cultural conventions. Instead, the fact that we can still understand one another is a function of the overall structure of the language; we know what a mother is because we know what a daughter is. Meaning is defined relationally and through difference.

The crucial shift to poststructuralism can be found in the work of Jacques Derrida; he criticized Saussure for imagining that the link between the signifier and the signified was stable. Derrida argued that because meaning is arbitrary then we should recognize that signs are empty of meaning; signifiers do not refer to signifieds – they only refer to other signifiers. The search for meaning is thus a constant movement from one sign to another, like using a dictionary: meaning is constantly deferred. This circularity of language means there is no final place to interpret the world from.

The significance of this is that Derrida asks us to redefine the notions of a *text* and *textuality* in a much broader way than simply the writing on this page. The entire world is a text because it is full of meanings and interpretation. We can only talk about and think about the world – and therefore act – through these interpretations. This means that we should think of the world itself as a discourse. It is important to recognize the radicalness of this position. Derrida very famously once said that there is nothing outside of the text: it is not just that there are different interpretations of reality (which exists independently of these interpretations), but that there is nothing but these interpretations; they *are* reality to us in the sense that we cannot comprehend reality outside discourse (contrast this with (→) *Theory Concept: Social Constructivism*; Zehfuss 2002).

But does this all mean that anything goes? Why do some things appear to be truthful and stable? Why can I not change international relations by declaring things to be different? As should be obvious, this is not possible, and this is because not all discourses are equal, some are much more powerful than others. The issue of (→) power is absolutely central to postmodern scholarship (Edkins 1999). The postmodern conception of power is quite different from all the other theoretical approaches. Traditional conceptions of power are most commonly material ones (→ *Realism*) and they often see power as a thing or a force that is held by actors whether these be individuals, states or classes. In contrast, the postmodern concept of power is greatly indebted to the work of Michel Foucault. Rather than the common saying that knowledge is power, he argued that it operates in both directions; power defines what counts as knowledge. Hence power is not something that is purely negative or something that distorts knowledge, but instead is productive as it helps to produce knowledge. This is one point where postmodernism and (→) Critical Theory sharply diverge. Critical Theory advocates a strategy for stripping away power relations – thereby removing ideological *'false consciousness'*. For postmodernists this is impossible: they would ask, how do we know what we know? They would point out that all knowledge comes from somewhere, and that this knowledge reflects the power struggles that were involved at that time and place. There cannot be any pristine knowledge that exists outside power.

3. METHODOLOGIES

Because of their focus on the representation of reality, postmodernists/poststructuralists use the analysis of discourse as their main methodology. They try to show how certain representations of reality prevail in a struggle over meaning, and how alternatives are marginalized. As the entry on discourse elaborates, one of the central problems in such an approach is the question of what constitutes discourse – is it only text in the narrow sense or does it involve a broader set of practices (see Hansen 2006)?

The search for the moments when these struggles over meaning are won and a new regime of truth is institutionalized is called *genealogy*. A genealogical approach is a historical one, but unlike traditional history it seeks to identify those ruptures where *power/knowledge* were contested and show how one interpretation won. Crucially the aim of this is to underline that what is now accepted as truth is only one possible way of doing things, it is arbitrary, and that there were feasible alternatives. It seeks to recover those alternatives and repoliticize things that are taken for granted. The use of history to explain why things are as they are now means that genealogy has been termed a 'history of the present'.

Deconstruction is another method used by poststructuralists to unsettle seemingly stable oppositions. Like the genealogical method its aim is to highlight the problems of using artificially 'truthful' categories. Because meaning is always deferred, terms depend upon the use of oppositions to invent or construct their meaning; for instance, male/female, good/evil, inside/outside. Identity is defined through articulating (discursively constructing) difference: we are not them. As it is obvious, there is always a moral hierarchy between terms; the former is always privileged over the latter. Despite being presented as complete and opposite this can never actually be the case; instead they are always mixed in together. Deconstruction is the method of reading a text – in the broader sense – to show that these oppositions are invented and the story that is told depends upon these created oppositions. It does this by highlighting the contradictions that are covered up in the text.

4. EMPIRICAL APPLICATIONS

One of the first and still important poststructural interventions in IR was Richard Ashley's deconstruction of International Relations' focus on (→) sovereignty and (→) anarchy. Ashley (1988) focuses on anarchy because it so profoundly shapes the study and practice of international relations, and he wants to ask what would happen if we were able to think about international relations differently. Ashley's deconstruction shows that the boundaries between anarchy and sovereignty are untenable. Rather than there being a difference between the two, it actually lies within them: there are spaces of sovereignty in anarchy, and spaces of anarchy in sovereignty. For instance, it is simply not true that life outside a state is chaotic and without rule, just as it is not true that it is orderly and safe inside. Ashley shows how internal difference is repressed and converted into external difference. The significance of this is absolutely crucial. Both the way international relations are thought about and the way that states, statesmen, and citizens live their lives are affected by this discourse. The discourse serves to shape the practices and therefore bring about the world it claims to only describe.

Another excellent example of poststructuralist work is that of David Campbell (1993, 1998). His study of US (→) foreign policy highlights how the US – as well as other states more generally – are made and remade through and by their foreign policy. In line with the concern for explaining stability, the idea is not to try and discover what the state *is* but *how* it can actually exist. Campbell highlights how a discourse of danger of a threatening Other – whether that be the Soviet Union, the drug trade in South America, the economic threat of Europe or east Asia, or terrorism – serves to provide the possibility of the state existing. As above, the possibility of a coherent identity is dependent upon the articulation of an oppositional Other. In this sense the state is said to be 'performed'. That is, the state does not exist as some pre-given foundation such as a national or political community, but by acting (performing) as a state – through attending diplomatic summits, maintaining and/or deploying a military, etc. – then the state comes into being. So again we can see how the discourses of statehood constitute the material reality of the world.

Other scholars, such as James Der Derian (1987, 1992, 2009), have focused more on the changing ways of representing international relations, (→) diplomacy and (→) security in the light of technological changes. But in Der Derian's work, too, the questions of power and marginalization remain central.

5. CENTRAL CRITICISMS

The most common criticism of postmodernism and poststructuralism is that they are politically conservative or even nihilistic. It can be argued that because postmodernism refuses to offer a concrete or coherent vision of society it is ethically and politically useless. While this is not necessarily the case it is a common cause for frustration among it critics. A postmodern response would be that they offer a constant ethical challenge to totalizing visions, the type of thought that leads to the gulags and Auschwitz–Birkenau. Another common criticism is that no matter how important interpretation is to social life there are things and events that are real and occur independently of their discursive construction. What, for example, is discursive about a volcanic eruption? Or, how discursively constructed were the planes that flew into the World Trade Center for the thousands that were killed and their families? Again, this tends to misunderstand the poststructural project. For example, one response would be to show how the US's involvement in the Middle East is a function of its massive dependence upon oil. Its dependence upon oil is in turn fuelled by a car culture that encourages the use of large and fuel-inefficient vehicles. This, in turn, is rooted in a self-understanding of 'America' that is based upon exceptionalism, individual liberty, and the frontier spirit, which, as a set of ideas, are causally effective; that is, discursive representations bring about real and material effects.

Further criticisms of poststructuralist and postmodernist work are that they are unnecessarily complicated; they use obfuscatory language and display an obsession with philosophical theory that is derivative of 'real world' problems. While, on occasion, certain texts do appear awfully long-winded and self-important, there is a reason for the complicated language. Because poststructuralists highlight how words are imbued with hegemonic meanings it is desirable to try and use less loaded terms (although, of course, even this cannot erase the problem entirely). And, on the other hand, while poststructuralism does require a degree of theoretical savvyness, the best work is also highly empirical, often a detailed and historical examination.

6. CORE READING

Campbell, David (1998) *Writing Security: United States Foreign Policy and the Politics of Identity* (Minneapolis: University of Minnesota Press; 2nd edn). Generally seen as one of the most exemplary works of postmodern IR scholarship, combining a highly sophisticated reinterpretation of foreign policy with an in-depth empirical study.

Der Derian, James and Michael J. Shapiro (eds) (1989) *International/ Intertextual Relations: Postmodern Readings of World Politics* (Lanham, MD: Lexington Books). The first compilation of postmodern writings in the discipline – no longer up to date, but a historical milestone.

Walker, R. B. J. (1993) *Inside/Outside: International Relations as Political Theory* (Cambridge: Cambridge University Press). A highly influential book that turned the relationship between International Relations and political theory upside-down and elaborated how the conception of the anarchical international system is constitutive for the imagination of the order of the sovereign state.

7. USEFUL WEBSITES

http://www.foucault.info/. Information on Michel Foucault, including an archive of writings and lectures.

http://poststructuralism.info/. This website aims to allow users to describe poststructuralist ideas, but also to create new ideas and concepts based on poststructuralist foundations.

http://pravda.gmxhome.de/pomobib.htm. Detailed bibliography on postmodernism in IR.

http://www.david-campbell.org/. David Campbell's website with videos, artwork and reports on past and ongoing research.

http://www.watsoninstitute.org/infopeace/index2.cfm. A website maintained by the Watson Institute of Brown University with James Der Derian, looking at how information technology changes the representation of world politics.

Power

1. CORE QUESTIONS ADDRESSED

- What are the different forms of power in international relations?
- What is the role of power in analysis of international relations?
- Is there a shift in the predominant forms of power in international relations?

2. DEFINITIONS

Power is one of the central, if not the most central, concept in International Relations. Yet despite, or perhaps exactly because of, its centrality, its meaning remains contested. Excluded in what follows is the notion of power as an actor, in the sense of 'great power' or 'superpower'. This still leaves a wide array of definitions.

A first distinction is between the concept of power as *capabilities* and power as a *relationship* (see Baldwin 2002: 185). If power is used as a relational concept, it signifies a situation in which an actor can bring another actor do something even against the latter's own will. This relational concept of power can be found in the work of Max Weber (and is thus also sometimes referred to as the Weberian concept of power, see Weber 1922). In political science, it was made particularly popular by Robert Dahl and his formulation that A can 'get B to do something that B would not otherwise do' (Dahl 1994: 290). Similarly, classical realist Hans Morgenthau (1961: 29) defines political power as 'control over certain actions of [those over whom power is exercised] through the influence which [those who exercise power] exert over the [former's] mind'. In all of these definitions of power, power is effectively equated with influence.

In Morgenthau's work, however, there is at least an ambiguity in the way the concept of power is used. While it denotes on the one hand a relationship, at the same time Morgenthau (1961: 110) refers to 'elements' or 'components' of national power, which include geography, natural resources, industrial capacity, military preparedness, population, national character, national morale, quality of diplomacy, and quality of government. These 'elements' clearly refer to capabilities rather than influence as such, and would have to be turned, through the 'exercise' of power in Morgenthau's terms, into influence. Often, then, power consists of a combination of capabilities and influence.

In these definitions, power is related to an actor who exercises power. Not all definitions of power would share this restrictive view, and some would add structural forms of power, in which power does not rest with an individual actor but in societal structures or (→) discourses that get actors to behave in particular ways without the necessary existence of an actor who consciously aims at such influence. Gender relations are often described in such terms (cf. Strange 1996: 26; → *Theory Concept: Feminism and Gender*). Similarly, the relationships in a globalized capitalist economy are not solely characterized by direct forms of the exertion of power, but are dependent on a system that makes them act in specific ways because their existence is bound up with the structures of that system (e.g. Cox 1992; → *Theory Concept: Marxism and Critical Theory*). Thus, actors are at least in part only able to act as actors because the systemic structures allocate this role to them. Such power is therefore not forcing actors to do something against their will; it rather forms their will in the first instance and as such *enables* actors to do something. In the reformulation of neorealism (→ *Theory Concept: Realism and Neorealism*) by Barry Buzan, Charles Jones and Richard Little (1993), the structure of the international system has a similar effect on the status and behaviour of states.

One of the most famous contributions to the analysis of power is Steven Lukes' notion of three 'faces' or dimensions of power (Lukes 1974). The relational notion of power thus only covers the most obvious and direct form of power. There are however more indirect forms of power, for instance in the ability to set agendas and steer the direction of a debate, and in the most radical, third notion of power, the power to determine the interests of actors. This last notion of power clearly has structural qualities, in that structures such as a capitalist or nationalist world system make actors define their interests in ways that make them ignore their 'true' interests and thus be willing, for instance, to die for 'their' nation instead of working towards global peaceful relations.

Taking such forms of power that are not tied to individual actors into account, Michael Barnett and Robert Duvall (2005: 12) have suggested two dimensions along which we can differentiate between different kinds of power. On one dimension, they distinguish between power that 'works through the interaction of specific actors' and power that 'works through social relations of constitution'. On the other dimension, they ask whether the effects of power concern specific actors directly, or whether they are diffuse in the sense that we may specify a broad group of people that may be affected, but not specific individuals. They characterize the traditional relational concept of power as 'compulsory' as it directly forces one actor to follow another actor's will. They note however that actors can choose to exercise power in a more diffuse way over actors that they are not in direct contact with by setting up institutions to enforce their will. They thus call such power 'institutional'. The term 'structural power' they reserve for constitutive social relations that directly affect particular actors, while they call the more diffuse variant 'productive', emphasizing the fact that social actors are 'produced' by such structures. Since such productive power first and foremost operates through discourse, it is otherwise often referred to as 'discursive power'. In contrast to Lukes' third face of power, such discursive power does not pretend there is a 'true' interest of people, but would see any meaning and all forms of knowledge also as instances of power (Foucault 1980; → *Theory Concept: Postmodernism and Poststructuralism*).

3. THEORETICAL PERSPECTIVES

It is obvious from the above that one's definition of power depends on one's broader theoretical perspective. We have seen how classical realism depends on a traditional power conception that focuses on power capabilities of states and relational power in direct interaction. Most of realism uses a concept of power that Barnett and Duvall would characterize as compulsory. Neoliberalism (→ *Theory Concept: Liberalism and Neoliberalism*) includes institutional power in its analysis of (→) international regimes and organizations. World systems and (→) dependency theories emphasize structural power, while discursive power is central to poststructuralist approaches. The definition of power epitomizes the broader ontological understanding of how international relations work in the respective theories. It is all the more astonishing that in Kenneth Waltz's version of neorealism, power, while playing a central role in the characterization of the systemic structure through its distribution, remains undefined so that he continues to use the old realist understanding with an emphasis on capabilities rather than resources (Guzzini 1993: 449; Schmidt 2007: 43).

Power is central to many International Relations theories and approaches because it is used to explain outcomes. Thus, agreements or the failure to agree are commonly put down to the power of a particular state. Yet as Guzzini (1993) has shown in an influential article, such arguments are hugely problematic because they include a tautological fallacy: if power is relational then we see power at work if an actor does something s/he would not have otherwise done. Yet at the same time, we then attribute the change of behaviour that is used as an indication of power to power itself – clearly a circular argument. Following Anthony Kenny, Lukes (2007: 84) calls this problem the 'exercise fallacy' because it reduces power to its exercise. This leaves us with three options: first, we would have to not use power as the explanation of outcomes, but explain instances of power. Second, we could recognize that power does not lend itself to causal analyses but rather involves constitutive reasoning as it is prevalent in constructivist approaches. Third, we could investigate how the meaning of the concept of power has changed over time and which political consequences particular usages have had – or, as Guzzini (2007: 23) suggests, we could ask, 'How has "power" come to mean and be able to do what it does?'

The second and third options would draw the analysis of power clearly into a constructivist framework. From a positivist point of view, this will not be satisfactory. Yet if we want to rescue power as an explanation, we will have to specify the exact pathways through which influence takes place, including a differentiation between the different forms of power, and the conditions that facilitate or hinder such influence, and therefore look beyond power as a blanket explanation.

4. EMPIRICAL PROBLEMS

Such a more complex analysis of power raises a number of empirical difficulties. In *Power and Interdependence*, Robert Keohane and Joseph Nye (1989: 11–14) for instance suggest that in order to understand the workings of power, one would have to analyse the extent to which states are sensitive (in the sense that states are affected by a development or the actions of another actor to various degrees) and vulnerable (in the sense that states can meet the difficulties imposed on them by others), which leads us to the exploration of the conditions of influence. Others have used process-tracing to demonstrate different forms of influence, for instance in analysing the power of European integration in border conflict transformation (Diez, Stetter and Albert 2006). Even so, the more diffuse power is, the more difficult it is to trace, and the more our analyses will either problematize power or emphasize its constitutive effects rather than making causal claims.

In their work, Keohane and Nye have made another contribution to the analysis of power that is important to bear in mind, and that is that there are different empirical forms of power. While the realism of Morgenthau knew, as we have seen, a great variety of power resources or capabilities, neorealism, with a few exceptions such as Robert Gilpin, became increasingly concerned with political and especially military power. Keohane and Nye (1989: 16–17, 60) emphasized that there are both military and non-military forms of power and that their effectiveness varies across issue areas. To put it simply: one may have the biggest and technologically most advanced army in the world, but this will be of little use in sorting a financial crisis or global warming.

Nye (1990) has also developed the now-widespread concept of 'soft power'. This was evidently set against the notion of 'hard', military power, but echoing the more diffuse definition of power was primarily aimed at capturing the power of attraction (Nye 2007: 163). That there is power in attraction is, however, not new. A cultural notion of (→) hegemony would for instance emphasize the ability of the hegemon to attract a following. Thus, the hegemon exercises power but not against the will of those who are affected by this power – a power that can take on both actor-centred and structuralist characteristics, and which includes Lukes' three faces of power.

The idea that there are different forms of power has also sparked a debate about whether the predominant use of power in international relations is changing. The extent to which non-military issue areas become increasingly important under the conditions of complex interdependence would suggest so. Similarly, analysts have asked whether actors in international relations can be differentiated according to their 'preferred' exercise of power. Of particular importance in this context is the debate over whether the European Union represents a new form of 'normative power' in that it relies primarily on 'its ability to shape conceptions of normal' (Manners 2002: 239), which would bear resemblances to Nye's notion of 'soft power', Lukes' third face of power, and Barnett and Duvall's 'productive power'. It will not come as a surprise though that this is a rather contested argument, which reiterates again the complexity of defining and analysing power.

5. CORE READING

Barnett, Michael and Raymond Duvall (eds) (2005) *Power in Global Governance* (Cambridge: Cambridge University Press). An outstanding investigation of the role of power in global governance, operating on the basis of the four-fold power scheme identified above.

Berenskoetter, Felix and Williams, M. J. (eds) (2007) *Power in World Politics* (London: Routledge). An edited collection of articles that brings together some of the major perspectives on power in IR.

Guzzini, Stefano (1993) 'Structural Power: The Limits of Neorealist Power Analysis', *International Organization* 47 (3), 443–78. A widely cited and lucid analysis of the analytical use of the concept of power in IR, especially neorealism.

6. USEFUL WEBSITES

http://vimeo.com/8913534. A lecture by Joseph Nye on his theory of soft power and its importance for today's governments and global societies at the first anniversary of President Obama's inauguration.

http://www.britannica.com/bps/additionalcontent/18/32767100/Hard-Power-Soft-Power-Toward-a-More-Realistic-Power-Analysis. Entry in the Britannica online encyclopedia about hard vs. soft power.

http://en.allexperts.com/e/p/po/power_in_international_relations.htm. Comprehensive overview regarding different concepts of power in international relations.

Theory Concept: Realism and Neorealism

1. CORE QUESTIONS ADDRESSED

- What are the fundamental assumptions of realism?
- What are the main differences between classical realism and neorealism?
- What are the main assumptions of neorealism with regard to the stability of the international system?

2. OVERVIEW AND BACKGROUND

Realism entered academic International Relations in the period between the late 1930s and the early 1940s, mostly as a theoretical answer to the liberal or 'idealist' tradition that dominated the discourse about world politics since the end of the First World War (→ *Theory Concept: Liberalism and Neoliberalism*). Realism accused liberalism of ignoring the fundamental question of (→) power in world politics while at the same time overestimating the capacity of humans and states to progress through learning and increased civilization towards intersubjectively shared reasoning. Instead of following some ideological assumptions or normative codes of conduct, realists called upon policy-makers to keep in mind the most basic challenge for each state in the international system: preserving the national security and survival within an anarchical self-help system, which in a realist logic can only be achieved through the constant struggle for maximizing power.

Realism claims to rest upon a much older tradition, starting with Thucydides' (*c.* 460–406 BC) account of the ancient Peloponnesian War that took place between the dominant regional powers of that time, the city-states of Athens and Sparta. Thucydides, who was an Athenian admiral and therefore took part in the war himself, not only describes the history of the participants, the war and its consequences, but also refers in his interpretation of the conflict's causes to Athens as having become too powerful not to be perceived as a threat by Sparta. The increase of Athens' power challenged the dominant status of Sparta in the region. This, combined with an already present drive for power in the calculations of Spartan politicians, led to the declaration of war against the rival. Further prominent examples of realist considerations can be found in the work of Niccolo Machiavelli (1469–1527), where power as a regulative and constitutive force in politics also plays an important role, as well as in the theoretical considerations of Thomas Hobbes (1588–1679), a contemporary witness of the English Civil War who elaborated a theory of states, based upon the legitimate use of violence through a central authority. Essential for subsequent realist considerations has been the Hobbesian depiction of anarchy, the famous 'state of nature', which he described as a condition where men are engaged in a war of all against all, constantly struggling for survival, although it should be noted that Hobbes himself did not think that relations between states operated on the same basis as relations between individuals, which is in effect what realists have inferred from his writings.

Classical realism

The most prominent authors of classical realism are Hans J. Morgenthau, Edward Hallett Carr and Reinhold Niebuhr. In *Politics Among Nations* (1948), Morgenthau elaborates a realist theory of world politics, starting with the premise that a theoretical approach towards politics should be considered as an approach towards human beings. Referring strongly to the anthropological considerations made by Hobbes in *Leviathan* (1651), Morgenthau conceptualized humans as rational and egoistic, constantly seeking to maximize power. According to Morgenthau, these anthropological premises can be transferred to the behaviour of states in the international system: 'politics, like society in general, is governed by objective laws that have their roots in human nature' (Morgenthau 1961: 4). Consequently, Morgenthau concludes that states as actors have to struggle for survival in world politics in the same way that men do in the theoretical considerations made by Thomas Hobbes. Morgenthau's international system is an anarchical self-help system composed of states which try to pursue their interests, defined in terms of power, against the interests of other states.

Neorealism

Neorealism, or structural realism, agrees with the realist conception of power as essential for understanding world politics. But in contrast to classical realism's focus on human nature, neorealism highlights the absence of a central authority in the international system and the relative distribution of power among the states as structural causes for a competition on security in the international system. According to Kenneth N. Waltz's *Theory of International Politics* (1979), it is not the motivation of the actors involved but the political structure in which they are embedded that helps explain how international politics works. This political structure is always characterized by an underlying ordering principle. Waltz differentiates between two ordering principles: in a state of hierarchy, units are in a relationship that can be described as authority or subordination. In consequence, Waltz strongly identifies hierarchy with domestic politics, arguing that, as already described by Hobbes, within a nation the war-prone state of anarchy is overcome by an authoritarian political structure. But, since this overarching authority is missing in world politics, Waltz associates international politics with (→) anarchy. As he argues further, anarchy eliminates functional differentiations between units. From a structural realist point of view, within an anarchical international system all states are like-units and in consequence what becomes relevant for explaining international politics is not unit-level variation, such as different types of regimes, but the distribution of capabilities between these units. Structural realism is interested in providing a rank ordering of states in order to be able to identify the great powers within an international system. This number of great powers determines the structure of the international system – the polarity (number of poles) of the system (Donnelly 2009: 36–7; Dunne and Schmidt 2007: 98). In consequence, states have to be aware of the distribution of power in the international system and be sensitive towards the relative gains of others, in order to ensure their own security.

To achieve the primary objective of survival within this self-help system, states have to enter into a competition concerning the distribution of capabilities and (military) power ($\rightarrow$ *Security Dilemma*), especially since they can never be certain about the intentions of other states. Once a state is confronted with an adversary who has become powerful enough to be perceived as a potential threat, Waltz argues that it can only choose the option of balancing ($\rightarrow$ *Balance of Power*) against this great power. According to neorealists, two options of balancing exist: a state at risk can either choose to increase its own military capacities, i.e. through military expenditures (internal balancing), or it can seek to build strategic alliances to jointly balance against the great power (external balancing). Hence, states are interested in balancing to correct a 'skewed distribution of relative power in the international system' (Layne 1993: 12). Because balancing against a great power, or ($\rightarrow$) a hegemon, is determined by the anarchical structure of the international system, it is considered an automatism. States have to balance because of the structural pressure of anarchy – they cannot help it. In consequence, neorealists see international political outcomes, such as conflicts between great powers, as caused by the specific structure of the international system at a particular time, or how Donnelly describes it: 'The Cold War, in this account, was not "caused" by anyone but was the "natural" result of bipolarity' (Donnelly 2009: 37; see also Mearsheimer 2007: 78–80).

Within the history of International Relations as a discipline, Waltz's structural realism is usually referred to as *defensive realism*, as opposed to the theoretical approach termed *offensive realism* by John J. Mearsheimer. Although Mearsheimer shares most of the basic assumptions made by Waltz, he disagrees in one particular point, the question about 'how much power states want' (Mearsheimer 2001: 21). According to Waltz, it is not conducive for states to attempt to maximize their power and become the leading world hegemon, since the structure of the international system will automatically produce counterbalancing activities, such as the creation of balancing coalitions by great powers which will finally lead to the decline of the hegemon. Therefore, Waltz argues, states should rather pursue the possession of an 'appropriate amount of power' (Waltz 1979: 40). In contrast, from an offensive realist point of view, it makes perfect sense to pursue as much power as possible, in particular hegemony, since it is 'the best way to ensure one's own survival' (Mearsheimer 2007: 72). *Offensive realists* do not 'buy' the argument that hegemony automatically produces successful counterbalancing activities – with reference to historical examples they rather conclude that most of these activities are not successful, in particular since the hegemon has a more advantageous position within such a conflict and therefore offence hardly ever pays. That it is indeed possible to become the world's hegemon is usually illustrated by the overwhelming military capacities of the United States in the nineteenth century and in particular since the end of the Cold War (Mearsheimer 2007: 76).

Neoclassical realism

A new, intermediate approach towards the realist study of International Relations emerged in the late 1990s. Although authors such as Gideon Rose (1998) or Randall L. Schweller (1996) admit that the structure of the international system provides a fruitful approach towards the understanding of world politics, they argue for the incorporation of additional explanatory variables on the individual or domestic level. In including these factors they refer back to variables already introduced by classical realism such as the perceptions of state leaders or the motivations of states. In this logic, factors on the domestic or individual level are intervening variables between the distribution of power (independent variable) in the international system and the foreign policy of states (dependent variable) (Donnelly 2009: 33; Dunne and Brian 2007: 99).

3. METHODOLOGIES

Realism is a rationalist approach to world politics referring in various applications to rational-choice theory. Rationalism is based on the concept of the egoistic individual who always seeks to maximize their individual benefits. Like other rationalist approaches to social behaviour, realism assumes that patterns of individual or state action can be understood as the result of a prior rational calculation of these actors. This logic of action is termed 'logic of consequentiality', as opposed to the 'logic of appropriateness', where actors are depicted as embedded into a specific social structure and therefore follow norms and rules because they are perceived as legitimate and rightful (→ *Theory Concept: Social Constructivism*). Furthermore, realism provides the actors involved with specific assumed priorities constraining the available options for action: actors in realism seek to maximize power. Moreover, the choices an individual can make are determined by the specific structures in which the actions take place: as the structure of the international system is assumed to be anarchical, states seek to maximize their relative power by increasing their capabilities, for instance through military expenditure or economic growth. In order to explain decisions made by actors in specific constellations, realism turns to rationalist (→) game theory (for an overview of rationalism see for instance Fearon and Wendt 2002).

4. EMPIRICAL APPLICATIONS

In realism, world politics are power politics and therefore it is no surprise that empirical applications of the theory usually refer to the politics of the great powers of the time. During the Cold War, this was naturally the rivalry between the two 'superpowers', the US and the Soviet Union, and mainstream debate in neorealism at that time analysed the consequences of bipolarity. This debate about the results of polarity is closely related to the previously mentioned discourse between *defensive* and *offensive realism*. But instead of focusing on the question about how much power states want, authors concentrate on the prospects of a particular international political structure for temporary peace.

Against the historical background of the Cold War rivalry between the US and the Soviet Union, and in addition to the relative decline of US hegemony in the 1970s, Kenneth N. Waltz reaches the conclusion that bipolar international systems with two major powers tend to be less conflict prone than uni- or multipolar ones. With polarity conceptualized as the number of major powers within an international system, he argues that in a bipolar constellation the distribution of capabilities between the two adversaries is quite predictable. This thought is based on the assumption that the probability of miscalculating the power of the rival, a perception that would trigger balancing activities, is rather unlikely. A balance of power, opening up opportunities for temporary stability, can be achieved relatively easily (Waltz 1979: 161–3). On the contrary, within a multipolar international system the situation is more complex, owing to the fact that every state is confronted with at least a few potential adversary states, trying to estimate their capabilities and intentions in the near future. Furthermore and as already mentioned, a unipolar system also tends to produce conflict due to the structural demand for balancing. Following Waltz, a bipolar system is thus more stable than a unipolar one, while a multipolar is the least stable of the aforementioned alternatives.

After the end of the Cold War a theoretical debate within neorealism started referring closely to the prospective stability of the unipolar system with the US as the sole remaining superpower: the majority of neorealist scholars like Kapstein and Mastanduno (1999), Wohlforth (1999) or Mearsheimer (2001) reversed Waltz's argumentation stating that a unipolar system is more stable and therefore more peaceful than any other. Wohlforth argues that the predominance of American hegemony in the post-Cold-War era should not only be recognized as historically unique, but also that the benefits of such unipolarity should be put into perspective. According to Wohlforth, the immense power advantage of the US makes a great power struggle for hegemony unlikely in the foreseeable future as its outstanding position offers no opportunity for counterbalancing, whether by individual states or by alliances. Additionally, its status of being the only remaining superpower provides the US with the possibility to constantly increase its capabilities, thus widening the gap between the hegemon and other states and making the unipolar structure of the international system enduring (Wohlforth 1999: 7–8).

These pro-unipolarity arguments have been opposed by Christopher Layne and others, pointing out that preserving the unipolar status of the US after the Cold War is impossible and therefore an illusion (Layne 1993: 7). This goes back to the arguments stated by Waltz – according to Layne, anarchy produces a further systemic constraint against unipolarity: sameness, i.e. the tendency of smaller states 'toward imitating their rivals' successful characteristics', in order not to fall behind (Layne 1993: 15; Waltz 1979: 127).

Other realist scholars, such as Michael Mastanduno, have emphasized the importance of 'perceptions of threat' for the decision of whether balancing is necessary. In his balance-of-threat logic, he argues that the decision of states to counterbalance a hegemon is based on the behaviour of the superpower itself, thus offering the interpretation of a so-called benign hegemon, who is apparently no threat to the immediate security of his neighbours (Mastanduno 1999: 146–51). A further addition to the balancing assumption was made by fellow neorealist Stephen M. Walt, who doubted the assumption of balancing as structural automatism. Walt reached the conclusion that it might be more attractive for weaker states to bandwagon, thus enjoying benefits such as protection or preferential trade agreements, than opposing the hegemon directly through balancing. Therefore, the antonym of balancing within neorealist theory is bandwagoning. Nevertheless, because bandwagoning always includes the risk of relatively losing power while strengthening the relative power of others, it is not considered as a preferable option by the majority of neorealist scholars.

Because realism has not only been involved in explaining international political outcomes, but additionally aims to provide practical advice to policy-makers particularly in the US, a number of realist scholars have been concerned with the rise of new great powers and especially the future role of China, since the beginning of its extraordinary economic growth in the 1980s. Realism focuses on the question of how the expanding economic capacities of China might translate into military potentials, thus leading to an increase of China's power and a change in the international order. More specifically, questions are raised about whether China can rise peacefully, and whether China's power capacities will become so great that they would re-establish a bipolar structure of the international system (Kaplan 2005; Deng 2001).

5. CENTRAL CRITICISMS

Realism has frequently been criticized for not providing a coherent and comprehensive theoretical framework: classical realism, according to its critics, accepts the anthropological premises made by Thomas Hobbes without questioning and simply translates them into world politics. In consequence, subsequent realist scholars referred to sociological or structural causes of violence, such as emphasized in the works of Niebuhr or John J. Herz. Furthermore, Morgenthau provides the reader neither with an explicit definition of power, nor with a precise distinction between power and interests. This close linkage between power and interests makes his interpretation of power tautological. Neorealism seeks to overcome this problem by defining power as measurable capabilities of states.

Moreover, neorealism has displayed a poor predictive record, in particular since it failed to forecast and explain major developments in international politics, such as the end of the Cold War, the development of regional integration, as well as the emergence of a (→) security community in Europe in the 1990s and the growing incidence of intrastate conflict, in particular in Africa.

In the discipline of International Relations, realism has become engaged in two main debates: the first, also referred to as the 'neo-neodebate', took place in the 1980s between neorealist scholars and neoliberals. While the majority of neorealists claimed that cooperation under anarchy can only be a temporary phenomenon and necessarily rests upon the support of a hegemonic power, it became evident after the relative decline of US hegemony in the 1970s that the theoretical answers provided by neorealism did not explain the reality. Although neoliberals started with the same assumptions as neorealists, such as the premise of rational actors and the state of anarchy in the international system, they came to a different conclusion, namely that cooperation can be rational behaviour. Neorealists, such as Grieco (1988), tried to provide a theoretical answer to this criticism by pointing to the importance of relative gains in an anarchical international system. Nevertheless, realism remains poorly equipped to explain the variety of international cooperation (→ *International Regimes*).

The second, most fundamental, criticism of realism was articulated by Alexander Wendt (1992) in his article 'Anarchy Is What States Make of It: The Social Construction of Power Politics'. According to Wendt, the anarchical state of the international system does not translate directly into a self-help system of power politics (Wendt 1994: 394). In contrast to the neorealist account of structure as being an exogenous factor to the study of world politics, Wendt argues that structure is something that is socially constructed by actors, through interaction, discourse and perception. In this logic, what neorealists claimed to be an inevitable force which determines the actors involved, is rather a socially constructed logic, which can be influenced and changed by the actors involved (→ *Social Constructivism*).

6. CORE READING

Morgenthau, Hans J. (1961) *Politics Among Nations* (New York: Alfred A. Knopf, 3rd edn, orig. pub. 1948). Defines the field of realist International Relations theory.

Mearsheimer, John J. (2001) *The Tragedy of Great Power Politics* (New York: W. W. Norton). An introduction to the main theoretical considerations of offensive realism.

Waltz, Kenneth N. (1979) *Theory of International Politics* (Reading, MA: Addison-Wesley). In this book, Waltz provides the most fundamental approach to neorealism.

7. USEFUL WEBSITES

http://globetrotter.berkeley.edu/conversations/. UC Berkeley produces an interesting series titled: 'Conversations with History'; here interviews with John. J. Mearsheimer, Stephen Walt and Kenneth Waltz can be downloaded.

http://walt.foreignpolicy.com/blog/2072. Blog by Stephen Walt called 'A Realist in an Ideological Age'.

http://www.theory-talks.org/2008/07/theory-talk-12.html. Interview with Robert Jervis on nuclear weapons, explaining the non-realist politics of the George W. Bush administration and US military presence in Europe.

Regional Integration

1. CORE QUESTIONS ADDRESSED

- What or who drives regional integration?
- To what extent is European governance different from governance within nation-states?
- Under what conditions can supranational governance be legitimate?

2. DEFINITIONS

Regional integration is the process of establishing a degree of supranational authority beyond the nation-state within a particular geographical region – that is, where the governments of nation-states decide to hand over some decision-making capacity to a new, higher level of governance. We speak of a supranational authority as opposed to intergovernmental cooperation (which we find on all sorts of issues) if decisions taken on the supranational level take direct effect, or have the status of law within the member states of the regional body. In contrast, in intergovernmental arrangements, any binding agreement needs to be ratified on the national level through the appropriate procedures (e.g. parliamentary assent). This means that intergovernmental cooperation does not result in the setting-up of a new level of government. In more advanced stages of regional integration, decisions taken on the supranational level no longer require the consent of all members, but often are decided by qualified majorities.

This definition focuses on the political aspects of regional integration (see Wiener and Diez 2009). This is, however, only one aspect of integration. 'Integration' can also mean the formation of a new identity beyond national boundaries through increased interaction (from trade to town twinning) between citizens of different states. We may then speak of social integration. Social integration is both a possible effect of as well as a possible condition for successful political integration. Likewise, we can speak of economic integration, with the increasing movement of labour, goods and capital across borders. Liberals argue that this is often the engine of other forms of integration.

While there are regional integration projects in many parts of the world, our understanding of regional integration has largely been shaped by the European integration process. Therefore this entry will concentrate upon European integration as it is the most advanced and truly supranational. However, there are also nascent integration processes in Asia (ASEAN and APEC), North America (NAFTA), and South America (MERCOSUR).

After the Second World War, there was a move in many European societies to find a new form of political authority to transcend the nation-state, which was seen as the root cause of the devastating wars experienced in the first half of the twentieth century. The first organizations to be formed, the Organization for European Economic Cooperation and the Council of Europe, were both essentially intergovernmentalist. With the European Coal and Steel Community (ECSC), however, which was agreed in 1952 in the Treaty of Paris (initially western) European states embarked on a more ambitious course of regional integration, installing a supranational authority to oversee and govern the new Community (Dinan 1999).

Despite several setbacks, European integration continued to expand into new policy areas and to enhance the integration of policies already within its frame (this is referred to as *deepening of integration*) as well as to attract new member states (*widening of integration*, commonly referred to as 'enlargement'). In the Treaties of Rome (1957), the European Economic Community and the European Atomic Energy Community were added to the ECSC. Together, the three communities were later simply called the 'European Community' (EC). In 1992, following the Maastricht Treaty, a Common Foreign and Security Policy as well as cooperation in Justice and Home Affairs were added as new pillars, besides the EC, to the integration project, although both of these new pillars remain largely intergovernmental in nature. The new three-pillar structure became the European Union (EU). It was abolished through the 2009 Lisbon Treaty, which replaced a failed attempt to provide the EU with a constitutional treaty. The contested nature of this process underlines just how difficult the processes of reconfiguring authority can be.

3. THEORETICAL PERSPECTIVES

Regional, and specifically European, integration has been both a puzzle for IR theorists to be explained (Why would states give up their sovereignty and embark on a process of integration?) and a *normative* challenge (Is integration a good thing? If so, how can further integration be achieved?). Broadly speaking, the overwhelming number of theoretical approaches dealing with integration come from, or are linked to, the liberal camp of IR theories. This is hardly surprising: after all, we are dealing with an advanced form of international cooperation and transnational links, the prime domain of liberalism (→ *Theory Concept: Liberalism and Neoliberalism*). This is not to say that there are no realist accounts of regional integration. They do exist, explaining integration with the geopolitical interests of the dominant member states (mostly France, Germany and the UK in the EU context) or the features of the international system at a particular historical juncture (the Cold War for European integration). Yet overall, regional integration is not a strength of realism (but see Pedersen 1998; Hyde-Price 2000) (→ *Theory Concept: Realism and Neorealism*).

For a long time, the dominant theory of regional integration was neofunctionalism (Haas 1968; Lindberg and Scheingold 1970). As the name suggests, this is a revised version of (→) functionalism. In a nutshell, neofunctionalism argues that once states have embarked on integrating a seemingly minor, technical field of integration (such as, in the European context, coal and steel), not only will they see the benefits of integration (a classic liberal argument), but also there will be functional linkages between the particular policy field integrated and other policy fields. Integration is therefore likely to 'spill over' from one field to another. A supranational authority (such as the European Commission) will in addition act as a driving force for further integrative steps.

Neofunctionalism not only dominated the theoretical field of regional integration studies, it was also something of a quasi-official ideology of European integration. Indeed, the basic ideas of neofunctionalism were set out not by academics, but rather by practitioners, above all Jean Monnet. He was a French civil servant who essentially wrote the plan, presented by French foreign minister Robert Schuman, on which the ECSC was based, and who became the first president of the High Authority of the ECSC. Over the years, as integration did not always proceed in the single direction predicted by neofunctionalism, the theory was revised again and again, and made more complex to account for setbacks brought about, most often, by resistances within member states towards integration. Yet it remains powerful to this day (Niemann with Schmitter 2009).

The main contender of neofunctionalism is intergovernmentalism, which explains integration as a result of the interests of member states. We have already encountered the realist version of this theory above, but more influential today is liberal intergovernmentalism. Andrew Moravcsik (1998), its main proponent, agrees that integration is not an effect of spill-over or the interests of a supranational agent, but of member states' interests. Yet he does not deduct these interests from objective geopolitical considerations. Building on the idea of international politics as a two-level game, he argues that the interests of member states are determined in a domestic bargaining process. Governments represent the outcome of these bargaining processes in their own bargaining on the EU level, although once they have reached an agreement, they are keen on preserving the outcome by enshrining it in supranational procedures.

There have been a series of criticisms of liberal intergovernmentalism, which cannot all be recounted here (see *Journal of European Public Policy* 1999). One of the most important ones is that it negates the informal integration taking place on a day-to-day basis when officials, politicians and people in general meet and interact – the social integration that often brings with it political integration. These processes are the focus of more recent, social constructivist approaches (→ *Theory Concept: Social Constructivism*) to European integration, which focus on how actor identities change within the context of integration (e.g. Christiansen et al. 2001).

4. EMPIRICAL PROBLEMS

We have dealt with a core empirical problem, the explanation of integration, above. Let us therefore concentrate on some of the normative issues raised by integration. The tendency in IR, especially from within a liberal perspective, is to see regional integration as a good thing. Federalists in particular regard integration as a necessary step to guarantee peace. They deal with integration therefore not so much as an issue to be explained, but as a desirable path towards peace. The problem becomes how to best achieve integration. For many federalists a constitutional treaty is at the core of integrationist efforts, rather than the piecemeal spill-over of neofunctionalism, although as the history of European integration shows, one can lead to another (Burgess 2000).

Federalists are often accused of assuming that the end state of integration is a new federal state. Yet so far, European integration has led to a much more complex political system, which is often characterized as a system of governance (→ *Global Governance*) without a central government. A lot of studies are devoted to trying to make sense of this system, which operates with different decision-making procedures according to policy (the three pillars above, but also within these pillars), and bases its decisions on complex systems of consultation between a variety of actors on different levels (subnational, national, European) and cross-cutting these levels along functional lines (Marks et al. 1996). A core question is whether this new form of governance challenges the predominant position of the modern state in international politics, or whether it will eventually either fail or replicate the state model on a higher level (Bull 1977).

One of the most pressing problems of regional integration is its legitimacy (e.g. Eriksen and Fossum 2004; Weale and Nentwich 1998). Unless there is a parliament with full control of policies on the regional level, supranational authority does not conform to the idea of democracy as we know it. The new system of governance is therefore seen as legitimized either indirectly (decisions are taken by elected governments among a series of other actors), or based on other sources than voter participation (for instance, the beneficial output generated by integration, or new forms of participation in expert committees). Others simply see supranational governance as legitimate only within very strict boundaries.

Indeed, this normative view is in stark contrast to the positive assessment of integration in the eyes of many scholars of international politics.

5. CORE READING

Eilstrup-Sangiovanni, Mette (ed.) (2006) *Debates on European Integration: A Reader* (Basingstoke: Palgrave). A selection of the most influential articles in the study of European integration.

Moravcsik, Andrew (1998) *The Choice for Europe: Social Purpose and State Power from Messina to Maastricht* (Ithaca, NY: Cornell University Press). The core statement of liberal intergovernmentalism and still the central reference point of the debates in integration theory.

Wiener, Antje and Thomas Diez (eds) (2009) *European Integration Theory* (Oxford: Oxford University Press, 2nd edn). A core compilation of articles discussing the various theoretical approaches to European integration.

6. USEFUL WEBSITES

http://www.cris.unu.edu/. The United Nations University on Comparative Regional Integration Studies' website contains useful studies comparing the integration process in different regions.

http://www.uneca.org/aria/. The UN Economic Commission for Africa provides insight into the (economic) integration in Africa.

http://aric.adb.org/. The Asian Regional Integration Centre is tracking Asian (economic and monetary) integration.

http://europa.eu/. Official website of the European Union.

Security

1. CORE QUESTIONS

- Whose security are we referring to in International Relations?
- What are the threats against which security in international politics needs to be guaranteed?
- What is the relationship between security and identity?

2. DEFINITIONS

There used to be a time when security was easily defined in International Relations. Security had to do with protecting the territorial integrity and the political system of a state, or what one may call the identity of a state, first and foremost by military means. Security policy was, and to a large extent still is, therefore closely linked with defence policy. It is broader than defence policy in that it includes other foreign policy means than recourse to the military to secure the survival of the state, such as the participation in collective security organizations, from the United Nations (UN) on the global level to the Organization for Security and Cooperation in Europe (OSCE) on the regional level. Yet the survival of the state as its specific aim also makes it narrower than foreign policy. The focus on military defence is ultimately a consequence of the anarchical character of the international system where the sovereign state needs to have the possibility in the absence of a monopoly of violence on the system level to defend itself against potential aggression, a situation that leads to the so-called security dilemma ($\rightarrow$ *Anarchy*, $\rightarrow$ *Sovereignty*). The anarchical character of the system makes security in the international realm very different from questions of internal security.

Today, the meaning of security is openly contested in academia but also in international politics, both in terms of the field in which security is supposed to operate and in terms of the reference group, i.e. regarding the question: security for whom? In terms of the field, both scholars and practitioners have pointed to increasingly virulent threats that do not concern politics or the military, but economics, the environment or other areas (Buzan, Wæver and de Wilde 1998). Why, one may ask, should security policy focus on military strategy and defence budgets if these are inadequate instruments to stave off global warming as the 'real' threat to security? While such a threat may well affect the territorial integrity of the state, for instance through the flooding of maritime areas, it also implies a shift in the referent object of security. Thus, in the debate about the meaning of security, a crucial point of contention is whether we ought to talk about the security of the state, or that of individuals, or sub- and transnational groups. The concept of 'human security', for instance, centres on the individual rather than the state (Kaldor 2007; Paris 2001). Indeed, states can themselves be a security threat to individuals if they neglect human rights and the basic needs of their population.

3. THEORETICAL PERSPECTIVES

Narrow conceptions of security are usually attached to realist approaches (→ *Theory Concept: Realism and Neorealism*), which is a consequence of the realist emphasis on states as the main actors of international relations, their geopolitical interests, and the anarchical system in which they operate and in which cooperation is always fragile if possible at all. Liberal approaches (→ *Theory Concept: Liberalism and Neoliberalism*) tend to seek security more through cooperation than military threat, and have therefore favoured systems of collective security in which states join common institutions to work together in enhancing each other's security on a global or regional level. Liberalism would principally be more open to a widening of the notion of security, but authors working in this tradition tend to reserve the term for military security issues and then argue in favour of the importance of other policy fields. The neoliberal classic, *Power and Interdependence* (Keohane and Nye 1977), for instance, makes a strong argument for the importance of non-military forms of power but associates security with military power.

It is with the rise of the various forms of constructivist and Critical approaches in the 1980s (→ *Theory Concepts: Social Constructivism; Marxism and Critical Theory*) that security became such a contested concept. One of the first advocates of a widening of the concept was Barry Buzan (1991), who argued in *People, States and Fear* that national security is poorly understood if one ignores the identity struggles below the state level. Buzan was close to the realist tradition at the time, so he thought of security as a core concept in International Relations; yet he was also what may best be called an 'unorthodox' realist who was open to other approaches and sought the dialogue across disciplinary boundaries. Others followed Buzan, adding further fields of security. Environmental security became a particularly popular notion in the context of increasingly scarce resources, mounting pollution and environmental scares from acid rain to the nuclear catastrophe of Chernobyl. Security was no longer automatically associated with the military and the political survival of the state; it became attached to threats that were increasingly defined as security issues not only by academics and activists but also in the world of summits and debates within the United Nations.

In a second but related development, activists and scholars alike increasingly questioned the idea that it was the state that had to be granted primary protection in international politics. Already in Buzan's work, identity struggles were not an issue between states but groups of people within and across states who saw security as a matter of their group rather than the state as a whole. Issues such as environmental security, however, even go beyond this. They know no clear boundaries, and developments such as global warming potentially affect the whole world, albeit to different degrees and in different ways. Likewise, if true security is not achieved through the protection of the state but rather the individual, the reference point of security becomes both the individual human being but through this also humankind as such. This led to the notion of human security, which can be understood both from a liberal-cosmopolitan point of view, stressing human rights and individual freedom, and from a more critical-cosmopolitan point of view, emphasizing rights with an explicit view to human emancipation in what is broadly called critical security studies (Krause and Williams 1997; Booth 2005). Advocates of human security tend to take a holistic view of security on the individual level that includes both the freedom from fear and the freedom from want, providing a standard of living beyond hunger and disease.

Needless to say the advocates of a narrow conception of security were not persuaded by the extension of the concept. In particular, they argued that such a broadening of what security means would render the concept useless for analytical purposes at it was becoming difficult to distinguish what counted as security and what did not. Buzan, for one, agreed with them. Together with Ole Wæver and other colleagues at the Copenhagen Peace Research Institute, he developed a new approach to security studies that became known as the 'Copenhagen School' (Buzan, Wæver and de Wilde 1998; Buzan and Wæver 2003). This was built on two core arguments. Firstly, that there are regional security complexes in which security interaction (both of the threatening and the cooperative kind) was denser between actors within the complex than actors in other complexes. In short, Buzan and Wæver argued in favour of the significance of regions in international security. More importantly for the present context, however, they claimed that one cannot objectively decide what counts as a security issue and what not. Instead, security was discursively constructed through speech acts in which something was *represented* as an existential threat to a particular group of people. If such representation became widely accepted, the issue was 'securitized'. Note that this does not mean that the issue did not exist before, but rather that it only became a specific security issue through a (→) discourse of securitization. Through such a formal-discursive rather than substantive definition of security, Buzan and Wæver were able to agree with the broadening of the concept without allowing everything to be called security by the analyst. Instead, they focused on what the actors they studied defined as security, and formulated strict rules that such definitions had to adhere to, thus providing boundaries to the concept.

4. EMPIRICAL PROBLEMS

The Copenhagen School has broadly a constructivist approach perhaps with poststructuralist elements. (→ *Theory Concept: Postmodernism and Poststructuralism.*) Those following a critical-emancipatory line criticized it in particular for its alleged conservative social ontology (e.g. McSweeney 1999). This has in part to do with the fact that Buzan and Wæver together with their team applied their approach first to what they called 'societal security', where non-state identities are represented as being threatened by the increased significance of transnational developments, including (→) regional integration and (→) migration. Because security discourses, once established, tend to be relatively stable, the work seemed to reify societal identities and even to reinforce the notion that migrants, for instance, are a security threat, which runs counter to the emancipatory ideals of critical security studies. Yet at the heart of this criticism seems to lie a misunderstanding: the Copenhagen School does not treat identities as given. Instead, following a poststructuralist argument, such identities are only constructed (and continuously reconstructed) through the representation of an 'other', a threat against which big collectivities with a diverse membership such as 'nations' can only acquire meaning. The argument that such identities rely on the representation of the other as an existential – a security – threat carries in itself emancipatory potential, although not quite in the same way as envisaged by the core of critical security studies.

Migration is an interesting empirical problem that nicely illuminates the development of the concept of security. It did not play much of a role in traditional security accounts. Yet at the same time, the argument that migrants are a security threat was not alien to the public debate. The Copenhagen School, rather than ignoring such arguments, recognizes them but also offers a platform for their systematic critique. This has led to further debates about what exactly is involved in the process of securitization. A group around Didier Bigo (2002; see also Aradau and van Munster 2007; CASE Collective 2006; Huysmans 2006), commonly labelled the 'Paris School', questioned the heavy emphasis on emergency language in the Copenhagen account. They proposed instead that securitization, in particular in the field of migration, is generated by technocratic expertise and bureaucratic routines, for instance in the development of new technology to screen visa applicants and border entrants.

These debates are a far cry from where the concept of security in International Relations set out initially, not least because they transverse the boundary between internal and external security. There can be no doubt however that in a context of (→) globalization such a widened notion of security seems eminently more applicable than the old focus on the survival of the state.

5. CORE READING

Buzan, Barry and Lene Hansen (2009) *The Evolution of International Security Studies* (Cambridge: Cambridge University Press). A first comprehensive account of the development of security studies.

Buzan, Barry, Ole Wæver and Jaap de Wilde (1998) *Security: A New Framework for Analysis* (Boulder, CO: Lynne Rienner). The core statement of the so-called Copenhagen School of security studies, centred around the concept of securitization.

Williams, Paul D. (ed.) (2008) *Security Studies: An Introduction* (London: Routledge). An excellent textbook compilation but also a good resource for advanced readers, representing all facets of the security studies debate.

6. USEFUL WEBSITES

http://belfercenter.ksg.harvard.edu/project/58/quarterly_journal.html. Home of *International Security*, one of the main journals in International Relations.

http://casecollective.org/. CASE stands for 'Critical Approaches to Security in Europe'; it is a collective of researchers working with different notions of securitization.

http://www.humansecuritynetwork.org/. The Human Security Network is an intergovernmental body whose members are governments supporting the idea of human security.

http://www.libertysecurity.org/. The website of Challenge, an international research project on the relationship between liberty and security.

www.iiss.org. The website of the London-based International Institute for Strategic Studies.

www.worldsecurityinstitute.org. A major US-based non-profit organization working on security.

http://www.watsoninstitute.org/globalsecuritymatrix/. An interactive security forum run by James Der Derian and colleagues.

security

1. CORE QUESTIONS ADDRESSED

- How can stable peace be achieved under the condition of anarchy?
- What types of security communities can be differentiated?
- Under which conditions are security communities established?

2. DEFINITIONS

The concept of a security community was introduced to International Relations by Karl W. Deutsch in 1957, describing a community of states in which violence or even war has become an inconceivable course of action among members. Starting with the fundamental question of how durable and stable peace can be possible on the international level under the condition of anarchy, Deutsch points to the simple mechanism of community-building observable on a personal or national level. Deutsch discerns that the sense of an integrative 'we-feeling', created by communicative processes such as shared knowledge, or the transaction of material or immaterial goods, is an essential precondition for the formation of a community. By stating that the emergence of a security community among states, based on mutual sympathy, trust and common interests, is possible under specific conditions, he then applied this sociological observation to the international level. Deutsch defines a security community as 'a group of people' believing 'that they have come to agreement on at least this one point: that common social problems must and can be resolved by processes of "peaceful change"', e.g. without reference to physical violence (Deutsch et al. 1957: 6).

According to Deutsch, there are two types of security communities: the amalgamated and the pluralistic security community. The former is characterized by the formal merger of more than two single units into 'some type of common government after amalgamation' (Deutsch et al. 1957: 6). Deutsch provides the US as an example for an amalgamate security community: although the single states remain to a certain degree sovereign as ordering units, the collective nation is governed by strong national institutions, such as the House of Representatives or the Senate, in addition to a national government. Alternatively, a pluralistic security community consists of shared values and interests among its members. The establishment of common institutions is possible but not obligatory. In contrast to an amalgamate security community, members of a pluralistic security community remain legally independent; they do not have to transfer specific rights related to their sovereignty to institutions of the community (Adler and Barnett 1998: 6–7). Deutsch provides the US and Canada after 1815, and Sweden and Norway after 1905, as examples of pluralistic security communities.

The study of security communities was only elaborated further in 1998 by Emanuel Adler and Michael Barnett, who focus more specifically on the development of pluralistic security communities and the conditions under which these security communities are established. Adler and Barnett define a pluralistic security community as 'a transnational region comprised of sovereign states whose people maintain dependable expectations of peaceful change' (1998: 30). Pluralistic security communities differ in certain categories, such as the degree of institutionalization or the depth of mutual trust between the partners, and can therefore be categorized into the ideal types of loosely and tightly coupled pluralistic security communities. The former merely meets the minimal definitional requirements, such as common meanings and identity, which translate into the trust of not being attacked while states do not have additional, affirmative expectations about the behaviour of their partners. The latter, a tightly coupled pluralistic community, consists firstly of a 'mutual aid society', facilitating the further construction of collective arrangements and institutions among the partners. The second distinctive feature is a specific system of rule 'that lies somewhere between a sovereign state and a regional, centralized, government', composed of supranational, transnational as well as national institutions and some type of collective security mechanism (Adler and Barnett 1998: 30). To illustrate these conceptualizations, the authors turn to the North Atlantic Treaty Organization (NATO) as an example of a loosely coupled pluralistic security community, while the European Union provides an example of a tightly coupled one.

3. THEORETICAL PERSPECTIVES

Although the concept of security communities might not appear to be radically new at first glance, Deutsch introduced some highly interesting inputs to the study of world politics at a time where all theoretical conceptualizations differentiated between domestic and international politics. In domestic politics, the umbrella of the nation-state, with its legitimate use of violence and legal restrictions, allows the establishment of different types of social and political communities, while in international politics, characterized by an (→) anarchical self-help system, states were supposed to be only concerned about their survival, making the development of a community unthinkable. Consequently, in answering Deutsch's original question about the possibility of peace in an anarchical system, neither of the mainstream theoretical approaches of his time – realism and liberalism – refer to normative or social explanations. (→ *Theory Concepts: Realism and Neorealism; Liberalism and Neoliberalism.*) According to neorealism, war is an omnipresent phenomenon induced by the anarchical structure of the international system. The temporary absence of war can be either explained as a result of a balance of power, as a result of the establishment of temporary alliances, or as a consequence of (→) hegemonic deterrence. Alternatively, neoliberalism stresses that the consequences of anarchy can be overcome by the establishment of international organizations, facilitating international cooperation by reducing transaction costs, creating binding agreements and establishing mechanisms of sanction. Nevertheless, neoliberal approaches failed to explain integrative processes, such as the gradual creation of the European Union. It was thus not until constructivist approaches (→ *Theory Concept: Social Constructivism*) stated that the structure of world politics cannot be constructed only by material factors but also by social processes, that some of Deutsch's ideas about the development of an international political community, based on common identities and shared values, became popular again (Adler and Barnett 1998: 10–12).

The most challenging theoretical question that has to be answered with regard to security communities is under which conditions they are created. Deutsch himself stressed four basic conditions for the establishment of an integrative process that consecutively build on each other: firstly, security communities only develop between states that are relevant to each other, e.g. in terms of trade or travel. Secondly, these countries need to be able to communicate. Thirdly, they have to believe that both sides can gain advantages through cooperation. And finally, they have to share certain knowledge about the other's identity, which might be induced by media coverage, and results in a feeling of loyalty towards the other. Deutsch stressed 12 further societal and economical conditions for the successful performance or the creation of an amalgamate security community. Three political conditions will be mentioned examplarily: acceptance of common institutions, political loyalty, as well as the establishment and function of common institutions in a way conducive to the public good and not a particular interest. Deutsch discerns alternative political conditions for the success of pluralistic security communities: the compatibility of political norms of the partners, the capacity to react towards changes in the partner's anticipation and demands in an effective and peaceful manner, and finally a level of reliability towards the other (Deutsch et al. 1957: 115ff.). Unfortunately, Deutsch's initial impetus towards formulating the concept of a security community was not to elaborate a comprehensive theoretical approach but rather to encourage academic debate and start a new research agenda. Therefore, his line of argument often resembles a description of observable facts and developments rather than providing a broad theoretical foundation for his concept.

Aiming to specify the conditions under which the development of security communities might foster peace, Adler and Barnett developed a theoretical framework based upon three tiers. The first tier consists of material and immaterial precipitating conditions, such as a change in technologies, external threats or the development of new interpretations of social reality, animating states to desire a coordination of relations. The second tier is characterized by ongoing social interaction between the respective partners, leading to a steady transformation of their environment. Here, the authors differentiate between structural elements, such as power and ideas, and process elements of transactions, such as social learning. This stimulates a dynamic process, leading to the third tier, which consists of the development of trust and collective identity formation (Adler and Barnett 1998: 29–48). Furthermore, Adler and Barnett identify a number of stages in the development of a security community: they call the initial stage of a security community 'nascent', where the actors involved do not intentionally seek to create a structure for regional integration. The second phase is described as 'ascendant' and defined by an increasing number of transactions as well as institutions and organizations. Furthermore, cognitive structures have been established, allowing for a better understanding and discourse with each other, and thus deepening the mutual trust of the partners. In the third, 'mature', tier regional actors have developed a common identity and institutionalized their transactions through a variety of domestic and supranational settings – in the mature stage the outbreak of war in the region becomes unthinkable (Adler and Barnett 1998: 49–55).

4. EMPIRICAL PROBLEMS

Deutsch's original intention in introducing the concept of security communities into the study of world politics was to induce a broader academic discussion about the origins and establishments of these communities. In consequence he did not elaborate further on the theoretical framework his concept is based on, which on the one hand makes it relatively easy to interpret his intention but on the other hand hinders precise theoretical critique. Adler and Barnett's advancement of the concept relies most evidently on theoretical assumptions made by social constructivism. In consequence, this approach tends to underestimate materialistic factors such as the distribution of economic and military power for the establishment. Raimo Väyrynen, however, highlights the importance of trust as an important factor in creating communities, and discusses some of the methodological and theoretical problems stated in the literature with the security communities approach by Adler and Barnett. So for instance he emphasizes that the concept appears somehow redundant to a wider definition of (→) peace as the absence of physical violence between states. Furthermore, it is evident that the concept is defined in the context of interstate relations and thus has little to say with regard to intrastate security problems, while at the same time rests upon western liberal premises, assuming that a common identity and mutual trust can be achieved more easily amongst democracies. From the perspective of (→) discourse analysis, referring to security as a socially constructed concept, it would be interesting to elaborate the discursive processes leading to the securitization of particular issues (Väyrynen 2000: 113–120).

With reference to the normative claim of security communities as facilitating peaceful relations in world politics made, particularly by Adler and Barnett, Alex J. Bellamy raised the subsequent question about the relationship between security communities and their neighbours. Based on evidence from three case studies, Bellamy concludes that the type of security communities matters: tightly coupled security communities are in less danger of becoming what he calls a 'regional fortress', excluding the environment intentionally from prospective benefits of the community. Bellamy (2004) argues that, through learning processes and socialization, members of tightly coupled security communities tend to internalize the way security politics are ordered within the community, which furthermore shapes their worldview and the way they react to the environment, leading to the proliferation of institutions and cooperation. In contrast, in two of his case studies he found evidence that loosely coupled security communities tend to reproduce realist security problems on their borders (Bellamy 2004: 178–88).

The two most prominent for security communities in literature are, as already mentioned, the Association of Southeast Asian Nations (ASEAN) and NATO. ASEAN was established in 1967 to promote regional peace and economic and social cooperation among its member states. Within the literature, scholars such as Amitav Acharya (2001) tend to interpret the organization as an emerging pluralistic security community, resting on a common identity and common values, although the inclusion of new members, such as Cambodia, brought in new sources of conflict and additional demand for a conflict resolution mechanism. In contrast, Allan Collins (2007) questions the assumption that the presence of norms is sufficient for the consideration of ASEAN as a pluralistic security community. Instead he argues that if ASEAN would be a pluralistic security community, the emergence of new socializing norms should be observable as well as a constant involvement of civil society into decision-making processes in order to guarantee the participation of the people of ASEAN into the process.

However, the evolution of NATO after the end of the Cold War made the alliance an empirically interesting case for the following reasons: the members of the treaty, established in 1949, agreed to collective defence in response to an attack by an external party, thus guaranteeing the security of each of them. Established during a time of constant rivalry between the two superpowers, NATO was, in particular by neorealists such as John Mearsheimer, never considered to be more than a strategic military alliance, created for a specific purpose. Consequently, neorealists expected the alliance to dissolve once the Cold War was over (Mearsheimer 1990). But NATO continued to exist, and what is even more interesting, enlarged the number of its members, developing into the dominant institution in contemporary security relations (William and Neumann 2000: 2). Here it became evident that the mainstream neorealist approach to IR failed to understand the persistence and development of international security alliances, a subject on which neorealist theory claimed to be most evident. However, the development of NATO became more comprehensible, once the alliance was analysed through a more constructivist theoretical approach, considering NATO as a security community. According to a constructivist point of view, here represented by Thomas Risse, NATO still exists because the members of the treaty share democratic norms and identities and therefore continue to not perceive each other as threats, although the external threat, the Soviet Union, has ceased to exist. This development has been supported by constant and institutionalized cooperation as well as the establishment of 'regulative' and 'constitutive' norms and values (Risse-Kappen 1996).

5. CORE READING

Adler, Emanuel and Michael Barnett (eds) (1998) *Security Communities* (Cambridge: Cambridge University Press). Elaborates a comprehensive theoretical approach towards understanding security communities, illustrated with examples such as OSCE or NATO.

Deutsch, Karl W. et al. (1957) *Political Community and the North Atlantic Area: International Organization in the Light of Historical Experience* (Princeton, NJ: Princeton University Press). Classic introduction to the study of security communities.

Väyrynen, Raimo (2000) 'Stable Peace Through Security Communities? Steps Towards Theory Building', in Arie M. Kacowicz, et al. (eds), *Stable Peace amongst Nations* (Boston: Rowman & Littlefield), 108–29. Provides a brief introduction to the theoretical and methodological problems of the concept of security communities.

6. USEFUL WEBSITES

http://www.aseansec.org/16826.htm. Asian Security Community Plan of Action, sometimes considered as an indication that ASEAN is a nascent security community.

Security Dilemma

1. CORE QUESTIONS ADDRESSED

- What is the 'dilemma' of security?
- How can the security dilemma be overcome?
- Does the security dilemma apply to non-traditional threats?

2. DEFINITIONS

The security dilemma describes a situation in which one state increases its means of defence in order to achieve a higher degree of security, which, however, is interpreted by another state as an act of aggression and thus countered with security measures on its side, thus possibly leading to an armament spiral. The dilemma consists in a choice between two options, both of which may lead to a lower degree of security: not to invest in defence and thus risk an attack, or to invest in defence and risk counter-measures by the other state, leading to potentially greater insecurity through the deployment of weapons with greater destructive capacity. It therefore constitutes a classical 'tragic' situation (Roe 1999: 183) in which an actor has two choices, both of which may lead to disaster, even though all actors involved may have acted in order to avoid such a disaster (Butterfield 1951: 21). The term itself was introduced in the United States by John Herz (1950, 1951), but Herbert Butterfield (1951: 20–1) developed similar thoughts at the same time on the other side of the Atlantic.

The security dilemma relies on two main assumptions. Firstly, states, following the model of realism (→ *Theory Concept: Realism and Neorealism*), are power-seeking and relatively isolated so that they face a Prisoner's Dilemma (→ *Game Theory*) in that they cannot make any judgement on the intentions of other states. Secondly, the technology of defensive weapons can also be used for aggression (Roe 1999: 184), their varying degrees of utility for offensive use notwithstanding (Posen 1993: 29–30). Both assumptions mean that it is unclear to a state whether another state behaves defensively or offensively – in other words, the dilemma relies on uncertainty, which is difficult or even impossible to overcome under conditions of anarchy (Montgomery 2006; see Jervis 1978 for a discussion). As Ken Booth and Nicholas Wheeler (2008: 4–5) have pointed out, the security dilemma is in fact a twofold dilemma of uncertainty: it is firstly a dilemma about how to interpret the action of other states, and secondly a dilemma about how to respond to the action of other states.

The concept of a security dilemma has been further subdivided, depending on where authors located the main source of uncertainty. Jack Snyder (1985), for instance, distinguishes between a 'structural', a 'perceptual' and an 'imperialist' security dilemma. In the structural security dilemma, the uncertainty is a result of the anarchical structure of the international system (→ *Anarchy*). In the perceptual security dilemma, in contrast, the dilemma arises mainly because of state actors' perceptions of the actions of other states (→ *Foreign Policy Analysis*). An imperialist security dilemma occurs when states pursue offensive strategies to increase their security. It is not a 'classic' security dilemma because while the main state intention is security and the preservation of the status quo, the state seeks to achieve this by clearly offensive means (→ *Theory Concept: Realism and Neorealism*; see Collins 2004: 32). However, the dilemma re-occurs in the sense that no state can exclude the possibility that another state may pursue such offensive means in the future, and thus it needs to guard against this. Note that the imperialist dilemma can in itself be seen as an effect of the structure of the international system (e.g. Posen 1993) or of perception, or some mixture of both (e.g. Jervis 1976: 58–113).

In principle, the security dilemma is not confined to states but, in a Hobbesian world of human beings always having to fear that others may do harm to them and violate their property, applies to all relationships between humans (Butterfield 1951: 21; Herz 1950: 157–8). Within the state, this fear has been largely mitigated by the monopolization of legitimate violence (→ *Sovereignty*). Fear remains however a feature of the anarchical international system where such a monopolization of force has not (yet) been achieved (Herz 1951: 200).

3. THEORETICAL PERSPECTIVES

It is clear from the above that the security dilemma is first and foremost a 'realist' concept in the sense that it depends on assumptions common to realism, although it should be noted that neither of its two inventors, Butterfield and Herz, was realist in the strict sense of the term. Herz (2003: 413) explicitly argued, for instance, that international institutions, cautiously approached, provide a possibility to mitigate the security dilemma. It is probably fair to say, however, that realists appropriated the concept, and one can even relate its variations to variations within realism, such as offensive and defensive realism (see Glaser 1997; Montgomery 2006). In this view, the security dilemma is a constitutive characteristic of the international system, induced by its anarchical structure, and consequently there is no escape from it. Authors writing in the liberal tradition, in contrast, have tried to show that even in an anarchical world, the building of common institutions is possible, and that through such institutions, one can successfully tackle the Prisoner's Dilemma and thus the security dilemma (→ *Theory Concept: Liberalism and Neoliberalism*, → *International Regimes*).

Beyond, one can note that the security dilemma today is a widely used concept that has found its way into most theoretical perspectives, which differ in their view of the sources of and possible solutions to the dilemma. For Alexander Wendt, from a social constructivist perspective (→ *Theory Concept: Social Constructivism*) for instance, the security dilemma is a 'social structure' that consists of 'intersubjective understandings' which create the uncertainty that makes states distrust each other (Wendt 1995: 73). Yet for social constructivists, social structures and intersubjective understandings are not immutable. Thus, the security dilemma, as much as anarchy, can be overcome through socialization into more cooperative institutions and the development of common cultures. This however is not the only possible development – over time, actors engaged in a security dilemma may also internalize the role of the competitor rather than the security-seeker and see it as part of their identity, thereby entrenching conflict (Mitzen 2006). Even authors writing from a more critical perspective such as Booth and Wheeler (2008) think of the security dilemma as core to international relations, although, like Wendt, they are predominantly interested in the conditions that enable the dilemma to persist, informing the possibilities of its transcendence, for instance through trust-building (Booth and Wheeler 2008: 296–9).

4. EMPIRICAL PROBLEMS

We have noted above that the security dilemma does not only apply to states, although the anarchical structure of the international system makes the dilemma most pertinent in such a system. A number of authors have however noted that a security dilemma also occurs in relation to non-traditional in the sense of non-state security problems. A primary focus in this research has been ethnic conflict (e.g. Posen 1993). As John Herz already noted in 1950, the security dilemma applies to a situation 'where groups live alongside each other without being organized into a higher unity' (Herz 1950: 157) – this should of course apply to states and ethnic groups in failed states and similar situations alike (Kaufman 1996). In the application of Paul Roe (1999, 2005), the focus of the security dilemma on military security is extended to identity issues or what the Copenhagen School of (→) security studies calls 'societal security'. This allows Roe and others to apply the security dilemma to situations that do not involve states and traditional military threats.

Similarly, one can make the argument that the 'war on terror' presents an instance of the security dilemma that involves states and non-state actors alike (Herz 2003: 415; Booth and Wheeler 2008: 271; Cerny 2005). Extending the argument across various policy fields and actors on different levels, Philip Cerny (2000) suggests that the post-Cold-War world is characterized by new security dilemmas, which are more complex than the old ones, given that the greater variety of policy fields allows for a greater variety of policy choices and a greater number of actors. Such a world would be rife with uncertainties and disorder, so one can only hope that trust finds a way back into it.

5. CORE READING

Booth, Ken and Nicholas J. Wheeler (2008) *The Security Dilemma: Fear, Cooperation and Trust in World Politics* (Basingstoke: Palgrave). A book-length exploration of the different meanings of empirical applications of and possible solutions to the security dilemma.

Jervis, Robert (1978) 'Cooperation under the Security Dilemma', *World Politics* 30 (2), 167–214. A classic text that explores the offensive/defensive dimension of the security dilemma.

Roe, Paul (1999) 'The Intrastate Security Dilemma: Ethnic Conflict as "Tragedy"?', *Journal of Peace Research* 36 (2), 183–202. One of the first consistent theoretical re-articulations of the security dilemma in order to apply it to non-state actors in the post-Cold-War world.

6. USEFUL WEBSITES

http://securitydilemmas.blogspot.com/. Blog by a professor of International Relations and political philosophy at the University of Puget Sound who writes about international and national security and its dilemmas.

Theory Concept: Social Constructivism

1. CORE QUESTIONS ADDRESSED

- How do structure and agency interact in international relations?
- What is the role of norms in international relations?
- How are international identities constructed, maintained and transformed?

2. OVERVIEW AND BACKGROUND

For much of the 1980s, the discipline of International Relations was polarized between rationalist approaches on the one hand and 'reflectivist' approaches on the other (Keohane 1988). Core to rationalism was the 'neo–neo synthesis' between neorealism and neoliberalism (Wæver 1997a). (→ *Theory Concepts: Realism and Neorealism; Liberalism and Neoliberalism*.) On the opposite side, various critical theories, including post-Marxism/Critical Theory and postmodernism/poststructuralism, criticized this synthesis through questioning the purpose of its approaches: in their view, social science was not to function like the natural sciences but to problematize the dominant configuration of I/international R/relations both as a discipline and as its empirical focus, and possibly to develop alternatives or guidance on the way towards a more just world order. (→ *Theory Concepts: Marxism and Critical Theory; Postmodernism and Poststructuralism*.) These approaches were called 'reflectivist' because they saw their own work as integral to broader social and political life rather than as an objective observation and explanation of what was going on. If rationalists clung to a positivist notion of science, the discussion in the 1980s was about moving beyond positivism (see Smith et al. 1996).

Not all critics of the rationalist camp, however, agreed with such a radical step. For many, the focus on rationalist, interest-based explanations and the dichotomy of structure and agency in these explanations was unsatisfactory and misguided. At the same time, many did not want to be caught up in epistemological questions of knowledge and the possibility of 'objective' science, and still wanted to explain or at least understand outcomes in international relations rather than focus on critique and problematizations. One of their core arguments was that the international system is not simply given but socially constructed: while the structure of the system provides a particular context for action, it is only through such action that this structure can be maintained. They were thus called social constructivists, and their approach has entered International Relations as the 'via media' (Wendt 2000) or 'middle ground' (Adler 1997) within the discipline.

The main arguments of social constructivism may be summarized as follows:

1) *International structure and agency are co-constituted.* This is essentially an idea that constructivists took from sociologist Anthony Giddens (1986) and his theory of structuration. As outlined above, agents are always already situated in a particular structural context but this structural context is also reproduced by them, and therefore subject to change. In International Relations, the main target of this argument was the idea that the international system is (→) anarchical, accepted in principle by both neorealists and neoliberals. In an often quoted title of a seminal article, Alexander Wendt (1992) claimed instead: *Anarchy is what states make of it.* Yes, states do exist under conditions of anarchy, Wendt argued, but only in the sense that there is no higher authority above them. States can shape this anarchy however, and thus anarchy has evolved from its Hobbesian form (which best approximates what is usually considered as anarchy in the discipline) to Lockean versions (regulated through (→) international law and institutions) and possible Kantian ones (where (→) security communities prevail even though formally there is still no central 'world government') (see Wendt 1999).

2) *Norms and institutions matter in international relations.* For rationalists, norms and institutions only matter to the extent that they serve the interests of the most powerful actors in a particular setting. International organizations or regimes can therefore only be maintained as long as they are seen to benefit their members. At the core of the debate between neorealism and neoliberalism was therefore the question of whether cooperation between states was possible on the basis of relative gains ('we gain more than others') or absolute gains ('we all benefit if not necessarily to the same extent'). From a social constructivist point of view, norms and institutions have an effect that cannot be reduced to the objectives of involved actors (→ *Ideas and Norms*). In relation to

norms, one important reference point in this debate is the work of James March and Johan Olsen (1989) on different types of action. In rationalist accounts, actors are presumed to follow what March and Olsen termed *logic of consequentiality*, which is to say that they reflect on the consequences of their doing and calculate their benefits on this basis. In contrast to this, March and Olsen argue that often actors do not perform such calculations and instead simply follow established norms: they do what is expected of them. They called this the *logic of appropriateness*. In the international realm, actors, including states, will also often do what seems appropriate. As other approaches, most notably the 'English School' of international relations, have pointed out, there are norms in (→) International society (they identify in particular sovereignty and non-intervention), and states do follow these norms most of the time so that violations are often clearly identified as such and lead to debates about sanctions (which is when the logic of consequentiality sets in, as actors then need to consciously reflect on the impact of sanctions).

Social constructivists define institutions in a rather broad sense as stable patterns of behaviour. Thus, institutions are not only more or less formal forms of cooperation such as international organizations or regimes but any kind of action that is repeated by a set of actors over a longer period of time. In the case of the European Union's foreign policy, for instance, social constructivists have argued that the formal development of institutions such as the Common Foreign and Security Policy (CFSP) is only one part of the story. They have pointed to the so-called 'coordination reflex', among others, to demonstrate that there is a degree of integration outside the formal institutional context (e.g. Glarbo 1999). Core to this 'reflex' is that foreign ministries of EU member states tend to call their counterparts in other EU capitals to hear their views on a specific policy, even though this does not necessarily mean that they will stop the policy if there are objections.

Given the wide definition of institutions, social constructivist work tends to be problematic when it comes to the differentiation of institutions and norms, and indeed other related concepts such as culture. The coordination reflex could for instance be seen as both a norm and an institution. Generally speaking, norms will guide the pattern of behaviour, but in practice the usage of these terms often remains confusing. Many scholars therefore deal with institutions that have at least some degree of formality so that membership for instance can be easily determined. Institutions then have a *socializing* effect on their members: over time, the norms underpinning the institutions tend to become more accepted, and thus the logic of appropriateness becomes more important. Institutions therefore are not simply shaped by – they also shape – their members.

3) *Identities are important factors in understanding policy, but they are not unchangeable.* Identity and culture are categories that played hardly any role in both neorealism and neoliberalism. For social constructivists, they are highly relevant to international relations (see Lapid and Kratochwil 1995). To some extent, this relevance follows the argument of structure and agency: culture and identity are important parts of the context in which actors are situated. On the one hand, this means that culture and identity become core factors in understanding (→) foreign policies and policies on the international level more generally (e.g. Hopf 2002; Hudson 1998). On the other hand, cooperation on an international level needs to take into account the different understandings that parties bring to the negotiation table, which even if they act according to the logic of consequentiality may lead to different rationalities. This does not mean that culture and identities are treated as unchangeable by social constructivists; after all, as discussed above, structure and agency are interdependent. The socialization process within institutions, for instance, also transforms identities. Questions can again be asked about the definition of culture and identity, which often remain vague and differ between scholars and their works. None the less, the core argument is clear and has sparked a good deal of scholarship.

4) *Interests need to be understood with reference to other factors.* Despite their focus on culture, identities, institutions and norms, social constructivists do not deny the relevance of interests. However, they do not see interests as the primary explanatory variable, and they argue that interests cannot be taken as given independent variables but need to be 'endogenized', that is, their construction needs to be part of the research agenda. One important strand of social constructivist work has therefore focused on the question of how identities, norms and institutions shape interests. In this context, national interests are often only formed within international contexts (e.g. Finnemore 1996).

3. METHODOLOGIES

In a core contribution to the analysis of (→) international regimes and organizations, Friedrich Kratochwil and John Gerard Ruggie (1986) paved the way to a social constructivist analysis. If such forms of international cooperation are supposed to change the behaviour of their participants, they argued, a change in ontology is needed away from the notion of international actors that are purely seeking to maximize their benefits in relation to given interests. With this change of ontology, the methods of statistical analysis and positivist explanation may no longer be appropriate. Kratochwil and Ruggie were not advocating a move to poststructuralist approaches (Ruggie (1993) explicitly rejected them). Instead, they and other social constructivists argue for an understanding of policies from the inside: drawing on Max Weber's differentiation between explaining and understanding (see Hollis and Smith 1990), the point is not to objectively explain behaviour but to understand the subjective point of view of the policy-maker or other actor. To do so, social constructivists use a variety of approaches although often they resort to (→) discourse analysis without buying into the broader epistemological arguments of many discourse analysts with more poststructuralist leanings.

4. EMPIRICAL APPLICATIONS

Some of the empirical puzzles addressed by social constructivists have already been introduced above. In addition, one of the most often cited social constructivist studies deals with the impact of international (→) human rights on domestic political contexts (Risse et al. 1999b). The argument put forward in what the authors call the 'spiral model' of human rights is that regimes violating human rights will often make concessions on paper to demands to change their behaviour in order to obtain other benefits, such as financial aid – an example of the logic of consequentiality. However, such deals can then be used by local nongovernmental organizations to legitimize claims against their rulers. Together with a supportive international network, this may lead to regime change so that human rights become accepted norms. Initially, rulers may continue to adhere to such rights only to obtain further benefits, but their institutionalization and the subsequent socialization process may ultimately lead to a new generation of politicians for whom human rights norms become the standard, where the logic of appropriateness sets in. In other work, scholars have studied the importance of identities in regional integration contexts as well as their transformation, particularly in the context of European integration (e.g. Risse et al. 1999; Risse 2001) or the role of cultural factors in security policy (e.g. Katzenstein 1996).

5. CENTRAL CRITICISMS

Apart from the sometimes imprecise definition of core concepts and how they relate to each other, mentioned above, the main criticisms of social constructivism result from its self-selected position in the 'middle ground'. In its most radical form, the question is whether such a middle ground is tenable. If one does accept that the cultural context in which actors are operating is important, would this not also apply to the scholar who analyses international relations, and if so, does this not mean that one cannot avoid the epistemological questions that social constructivism is putting to one side? Or on the opposite side, does one not have to demonstrate the relevance of identities, norms and culture through much the same methods as those used by so-called positivists so that one knows that their influence is indeed true and not only presumed? Constructivists have given different answers, especially to the latter question, in part exploring more rigorous scientific methods (e.g. Checkel 1998, 1999), in part reverting back to the arguments of Kratochwil and Ruggie and insisting that there is no simple 'dependent' and 'independent' variable in the effect of culture on agency. As one of the most visible social constructivists, the work of Alexander Wendt has attracted a particularly huge amount of criticism, most importantly about consistency. Thus, his work has been seen as too state-centrist given that the state is only one particular construction in international politics, and there have been charges against him (and other constructivists) of either being too structuralist or too agency-centred. One should in fairness note that if one wants to adopt a middle-ground position, research is complicated by the sheer number of relevant factors and the fact that researchers will therefore always tend to bracket some factors in order to focus on others.

6. CORE READING

Adler, Emanuel (1997) 'Seizing the Middle Ground: Constructivism in World Politics', *European Journal of International Relations* 3 (3), 319–63. An influential summary of social constructivism in International Relations, advancing the idea of social constructivism as the middle ground between major theoretical approaches.

Risse, Thomas, Stephen C. Ropp and Kathryn Sikkink (eds) (1999) *The Power of Human Rights: International Norms and Domestic Change* (Cambridge: Cambridge University Press). An often cited example for the application of a social constructivist framework.

Wendt, Alexander (1999) *Social Theory of International Politics* (Cambridge: Cambridge University Press). The most famous work from a conventional constructivist viewpoint, a modern classic.

7. USEFUL WEBSITES

http://duckofminerva.blogspot.com/2008/08/introduction-to-constructivist-ir.htm. Blog containing a number of videos introducing social constructivism.

http://irdebate.blogspot.com/2006/02/constructivism.html. Blog about IR debates on social constructivism.

http://www.e-ir.info/?p=2570. Hub of information and analysis on some of the key issues in international politics, created by students of UK universities, including a comprehensive essay about the 'Great Debates' that structured International Relations theory.

http://www.theory-talks.org/2008/04/theory-talk-3.html. Interactive forum for discussion of debates in International Relations with an emphasis on the underlying theoretical issues, including interviews with leading scholars, e.g. Alexander Wendt.

Sovereignty

1. CORE QUESTIONS ADDRESSED

- What are the constituent elements of sovereignty?
- What makes the matter of defining sovereignty crucial?
- What are the main empirical challenges to understandings of sovereignty?

2. DEFINITIONS

Sovereignty is understood as the supreme or final authority of a political entity over its own affairs, frequently associated with a given territory (Shorten 2008: 39; Biersteker and Weber 1996: 2). This authority is the source of all binding commands within the political entity – a right which is recognized externally.

Since the Treaty of Westphalia (1648), sovereignty has been closely tied to the nation-state, which combines the population–territory–authority triad and has long displayed qualities of a 'sacrosanct' doctrine in international relations (Jellinek 1922). Reciprocal recognition of sovereign statehood has been characterized as the basic institution governing interstate relations and thus enabling their co-existence within the state system (Bull 1977: 36). The character of the state as the legitimate sovereign authority thus constitutes the very basis of (→) international law, such as the Charter of the United Nations, which even prescribes that its violation justifies the use of force in international relations (Biersteker and Weber 1996).

The concept of sovereignty entails a number of contested assumptions. First, the notion of authority infers the ability to legitimately exercise power, comprising both the right to issue commands and the duty to be obeyed (Wolff 1970). The source of that legitimate authority and its attribution to the state have long been the subject of philosophical debate: it is thought to stem, among others, from natural law, the public good and the consent of the people. The direct or indirect consent of those subject to it, also termed popular sovereignty, is the most recent and widely accepted version of sovereignty. Second, sovereignty contains the notion of supremacy. The sovereign actor's authority is wide in scope for the territory it governs – the state literally has 'the last word' in relation to other, subordinate authoritative domestic and also international bodies. With a number of exceptions, such as the supranational bodies of the European Union, the state is not commanded by any superior international body. It follows, third, that sovereignty has both an internal and an external dimension: internally, it refers to the possession of supreme authority over a particular domain, and externally that authority is recognized by others (Biersteker and Weber 1996: 2). Recognition is the key term here as prescriptions of sovereign recognition or rather the norms of recognition associated with the institution of sovereignty have changed over the years. Criteria for recognition commonly include the combination of effective control over territorial space, states' ability to fulfil international commitments, and the aforementioned consent of the governed in combination with democratic governance – a criterion which has arguably gained primary significance since its institutionalization in the United Nations Charter (Biersteker 2002: 164).

3. THEORETICAL PERSPECTIVES

It is hardly possible to separate the task of defining sovereignty from diverging International Relations theories' perspectives on the matter.

Classical realists such as Hans Morgenthau and E. H. Carr had been acutely aware of sovereignty's blurry outline – Carr went so far as to term sovereignty merely a 'convenient label' (2001: 212). In contrast, owing to their emphasis on structural factors, so called neorealists (→ *Theory Concept: Realism and Neorealism*) considered the sovereign state 'the' international actor and did not question its sovereign authority in any way (Mearsheimer 2001). The narrative of absolute sovereignty began to crumble with the liberal (→ *Theory Concept: Liberalism and Neoliberalism*) recognition of states' co-existence with transnational actors in complex interdependence in the early 1970s (Keohane and Nye 1977). While liberal theorists did not concern themselves with providing theoretically useful re-evaluations of sovereignty, their empirical description of eroding state sovereignty through the increasing global importance of transnational actors pointed to loci of authority outside the nation-state and prepared the grounds for more comprehensive conceptual work that evolved throughout the 1990s.

In the context of the fourth debate, social constructivists (→ *Theory Concept: Social Constructivism*) began to claim that sovereignty was socially constructed in a two-fold process. On the structural side, states' claims to sovereignty construct a social environment, i.e. the (→) international society of states, while at the same time, on the agents' side, the mutual recognition of states' claims to sovereignty constitutes an important element in states' self-construction (Biersteker and Weber 1996: 2). The theoretical realization that sovereignty is disputed constitutes not so much a new scholarly beginning but rather a return to excavating the concept's rich and contested history. International Relations theorists from the 1990s onwards began to understand sovereignty very much as an ideal that was never fully realized and is, as constructivists argue, best understood as a social product that can be and has been subject to change. Analysing state and international relations (→) discourse, J. Samuel Barkin shows that there have been changes in sovereignty's required sources of legitimacy from its 'inception' in the seventeenth century. Legitimacy sources of sovereignty changed from religion in the post-Westphalian era, to monarchical solidarity after the Vienna conference of 1814, to territorial legitimation after the Second World War, and finally to the idea of the individual citizen in possession of formal political rights after the end of the Cold War (1998: 236–249). Connected to these changes in what legitimately constitutes a sovereign state are changes in sovereignty's operational definition – a main research focus of constructivists in the field of sovereignty.

Poststructuralist theorists (→ *Theory Concept: Postmodernism and Poststructuralism*) go even further in concluding that 'the very attempt to treat sovereignty as a matter of definition and legal principle encourages a certain amnesia about its historical and culturally specific character' by freezing its meaning in the present (Walker 1993; Bartelson 1995). In light of this, constructivists contend that not only the concept of sovereignty, but the entire Westphalian ideal, i.e. the normative linkage of authority, territory and population, is constructed and upheld with great effort and dedication by the practices of a group of powerful agents at the expense of alternative conceptions (Biersteker and Weber 1996: 3). To F. H. Hinsley, the motivation supporting this effort is quite clear: safeguarding a fictional concept of absolute sovereignty logically follows from equating sovereignty with the 'assertion or the justification of the independence of a state' (1986: 226). Constructivist authors seek to look behind this assertion in uncovering how the construction and redefinition of sovereignty and its constitutive elements is possible through the practices and justifications for practices of both states and non-state actors. Indeed, discursive justifications serve to define the very meaning of sovereignty by constructing or reconstructing it (Weber 1995).

These practices and justifications can be and often are contradictory, an observation that is echoed in Stephen Krasner's sovereignty as 'organized hypocrisy' (1999). Krasner argues that although the institution of sovereignty firmly includes the principle of non-intervention, breaches of this have long been a regular, planned feature of international relations. Yet, Krasner does not go beyond this assumption and remains, in contrast to constructivist contributions, firmly within a static conception of sovereignty.

4. EMPIRICAL PROBLEMS

The attention dedicated to sovereignty within International Relations skyrocketed following the end of the Cold War. Triggered by the fragmentation of states such as the Soviet Union and Yugoslavia and the advent of so-called failed states in Africa, the 'traditional' conception of sovereignty came under fire. Three questions referring to sovereignty's internal and external dimensions gained particular empirical significance in this context: first, is the state the legitimate locus of sovereignty?; second, how far is (→) globalization contributing to the erosion of sovereignty?; and third, under what conditions should a state be recognized as sovereign?

First, the modern state system has consistently excluded cultural, ethnic and racial 'others' by denying them sovereign recognition. Should the locus of sovereignty therefore lie with the nation, i.e. a homogenous people, the residents of a territorially bounded entity, or elsewhere entirely? The second question stands in direct connection to this first observation – is sovereignty 'as we know it', i.e. territorial authority, endangered by the processes of globalization, enabling companies to operate across borders easily without state consent (Sassen 1996)? Environmental concerns, global communication systems, nuclear weapons, terrorism and drug trafficking all call into question the idea of an autonomous sovereign state in full control of what happens within its borders. The consequences of these 'transsovereign problems' (Cusimano 2000) have been captured by a variety of metaphors: state sovereignty is 'eroding', 'diminishing' or 'at bay', seemingly implying that sovereignty is a limited good. Scholars have pointed to the emergence of non-state-based authority, which has been mainly researched in studies on (→) global governance and the international political economy, but also draws attention to the potential moral authority of non-governmental organizations (Strange 1996; Cutler et al. 1999; Lipschutz 1996).

Third, when should a state be recognized as sovereign? This question points to two empirical problems inherent to sovereign recognition that became apparent in the 1990s. First, failed states such as Somalia illustrated a growing divide between *de jure* claims to sovereign statehood and a state's actual, *de facto* capability to act on these claims. If states are neither able to enforce their monopoly on the legitimate use of force, nor able to meet the economic needs of their citizens, can they still be considered sovereign? Robert Jackson integrates this problem analytically in distinguishing between positive and negative sovereignty: whereas positive sovereignty indicates the freedom to act or not to act in world politics, negative sovereignty indicates the freedom from the actions of others in world politics – in other words, the principle of non-intervention (Jackson 1990; Biersteker and Weber 1996: 10). 'Quasi-states' or failed states thus possess negative sovereignty rather than positive sovereignty: they are legally recognized through membership of the United Nations but lack the capacity to govern their own affairs without outside assistance (Jackson 1990). The second recognition problem refers to the non-intervention principle or negative sovereignty. In the face of omissions to provide security to their own citizens, scholars challenged the view of sovereignty as a right and instead encouraged an understanding of sovereignty as a responsibility. Sovereignty as responsibility requires states to uphold an appropriate standard of political goods and services, such as, most importantly, the provision of security, and ensuring the protection and well-being of their citizens (Deng 1993; Etzioni 2006). Should states refuse to provide this standard or negatively impact on it, scholars have argued that it then becomes the international community's responsibility to react and protect said states' citizens. This thinking is labelled the 'Responsibility to Protect' (R2P), a concept that originated in the work of the independent International Commission on Intervention and State Sovereignty (ICISS) and became enshrined in the UN General Assembly's World Summit Outcome 2005 (ICISS 2001; United Nations General Assembly 2005).

While understandings of sovereignty are in constant flux, it remains to be added that there is no operational understanding of sovereignty shared universally across all regions of the world. Rather, varied understandings co-exist. Generally, the main fault line opens up between understandings in advanced, postindustrial states perceiving of sovereignty as 'conditioned' and intervention as legitimate to secure democracy, and those in developing countries upholding non-intervention in domestic affairs as an inviolable norm. The latter understanding is also shared by a number of developed states such as Russia and China. Criteria for sovereign recognition remain crucially important as they define the identity of the principal agents of international relations – 'changes in these norms have important implications for the nature of states themselves' (Biersteker 2002: 164).

5. CORE READING

Barkin, J. Samuel (1998) 'Sovereignty and the Emergence of Human Rights Norms', *Millennium: Journal of International Studies* 27 (2), 229–52. Presents an accessible overview on historical changes in the legitimate constitution of sovereignty.

Biersteker, Thomas J. and Cynthia Weber (eds) (1996) *State Sovereignty as Social Construct* (Cambridge: Cambridge University Press). Collects analyses on sovereignty and its constitutive elements as social constructs.

Jackson, Robert (1990) *Quasi-States: Sovereignty, International Relations and the Third World* (Cambridge: Cambridge University Press). Classic study on the empirical challenges to sovereignty after the end of the Cold War.

6. USEFUL WEBSITES

http://www.iciss.ca/menu-en.asp. Website of the International Commission on Intervention and State Sovereignty.
http://sovereigntyblog.com/. Companion blog to the book Bothe et al. (2005) *Redefining Sovereignty*.

Territoriality and Borders

1. CORE QUESTIONS ADDRESSED

- How did the territorial state emerge as the main form of political order?
- What functions do borders perform in the international system?
- To what extent are territoriality and borders changing in globalization?

2. DEFINITIONS

Territoriality is the principle that political order is tied to a particular territory. Most of the time we take territoriality for granted. Indeed, one of the core elements of what constitutes a state according to the Montevideo Convention of 1933 is the existence of a clearly defined state territory. Secessionist movements therefore strive to gain control over a particular patch of land, and state borders take on a particularly significant role in defining what a state is and marking the outer edges of a government's legitimate control and monopoly of violence (→ *Sovereignty*).

Given this seemingly self-evident nature of territoriality in international relations, it is easy to forget that there are alternative ways of organizing political and social order. We can still have a glimpse of some of them when considering, for instance, that the Holy See as the representation of the Catholic Church without a corresponding territory has a special observer status at the United Nations and can enter international agreements as an equal to states (Kunz 1952; Abdullah 1996). Also, many functional international organizations, while based on state membership, primarily focus on the governance of a particular functional area, say the transportation of letters in the Universal Postal Union, rather than of a particular territory. And increasingly, private actors take on limited governing roles in 'inclusive institutions' (Rittberger et al. 2008) or global 'public–private partnerships' (Börzel and Risse 2005), where again functionality rather than territoriality is the main organizing principle. Territoriality is therefore by no means the only possible way of organizing political order; both historically and at present, alternatives have included personal, functional and belief-based relationships.

A particular territory requires borders that delineate it from other borders. Confusingly, there are two other concepts, 'boundaries' and 'frontiers', that are used alongside the notion of 'borders', and unfortunately they are distinguished in many different ways in the literature so that their usage has become highly inconsistent and often interchangeable (Donnan and Wilson 1999: 4). Thus, Anderson (1996: 9) comes to the assessment that 'frontier' is the broadest term in the sense of referring to a space at the border, whereas he takes 'boundary' to refer to the concrete line demarcating territories, with 'border' used for both purposes. Cohen (1998: 26), in contrast, argues that 'boundary' is the broadest term, especially in an anthropological understanding, whereas 'frontier' has 'limited geopolitical and legal' applicability. This confusion is exemplified in the following citation on the development of borders in Africa: 'Once the basic *frontiers* were established, the Europeans implemented some minor *border* adjustments in an effort to make a little more sense of the *boundaries* that they had established' (Herbst 1989: 685; emphases added).

It is impossible on this basis to provide a conclusive definition of these three terms. In International Relations, it is fair to say that Anderson's notion of boundary as the actual demarcation line prevails; that 'border' often, but not always, includes references to the institutions of border management (such as passport and customs control); and that frontier implies a broader border zone, but also one that carries with it allusions to the uncharted, the explorative and unknown. Thus, for instance, US-American identity is often seen as characterized by a frontier mentality that is tied up with the historical experience of a Western frontier that was successfully pushed to the Pacific (classic: Turner 1953). 'Borderland' has also become a popular term to denote the zone around a border (see e.g. Newman 2006a: 150), with perhaps more neutral connotations, but allowing for a broader study of the variety of practices of negotiating a border in its neighbourhood (Anzaldúa 1987).

3. THEORETICAL PERSPECTIVES

Most traditional theories in International Relations take borders and territoriality to be unproblematic. For realists (→ *Theory Concept: Realism and Neorealism*), borders matter only as properties of the state that need to be protected. Neoliberalism (→ *Theory Concept: Liberalism and Neoliberalism*) recognizes the challenge of transnational (read: transborder) problems, but seeks to answer this challenge predominantly in the form of international institutions. These institutions, as argued above, have a functional purpose, but this does not lead to a general questioning of borders and the territorial foundations of politics. The (→) functionalism of the interwar years and immediate aftermath of the Second World War developed a more consistent model of a world order that was not based on territoriality, but this was predominantly related to the problems of (→) anarchy and (→) sovereignty and not to borders and territoriality as such. Likewise, Hedley Bull (1977: 264) discusses 'a new mediaevalism' with 'overlapping' and 'segmented' authority as a possible alternative to the present order of the society of (territorial) states (→ *International Society*), but this does not lead him to a sustained reflection on territoriality as a defining feature of the international system.

The main impetus for the analysis of territoriality and the problematization of borders in International Relations has therefore come from critical and constructivist works (→ *Theory Concept: Social Constructivism*), and has only really gained ground in the 1990s under the impressions of globalization and the changing border of the post-Cold-War world (Newman and Paasi 1998: 190). Thus, as Newman (2006b) argues, the construction, management and impact of borders on human practices have become a focus of research. Borders are no longer taken as a given but seen as being shaped by the 'borderwork' of politicians as much as citizens and non-citizens (Rumford 2009). Likewise, territoriality is seen as emerging from particular historical developments, which are undergoing a process of change again, leading to perhaps new types of political order (Ruggie 1993).

4. EMPIRICAL PROBLEMS

This renewed interest in the construction of borders and territoriality has led to a great number of studies analysing the way specific borders are imagined, monitored and symbolized, and how they shape state and nation identities and regulate the flow of migration, among many themes (for overviews, see Donnan and Wilson 1999; Newman 2006b). Of particular importance in International Relations have been studies on how borders shape identities and political orders (e.g. Albert et al. 2001), why some borders are managed more successfully than others (e.g. Gavrilis 2008), how borders can lead to exclusion and violence (Ashley 1989) but also help the toleration of difference (Williams 2002), or how conflictive borders can be transformed (Diez, Albert and Stetter 2008).

To some extent, these works can be seen as a reaction to arguments about a 'borderless world' that some already saw emerging on the horizon in the context of globalization (see Newman 2006a). John Ruggie's insistence on the analysis of the processes that led to the emergence of the territorial state system (Ruggie 1993) remains hugely important in this respect. Ruggie identified material environments (such as economic expansion), strategic behaviour (such as the rise of new types of economic and political entrepreneurs), social epistemes (such as the rise of the single-point perspective), and social empowerment (above all in the form of new types of administration) as the core elements of the rise of territoriality. Others have since provided longer in-depth studies (e.g. Spruyt 1994; Teschke 2003), but more is needed, also in relating the findings to today's challenges (see Buzan and Little 2000).

5. CORE READING

Donnan, Hastings and Thomas M. Wilson (1999) *Borders: Frontiers of Identity, Nation and State* (Oxford: Berg). A good overview of the literature as well as an investigation of how borders relate to the construction of state and nation.

Newman, David (2006b) 'Borders and Bordering: Towards an Inter-disciplinary Dialogue', *European Journal of Social Theory* 9 (2), 171–86. An overview article of the treatment of borders in different disciplines and a plea for interdisciplinarity.

Ruggie, John Gerard (1993) 'Territoriality and Beyond: Problematizing Modernity in International Relations', *International Organization* 47 (1), 139–74. A core article calling for the analysis of the developments that led to the territorial state system and to compare these to present developments.

6. USEFUL WEBSITES

http://www.dur.ac.uk/ibru/. International Boundaries Research Unit offers practical expertise in boundary-making, border management and territorial dispute resolution;

and academic leadership in the study of boundaries and their impact on international relations and borderland development.

http://www.absborderlands.org/. Association for Borderland Studies is the leading international scholarly association dedicated exclusively to the systematic interchange of ideas and information relating to international border areas. The website hosts a journal, resources, and a borders bibliography.

http://www.borderlands.com/. The Borderland Sciences Research Network is home to the *Journal of Borderland Research*.

http://www.mapreport.com/subtopics/p/b.html. Provides an overview of all border conflicts and incidents from 2000 onwards.

https://www.cia.gov/library/publications/the-world-factbook/fields/2070.html. Detailed CIA factbook listing of all territorial conflicts after the Second World War.

Terrorism

1. CORE QUESTIONS ADDRESSED

- What makes terrorism a highly contested concept in International Relations?
- What are the central theoretical approaches towards analysing terrorism?
- How do the United Nations seek to combat terrorism in the twenty-first century?

2. DEFINITIONS

Since the start of the new millennium terrorism has been cast as the most vital security problem of western societies by media, political representatives and also by some scholars. Nevertheless, terrorism is by no means a modern phenomenon, but has in fact posed a threat to human life and societies since the ancient world: ancient examples of terrorism, mainly motivated by religious goals, are the Jewish Zealots in Palestine aiming to eliminate Roman rule, or the Muslim Assassins in the Middle East, operating for over two hundred years in order to 'purify' Islam and reconstitute it as a religious entity (Richardson 2006: 23–8). Historically, the term 'terrorism' was first mentioned during the French Revolution and described the violent use of state power against its citizens. Following the American lead, the French Revolution wanted to break the absolute power of monarchy and establish a republic where citizens were free and equal under public law. In order to prevent a counter-revolution re-establishing the *ancien régime*, the leaders of the revolution, such as Maximilien de Robespierre and Louis Antoine de Saint-Just, declared that the enemies of the revolution had to be removed, and thus started to execute suspicious citizens publicly on behalf of the people.

Today's literature highlights a 'new era of terrorism', a shift of terrorism from a transnational phenomenon (in)to a global one, not only endangering national security, but also becoming a threat to major powers and western societies (Martin 2008: 37; see also Dunne 2005). In particular since Al-Qaeda's terrorist attacks in the United States many authors argue that today's global terrorism is characterized by a flexible organizational structure and the purposeful use of mass media and new technologies for the creation of 'spectaculars', aiming to create fear and horror (Dunne 2005: 264).

The concept of terrorism is highly contested in today's International Relations, a situation strongly reflected by the facts that over a hundred definitions of terrorism can be found within the literature, and a generally accepted definition is missing (Dunne 2005: 260; Hoffman 2006; Laqueur 1977, 1987). Authors such as Tim Dunne or James D. Kiras argue that this is mainly due to the fact that there are diverse types of terrorist groups pursuing a variety of goals and using different methods which make it challenging to subsume them all under one definition (Dunne 2005: 258–69; Kiras 2008: 372–4). Bruce Hoffmann provides an additional explanation for this variety, stating that terrorism is a subjective term, used over centuries in political disputes to discredit the actions of a political opponent or enemy as violent and illegitimate. In consequence, he argues that the notion of terrorism has an indisputable negative connotation, particularly with the public, and that no political activists of today will deliberately identify themselves with the term (Hoffmann 2006: 20). Distinguishing clearly between guerrilla warfare, separatist movements and terrorism is thus not an easy task. This dilemma is most prominently summarized by the statement: 'One person's terrorist is another person's freedom fighter' (Martin 2008: 11). Contested elements of a widely recognized definition of terrorism are firstly the nature of the act, i.e. the questions of the necessity to distinguish between state terror and substate terrorists as well as the question of whether terrorism should rather be considered as an act of warfare or a crime; secondly, the exact and already mentioned distinction between terrorism and other forms of political violence; and thirdly, the inclusion of aims or targets of terrorism as defining the character of the act.

Probably the most basic definition of terrorism has been given by Walter Laqueur, defining it as 'illegitimate use of force to achieve a political objective when innocent people are targeted' (Laqueur 1977). Ken Booth and Tim Dunne define terrorism as 'a method of political action that uses violence . . . against civilians and civilian infrastructure in order to influence behaviour, inflict punishment or to exact revenge' (Booth and Dunne 2002: 8). Paul Wilkinson differentiates between internal and international terrorism, describing the distinction as follows: 'Internal terrorism is confined within a single state or region while international terrorism . . . is an attack carried out across international frontiers or against a foreign target in the terrorists' state of origin' (Wilkinson 2001: 13). In 2004, United Nations Security Council Resolution 1544 defined terrorist attacks as 'criminal acts, including against civilians, committed with the intent to cause death or serious bodily injury, or taking of hostages, with the purpose to provoke a state of terror in the general public or in a group of persons or particular persons, intimidate a population or compel a government or an international organisation to do or to abstain from doing any act, which constitute offences within the scope of and as defined in the international conventions and protocols relating to terrorism' (UNSC/Res.1544/ 2004).

A critical perspective towards these mainstream definitions of terrorism has been introduced into the debate by representatives of critical terrorism studies, such as Richard Jackson or Andrew Silke. These authors argue that the definitional confusion does not come by surprise, but rather illustrates how the concept of terrorism is a socially constructed reality: 'Terrorism is fundamentally a social fact rather than a brute fact; while extreme physical violence is experienced as a brute fact, its wider cultural-political meaning is decided by social agreement and intersubjective practises' (Jackson 2007: 4). According to this interpretative approach, similar to the aforementioned point made by Bruce Hoffmann, the term terrorism is understood as a political judgement discrediting the actions of a political opponent as illegitimate, while the act of terrorism as such is not a distinctive political phenomenon; it is simply an intentional use of violence as political strategy, an 'instrumental use of terror by actors' (Jackson 2007: 5).

terrorism

3. THEORETICAL PERSPECTIVES

Theoretical approaches towards terrorism strongly reflect the ontological and methodological confusions surrounding the concept.

Conventional theoretical approaches to the concept seek to analyse the origins and consequences of terrorism, in particular by trying to understand terrorist behaviour. One part of the existing literature seeks to approach terrorism by relating it to concrete major developments and challenges such as (→) globalization, questions of international order or (→) international law (see for instance Booth and Dunne 2002), or focus on the differences in political responses towards terrorism (see for instance Ankersen 2007). The majority of the literature seeks to understand the phenomenon inductively, attempting to generalize empirical observations from a range of historical cases, such as the terrorist attacks by the Red Army Faction (RAF) in Germany or the actions of the Irish Republican Army (IRA) in Northern Ireland, and providing a history of terrorism, including detailed descriptions of the phenomenon at the present status (Laquer 1977; Hoffman 2006; Martin 2010). While a comprehensive theory of terrorism is missing, psychologists, sociologists as well as political scientists found different explanatory factors for the causes of terrorism on the individual, group, national and transnational levels (for an overview see Martin 2010 or Richardson 2006).

However, these conventional approaches have been met with severe criticism by authors such as Jeroen Gunning, Charles Tilly and Richard Jackson. In his article 'A Case for Critical Terrorism Studies?', Gunning elaborates the core problems with conventional terrorism analysis, emphasizing that in particular the focus on 'problem-solving approaches' leads to a state-biased, uncritical approach resulting in practical advice mainly supporting coercive counter-terrorism policies, based on over-reliance on secondary information (Jackson 2007: 1; Silke 2004: 61–5). Critical terrorism studies start from a number of different ontological and epistemological premises in comparison to traditional terrorism studies, such as the assumption of terrorism, knowledge as socially constructed through language and discourse, the rejection of neutral or objective approaches towards terrorism, as well as the methodological primacy of interpretative methods. As a result, it calls for an analysis of critical questions, in particular with regard to the audience, such as 'Who is terrorism knowledge for, and what functions does it serve in supporting their interests?' (Jackson 2007: 3–5). With reference to their usage by the US State Department, Charles Tilly exemplarily elaborates on the elusive character of these notions and urges that their analysis should be applied with a careful understanding of implicit assumptions and relations. As a result, knowledge about terrorism should always be analysed in a wider historical and political context (Tilly 2004).

4. EMPIRICAL PROBLEMS

As a consequence of terrorism's place among the major threats to international security in the twenty-first century, policy-makers around the globe remain focused on how terrorism can be combated appropriately. It has become evident that the acute prevention of international terrorism can only be achieved by multilateral measures since its network character necessitates a coordination of financial, intelligence and military capacities. The fundamental constraint towards meaningful international action against terrorism has been the agreement on a common definition of terrorism. Further practical problems include the identification and localization of terrorists as well as the isolation of terrorists from their financial and practical supporters. Despite the fact that information technologies today facilitate the process of collecting and analysing information, this remains a time- and resource-consuming process (Kiras 2008: 382–3). In the course of counter-terrorism strategies adopted by various actors such as states, substate institutions as well as international organizations in the wake of 9/11, the conflictive relationship between core liberal values – such as respect for human rights and the rule of law – and military and political measures as part of the 'global war on terror' became virulent. In this context, fundamental human rights, such as the prohibition of torture, were suddenly questioned by actors such as representatives of the George W. Bush administration. Furthermore, within liberal states, in particular in Europe, counter-terrorism measures adopted by national or international institutions aiming to improve the transparency of communication and transaction flows between individuals in order to identify terrorist activities provoked a vital public discussion about the appropriateness of these policies with regard to civil rights and legitimacy (see for instance Wilkinson 2001: 218ff.).

After years of fruitless dialogue with regard to defining and adopting measures to combat terrorism, the international community finally adopted two major steps for an international response towards terrorism in the aftermath of 9/11: the aforementioned 2004 Security Council definition of terrorism and the United Nations Counter Terrorism Strategy, adopted by the General Assembly in 2006. The UN Counter

Terrorism Strategy rests upon four pillars, including measures addressing the conditions conducive to the spread of terrorism as well as measures to prevent and combat terrorism. Particularly interesting with regard to the above discussion concerning the conflictive relationship between human rights and counter-terrorism activities is pillar number four, including measures for ensuring the respect for human rights and the rule of law, such as the reaffirmation that states 'must ensure that any measures taken to combat terrorism comply with their obligations under international law, in particular human rights law, refugee law and international humanitarian law' (A/RES/60/288).

5. CORE READING

Booth, Ken and Tim Dunne (eds) (2002) *Worlds in Collision: Terror and the Future of Global Order* (Houndmills: Palgrave Macmillian). Useful introduction to debates about terrorism and problems with fighting terrorism.

   Gunning, Jeroen (2007) 'A Case for Critical Terrorism Studies', *Government and Opposition*, 42 (3), 363–93. Summarizes the major critiques concerning conventional terrorism studies and introduces prospective critical questions with regard to the analysis of terrorism.

   Hoffmann, Bruce (2006) *Inside Terrorism*, second edition (New York: Columbia University Press). Identifies major historical trends in the evolution of terrorism.

6. USEFUL WEBSITES

http://www.terrorism-research.com/. Includes research on terrorism, terrorist groups and a detailed glossary.

http://www.cfr.org/issue/135/. Section of the Council on Foreign Relations homepage dedicated to terrorism listing terrorist groups, state sponsors and havens, the causes and responses.

http://www.un.org/terrorism/. This official site presents the latest developments, and reports on the work of the General Assembly and the Security Council, conventions, declarations, and statements on the issue of terrorism.

http://www.ict.org.il/. The International Institute for Counter-Terrorism (ICT) is an independent thinktank for counter-terrorism in the world, facilitating international cooperation in the global struggle against terrorism.

http://www.tandf.co.uk/journals/titles/09546553.asp. Homepage of the journal *Terrorism and Political Violence* which aims to reflect the full range of current scholarly work on terrorism from many disciplines and theoretical perspectives.

references

Abbott, Kenneth O. W. et al. (2000) 'The Concept of Legalisation', *International Organization* 54 (3), 17–35.

Abdullah, Yasmin (1996) 'The Holy See at United Nations Conferences: State or Church?', *Columbia Law Review* 96 (7), 1835–75.

Acharya, Amitav (2001) *Constructing a Security Community in Southeast Asia: ASEAN and the Problem of Regional Order* (London: Routledge).

Ackerley, Brooke A., Maria Stern and Jacqui True (2006) *Feminist Methodologies for International Relations* (Cambridge: Cambridge University Press).

Adler, Emanuel (1997) 'Seizing the Middle Ground: Constructivism in World Politics', *European Journal of International Relations* 3 (3), 319–63.

Adler, Emanuel and Michael Barnett (eds) (1998) *Security Communities* (Cambridge: Cambridge University Press).

Akehurst, Michael (1995) *A Modern Introduction to International Law* (London: Routledge, 6th edn).

Albert, Mathias, David Jacobson and Yosef Lapid (2001) *Identities, Borders, Orders: Rethinking International Relations Theory* (Minneapolis: University of Minnesota Press).

Aldecoa, Francisco and Michael Keating (1999) *Paradiplomacy in Action: The Foreign Relations of Subnational Governments* (London: Cass).

Alesina, Alberto and David Dollar (2000) 'Who Gives Foreign Aid to Whom and Why?', *Journal of Economic Growth* 5 (1), 33–63.

Alker, Hayward R. (1996) 'Beneath Tit-for-Tat: The Contest of Political Economy Fairy Tales within SPD Protocols', in Hayward R. Álker, *Rediscoveries and Reformulations: Humanistic Methodologies for International Studies* (Cambridge: Cambridge University Press), 303–31.

Allison, Graham (1971) *Essence of Decision: Explaining the Cuban Missile Crisis* (Boston: Little, Brown).

Allison, Graham and Philip Zelikow (1999) *Essence of Decision: Explaining the Cuban Missile Crisis* (New York: Longman; rev. edn).

Amstutz, Mark (2005) *International Ethics: Concepts, Theories, and Cases in Global Politics* (London: Routledge, 2nd edn).

Anderson, Benedict (1991) *Imagined Communities: Reflections on the Origin and Spread of Nationalism* (London: Verso, 2nd edn).

Anderson, K. (2000) 'The Ottawa Convention Banning Landmines, the Role of International Non-Governmental Organisations and the Idea of International Civil Society', *European Journal of International Law* 11 (1), 91–120.

Anderson, Malcolm (1996) *Frontiers: Territory and State Formation in the Modern World* (Oxford: Polity).

Angell, Norman (1910) *The Great Illusion: A Study of the Relation of Military Power to National Advantage* (London: Heinemann).

Angell, Norman (1938) *The Great Illusion – Now* (Harmondsworth: Penguin).

Ankersen, Christopher (ed.) (2007) *Understanding Global Terror* (Cambridge: Polity Press).

An-na'im, Abdullah A. (ed.) (1992) *Human Rights in Cross-Cultural Perspectives: A Quest for Consensus* (Philadelphia: University of Pennsylvania Press).

Anzaldúa, Gloria (1987) *Borderlands/La Frontera: The New Mestiza* (San Francisco: Aunt Lute).

Aoi, Chiyuki, Cedric de Coning and Ramesh Thakur (eds) (2007) *Unintended Consequences of Peacekeeping Operations* (Tokyo: United Nations University Press).

Aradau, Claudia and Rens van Munster (2007) 'Governing Terrorism through Risk: Taking Precautions, (un)Knowing the Future', *European Journal of International Relations* 13 (1), 89–115.

Armstrong, David, Theo Farrell and Hélène Lambert (2007) *International Law and International Relations* (Cambridge: Cambridge University Press).

Aron, Raymond (1966) *Peace and War* (New York: Doubleday)

Ashley, Richard K. (1984) 'The Poverty of Neorealism', *International Organization*, 38 (2), 225–86.

Ashley, Richard K. (1988) 'Untying Sovereign State: A Double Reading of the Anarchy Problematique', *Millennium: Journal of International Studies* 17 (2), 227–62.

Ashley, Richard K. (1989) 'Living on Border Lines: Man, Poststructuralism and War', in James Der Derian and Michael Shapiro (eds), *International/Intertextual Relations: Postmodern Readings of World Politics* (Lexington: Lexington Books), 259–322.

Ashman, Sam (2009) 'Capitalism, Uneven and Combined Development and the Transhistoric', *Cambridge Review of International Affairs* 22 (1), 29–46.

Axelrod, Robert M. (ed.) (1976) *Structure of Decision: The Cognitive Map of Political Elites* (Princeton, NJ: Princeton University Press).

Axelrod, Robert (1984) *The Evolution of Cooperation* (New York: Basic Books).

Baines, Erin K. (1999) 'Gender Construction and the Protection Mandate of the UNHCR: Responses from Guatemalan Women', in Mary K. Meyer and Elizabeth Prügl (eds), *Gender Politics in Global Governance* (Lanham, MD: Rowman & Littlefield).

Balakrishnan, Gopal (ed.) (2003) *Debating Empire* (London: Verso).

Baldwin, David A. (2002) 'Power and International Relations', in Walter Carlsnaes, Thomas Risse and Beth A. Simmons (eds), *Handbook of International Relations* (London: Sage), 177–91.

Bali, Sita (2005) 'Migration and Refugees', in Brian White, Richard Little and Michael Smith (eds), *Issues in World Politics* (Basingstoke: Macmillan, 3rd edn).

Barash, David P. and Charles P. Webel (2002) *Peace and Conflict Studies* (Thousand Oaks, CA: Sage, 2nd edn).

Barash, David P. and Charles P. Webel (2009) *Peace and Conflict Studies* (Los Angeles: Sage).

Barber, Benjamin (2000) 'Jihad vs. McWorld', in Frank J. Lechner and John Boli (eds) (2000) *The Globalization Reader* (Oxford: Blackwell), 21–6.

Barkawi, Tarak and Mark Laffey (1999) 'The Imperial Peace: Democracy, Force and Globalization', *European Journal of International Relations* 5 (4), 403–34.

Barkin, J. Samuel (1998) 'Sovereignty and the Emergence of Human Rights Norms', *Millennium: Journal of International Studies* 27 (2), 229–52.

Barnett, Michael N. (2002) *Eyewitness to a Genocide: The United Nations and Rwanda* (Ithaca, NY: Cornell University Press).

Barnett, Michael and Raymond Duvall (eds) (2005) *Power in Global Governance* (Cambridge: Cambridge University Press).

Barrow, Kristie (2004) 'The Role of NGOs in the Establishment of the International Criminal Court', *Dialogue* 2 (1), 11–22.

Barston, R. P. (1988) *Modern Diplomacy* (London and New York: Longman).

Bartelson, Jens (1995) *A Genealogy of Sovereignty* (Cambridge: Cambridge University Press).

Baumann, Rainer, Volker Rittberger and Wolfgang Wagner (2001) 'Neorealist Foreign Policy Theory', in Volker Rittberger (ed.), *German Foreign Policy Since Unification: Theories and Case Studies* (Manchester: Manchester University Press), 37–67.

Baylis, John, Steve Smith and Patricia Owens (eds) (2008) *The Globalization of World Politics* (Oxford: Oxford University Press).

Behera, Navnita Chadha (ed.) (2006) *Gender, Conflict and Migration* (London: Sage).

Beisheim, Marianne, S. Dreher, G. Walter, B. Zangl and M. Zürn (1999) *Im Zeitalter der Globalisierung?* (Baden-Baden: Nomos).

Beitz, Charles (1979) *Political Theory and International Relations* (Princeton, NJ: Princeton University Press).

Bell, Duncan (2007) 'Humanitarian Intervention', in Mark Bevir (ed.) *Encyclopedia of Governance* (London: Sage), 422–3.

Bellamy, Alex J. (2002) 'Pragmatic Solidarism and the Dilemmas of Humanitarian Intervention', *Millennium: Journal of International Studies* 31 (3), 473–97.

Bellamy, Alex J. (2004) *Security Communties and their Neighbours* (Basingstoke: Palgrave Macmillan).

Bellamy, Alex J., Paul Williams and Stuart Griffin (2004) *Understanding Peacekeeping* (Cambridge: Polity Press).

Bennett, Peter G. (1995) 'Modelling Decisions in International Relations: Game Theory and Beyond', *Mershon International Studies Review* 39 (1), 19–52.

Bercovitch, Jacob, Victor Kremenyuk and Willim I. Zartman (eds) (2009) *The Sage Handbook of Conflict Resolution* (London: Sage).

Berenskoetter, Felix and M. J. Williams (eds) (2007) *Power in World Politics* (London: Routledge).

Berridge, G. R. (1995) *Diplomacy: Theory and Practice* (London: Prentice-Hall/ Harvester Wheatsheaf).

Berridge, G. R. (2002) *Diplomacy: Theory and Practice* (Basingstoke: Palgrave, 2nd edn).

Berridge, G. R., Maurice Keens-Soper and T. G. Otte (2001) *Diplomatic Theory from Machiavelli to Kissinger* (Basingstoke: Palgrave).

Bethke Elshtain, Jean (2004) *Just War against Terror: The Burden of American Power in a Violent World* (New York: Basic Books).

Betts, Alexander (2008) 'Global Migration Governance', *GEG Working Paper* 2008/ 43, www.globaleconomicgovernance.org/wp-content/uploads/BettsIntroduction GEGWorkingPaperFinal.pdf [7.05.2010].

Betts, Alexander (2009) *Forced Migration and Global Politics* (Oxford: Wiley-Blackwell).

Biersteker, Thomas J. (2002) 'State, Sovereignty and Territory', in Walter Carlsnaes, Thomas Risse and Beth A. Simmons (eds), *Handbook of International Relations* (London: Sage), 157–76.

Biersteker, Thomas J. and Cynthia Weber (1996a) 'The Social Construction of State Sovereignty', in Thomas J. Biersteker and Cynthia Weber (eds), *State Sovereignty as Social Construct* (Cambridge: Cambridge University Press), 1–21.

Biersteker, Thomas J. and Cynthia Weber (eds) (1996b) *State Sovereignty as Social Construct* (Cambridge: Cambridge University Press).

Bigo, Didier (2002) 'Security and Immigration: Toward a Critique of the Governmentality of Unease', *Alternatives: Global, Local, Political* 27 (special issue), 63–92.

Bloomfield, David (1995) 'Towards Complementarity in Conflict Management: Resolution and Settlement in Northern Ireland', *Journal of Peace Research* 32 (2), 151–64.

Boeckh, Andreas (1985) 'Dependencia und kapitalistisches Weltsystem, oder: Die Grenzen globaler Entwicklungstheorien', in Franz Nuscheler (ed.), *Dritte-Welt-Forschung* (Opladen: Westdeutscher Verlag), 56–75.

Bonham, G. Matthew, G. M. Jönsson, C. Persson and M. J. Shapiro (1987) 'Cognition and International Negotiation: The Historical Recovery of Discursive Space', *Cooperation and Conflict* 22 (1), 1–19.

Booth, Ken (ed.) (2005) *Critical Security Studies and World Politics* (Boulder, CO: Lynne Rienner)

Booth, Ken and Tim Dunne (eds) (2002) *Worlds in Collision: Terror and the Future of Global Order* (Houndsmills: Palgrave Macmillian).

Booth, Ken and Nicholas J. Wheeler (2008) *The Security Dilemma: Fear, Cooperation and Trust in World Politics* (Basingstoke: Palgrave).

Booth, Ken, Tim Dunne and Michael Cox (2000) 'Introduction: How Might We Live? Global Ethics in a New Century', *Review of International Studies* 26 (special issue), 1–28.

Booth, Ken, Tim Dunne and Michael Cox (2001) *How Might We Live? Global Ethics in the New Century* (Cambridge: Cambridge University Press).

Börzel, Tanja and Risse, Thomas (2005) 'Public–Private Partnerships: Effective and Legitimate Tools of Transnational Governance?', in Edgar Grande and Louis Pauly (eds), *Complex Sovereignty: Reconstituting Political Authority in the Twenty-First Century* (Toronto: University of Toronto Press), 195–216.

Bothe, Michael, Mary Ellen O'Connell and Natalino Ronzitti (eds) (2005) *Redefining Sovereignty: The Use of Force after the Cold War* (Ardsley, NY: Transnational Publishers).

Boulding, Elise (2000) *Cultures of Peace: The Hidden Side of History* (Syracuse, NY: Syracuse University Press).

Boulding, Kenneth (1959) 'National Images and International Systems', *Journal of Conflict Resolution* 3 (2), 120–31.

Boutros-Ghali, Boutros (1992) *An Agenda for Peace: Preventive Diplomacy, Peacemaking and Peace-Keeping* (New York: United Nations).

Brams, Steven J. (2000) 'Game Theory: Pitfalls and Opportunities in Applying It to International Relations', *Peace Economics, Peace Science and Public Policy* 6 (2), 1–9.

Breuilly, John (1982) *Nationalism and the State* (Manchester: Manchester University Press).

Brock, Lothar, Anna Geis and Harald Müller (eds) (2006) *Democratic Wars: Looking at the Dark Side of Democratic Peace* (Houndsmills: Palgrave).

Brown, Chris (1999) 'Universal Human Rights: A Critique', in Tim Dunne and Nicholas J. Wheeler (eds), *Human Rights in Global Politics* (Cambridge: Cambridge University Press), 103–27.

Brown, Chris (2002) *Sovereignty, Rights and Justice: International Political Theory Today* (Cambridge: Polity).

Brown, Chris and Kirsten Ainley (2009) *Understanding International Relations* (Basingstoke: Palgrave Macmillan).

Brubaker, Rogers (1992) *Citizenship and Nationhood in France and Germany* (Cambridge, MA: Harvard University Press).

Bueno de Mesquita, Bruce (1981) *The War Trap* (New Haven, CT: Yale University Press).

Bueno de Mesquita, Bruce (2002) *Predicting Politics* (Columbus, OH: Ohio State University Press).

Bueno de Mesquita, Bruce (2009) *The Predictioneer's Game* (London: Random House).

Bueno de Mesquita, B., J. D. Morrow, R. Siverson and A. Smith (1999) 'An Institutional Explanation of the Democratic Peace', *The American Political Science Review* 93 (4), 791–807.

Bull, Hedley (1977) *The Anarchical Society: A Study of Order in World Politics* (Basingstoke: Macmillan).

Bull, Hedley (1982) 'Civilian Power Europe: A Contradiction in Terms', *Journal of Common Market Studies* 21 (1), 149–70.

Bull, Hedley and Adam Watson (1984) *The Expansion of International Society* (Oxford: Oxford University Press).

Burgess, Michael (2000) *Federalism and European Union: The Building of Europe, 1950–2000* (London: Routledge).

Burton, John W. (1987) *Resolving Deep-Rooted Conflict* (Lanham, MD/New York/London: University Press of America).

Burton, John W. (ed.) (1990) *Conflict: Human Needs Theory* (London: Macmillan).

Burton, John W. and Frank Dukes (eds) (1990) *Conflict: Readings in Management and Resolution* (London: Macmillan).

Butler, Judith (1990) *Gender Trouble: Feminism and the Subversion of Identity* (New York: Routledge).

Butterfield, Herbert (1951) *History and Human Relations* (London: Collins).

Butterfield, Herbert (1966) 'The Balance of Power', in Herbert Butterfield and Martin Wight (eds), *Diplomatic Investigations: Essays in the Theory of International Politics* (London: Allen and Unwin).

Buzan, Barry (1991) *People, States and Fear: An Agenda for International Security Studies in the Post-Cold War Era* (Hemel Hempstead: Harvester Wheatsheaf, 2nd edn).

Buzan, Barry (1995) 'The Level of Analysis Problem in International Relations Reconsidered', in Ken Booth and Steve Smith (eds), *International Relations Theory Today* (Oxford: Polity Press), 198–216.

Buzan, Barry (2004) *From International to World Society? English School Theory and the Social Structure of Globalisation* (Cambridge: Cambridge University Press).

Buzan, Barry and Lene Hansen (2009) *The Evolution of International Security Studies* (Cambridge: Cambridge University Press).

Buzan, Barry and Richard Little (2000) *International Systems in World History: Remaking the Study of International Relations* (Cambridge: Cambridge University Press).

Buzan, Barry and Ole Wæver (2003) *Regions and Powers: The Structure of International Security* (Cambridge: Cambridge University Press).

Buzan, Barry, Charles Jones and Richard Little (1993) *The Logic of Anarchy. Neorealism to Structural Realism* (New York: Columbia University Press).

Buzan, Barry, Ole Wæver and Jaap de Wilde (1998) *Security: A New Framework for Analysis* (Boulder, CO: Lynne Rienner).

Byers, Michael (2008) 'International Law', in Christian Reus-Smit and Duncan Snidal (eds), *The Oxford Handbook of International Relations* (Oxford: Oxford University Press), 612–31.

Cahill, Kevin M. (ed.) (2000) *Preventive Diplomacy: Stopping Wars before They Start* (London: Routledge).

Callinicos, Alex (2002) 'Marxism and Global Governance', in David Held and Anthony McGrew (eds), *Governing Globalization: Power, Authority and Global Governance* (Cambridge: Polity), 249–66.

Cammack, Paul (2005) 'The Governance of Global Capitalism: A New Materialist Perspective', in Rorden Wilkinson (ed.), *The Global Governance Reader* (London: Routledge), 156–73.

Campbell, David (1993) *Politics without Principle: Sovereignty, Ethics and the Narratives of the Gulf War* (Boulder, CO: Lynne Rienner).

Campbell, David (1998) *Writing Security: US Foreign Policy and the Politics of Identity* (Minneapolis: University of Minnesota Press, 2nd edn).

Cardoso, Fernando Henrique (1977) 'The Consumption of Dependency Theory in the United States', *Latin American Research Review* 12 (3), 7–24.

Cardoso, Fernando Henrique and Enzo Faletto (1979) *Dependency and Development in Latin America*. Originally published as *Dependencia y desarrollo en América Latina in 1971* (Berkeley and Los Angeles: University of California Press).

Carr, Edward Hallet (1945) *Nationalism and After* (London: Macmillan).

Carr, Edward Hallet (1946) *The Twenty Years' Crisis, 1919–1939: An Introduction to the Study of International Relations* (London: Macmillan).

Carr, Edward Hallet (2001) *The Twenty Years' Crisis 1919–1939: An Introduction to the Study of International Relations* (London: Palgrave).

CASE Collective (2006) 'Critical Approaches to Security in Europe: A Networked Manifesto', *Security Dialogue* 37 (4), 443–87.

Cerny, Philip G. (2000) 'The New Security Dilemma: Divisibility, Defection and Disorder in the Global Era', *Review of International Studies* 26 (4), 623–46.

Cerny, Philip G. (2005) 'Terrorism and the New Security Dilemma', *Naval War College Review* 58 (1), 11–33.

Chan-Tiberghien, Jennifer (2004) 'Gender-Skepticism or Gender-Boom? Post-structural Feminisms, Transnational Feminisms, and the World Conference Against Racism', *International Feminist Journal of Politics* 6 (3), 454–84.

Checkel, Jeffrey T. (1998) 'The Constructivist Turn in International Relations Theory', *World Politics* 50 (2), 324–48.

Checkel, Jeffrey T. (1999) 'Social Construction and Integration', *Journal of European Public Policy* 6 (4), 545–60.

Chen, Shaohua and Martin Ravallion (2008) 'The Developing World Is Poorer Than We Thought, But No Less Successful in the Fight Against Poverty', *Policy Research Working Paper 4703* (Washington, DC: World Bank Development Research Group).

Christiansen, Thomas, Knuder Erik Jørgensen and Antje Wiener (eds) (2001) *The Social Construction of Europe* (London: Sage).

Chirot, Daniel and Thomas D. Hall (1982) 'World-System Theory', *Annual Review of Sociology* 8, 81–106.

Clarke, M. and B. White (eds) (1989) *Understanding Foreign Policy: The Foreign Policy Systems Approach* (Aldershot: Edward Elgar).

Cochran, Molly (1999) *Normative Theory in International Relations: A Pragmatic Approach* (Cambridge: Cambridge University Press).

Cohen, Anthony P. (1998) 'Boundaries and Boundary-Consciousness: Politicizing Cultural Identity', in Malcolm Anderson and Eberhard Bort (eds), *The Frontiers of Europe* (London: Pinter), 22–35.

Cohen, Raymond (1997) *Negotiating Across Cultures: International Communication in an Interdependent World* (Washington DC: United States Institute of Peace Press).

Cohn, Carol (1987) 'Sex and Death in the Rational World of Defense Intellectuals', *Signs: Journal of Women in Culture and Society* 12 (4), 657–718.

Collins, Alan (2004) 'State-Induced Security Dilemma: Maintaining the Tragedy', *Cooperation and Conflict* 39 (1), 27–44.

Collins, Alan (2007) 'Forming a Security Community: Lessons from ASEAN', *International Relations of the Asia-Pacific*, vol. 3, 203–25.

Colman, Andrew M. (1982) *Game Theory and Experimental Games: The Study of Strategic Interaction* (Oxford: Pergamon Press).

Commission on Global Governance (2005) 'A New World', in Rorden Wilkinson (ed.), *The Global Governance Reader* (London: Routledge), 26–44.

Connolly, William E. (1983) *The Terms of Political Discourse* (Princeton: Princeton University Press).

Connolly, William E. (1991) *Identity/Difference: Democratic Negotiations of Political Paradox* (Ithaca, NY: Cornell University Press).

Constantinou, Costas (1996) *On the Way to Diplomacy* (Minneapolis: University of Minnesota Press).

Conzelmann, Thomas (2006) 'Neofunktionalismus', in Siegfried Schieder and Manuela Spindler (eds), *Theorien der Internationalen Beziehungen* (Opladen & Farmington Hills, MI: Barbara Budrich Publishers), 145–74.

Cooper, Andrew F. (2002) 'Like-Minded Nations, NGOs, and the Changing Pattern of Diplomacy within the UN System: An Introductory Perspective', in Andrew F. Cooper, John English and Ramesh Thakur (eds), *Enhancing Global Governance: Towards a New Diplomacy* (Tokyo: United Nations University Press).

Cooper, Andrew F. (2007) 'Beyond Hollywood and the Boardroom: Celebrity Diplomacy', *Georgetown Journal of International Affairs* Spring/Fall, 123–32.

Cox, Robert W. (1981) 'Social Forces, States and World Orders: Beyond International Relations Theory', *Millennium: Journal of International Studies* 10 (2), 126–55.

Cox, Robert W. (1983) 'Gramsci, Hegemony and International Relations: An Essay in Method', *Millennium: Journal of International Relations* 12 (2), 162–75.

Cox, Robert W. (1986) 'Social Forces, States and World Orders: Beyond International Relations Theories', in Robert Keohane (ed.), *Neorealism and Its Critics* (New York: Columbia University Press), 204–54.

Cox, Robert W. (1987) *Production, Power and World Order: Social Forces and the Making of History* (New York: Columbia University Press).

Cox, Robert W. (1992) 'Multilateralism and World Order', *Review of International Studies*, 18 (2), 161–80.

Cueva, Agustín (1976) 'A Summary of "Problems and Perspectives of Dependency Theory"', *Latin American Perspectives* 11 (3), 12–16.

Cusimano, Maryann K. (2000) *Beyond Sovereignty: Issues for a Global Agenda* (Boston: Bedford/St. Martin's).

Cutler, A. Claire, Virginia Haufler and Tony Porter (1999) *Private Authority and International Affairs* (Albany, NY: State University of New York Press).

Czempiel, Ernst-Otto (1992) 'Governance and Democratisation', in James Rosenau and Ernst-Otto Czempiel (eds), *Governance Without Government: Order and Change in World Politics* (Cambridge: Cambridge University Press), 250–71.

Czempiel, Ernst-Otto (1996) 'Kants Theorem. Oder: Warum sind die Demokratien (noch immer) nicht friedlich?', *Zeitschrift für Internationale Beziehungen* 3 (1), 79–101.

Dahl, Robert A. (1994) 'The Concept of Power', in John Scott (ed.), *Power: Critical Assessments* (London: Routledge), 288–309.

Dal Bó, Pedro (2005) 'Cooperation under the Shadow of the Future: Experimental Evidence from Infinitely Repeated Games', *The American Economic Review* 95 (5), 1591–604.

de Rivera, Joseph (1968) *The Psychological Dimension of Foreign Policy* (Columbus, OH: Merrill).

de Wilde, Jaap (1991) *Saved from Oblivion: Interdependence Theory in the First Half of the 20th Century. A Study of the Causality between War and Complex Interdependence* (Aldershot: Dartmouth Publishing).

Deitelhoff, Nicole (2009) 'The Discursive Process of Legalization: Charting Islands of Persuasion in the ICC Case', *International Organization* 63 (1), 33–65.

Deng, Francis (1993) *Protecting the Dispossessed: A Challenge for the International Community* (Washington DC: Brookings Institution).

Deng, Yong (2001) 'Hegemon on the Offensive: Chinese Perspectives on US Global Strategy', *Political Science Quarterly* 116 (3), 343–65.

Der Derian, James (1987) *On Diplomacy* (Oxford: Blackwell).

Der Derian, James (1992) *Antidiplomacy: Spies, Terror, Speed and War* (Oxford: Blackwell).

Der Derian, James (2009) *Virtuous War: Mapping the Military-Industrial Media-Entertainment Network* (London: Routledge; 2nd edn).

Der Derian, James and Michael J. Shapiro (eds) (1989) *International/Intertextual Relations: Postmodern Readings of World Politics* (Lanham, MD: Lexington).

Detter, Ingrid (1994) *The International Legal Order* (Aldershot: Dartmouth Publishers).

Deutsch, Karl W., et al. (1957) *Political Community and the North Atlantic Area: International Organization in the Light of Historical Experience* (Princeton: Princeton University Press).

Devetak, Richard. (2009) 'Critical Theory', in Burchill, Scott, et al., *Theories of International Relations* (London: Palgrave Macmillan, 4th edn), 159–82.

Dickinson, G. Lowes (1926) *The International Anarchy: 1904–1914* (London: Allan and Unwin).

Diehl, Paul F. (2008) *Peace Operations* (Cambridge: Polity Press).

Diez, Thomas (1999) 'Speaking "Europe": The Politics of Integration Discourse', *Journal of European Public Policy* 6 (4), 598–613.

Diez, Thomas (2001) 'Europe as a Discursive Battleground: Discourse Analysis and European Integration Studies', *Cooperation and Conflict* 36 (1), 5–38.

Diez, Thomas and Jill Steans (2005) 'A Useful Dialogue? Habermas and International Relations', *Review of International Studies* 31 (1), 127–40.

Diez, Thomas and Richard G. Whitman (2002) 'Analysing European Integration, Reflecting on the English School: Scenarios for an Encounter', *Journal of Common Market Studies* 40 (1), 43–67.

Diez, Thomas, Stephan Stetter and Mathias Albert (2006) 'The European Union and Border Conflicts: The Transformative Power of Integration', *International Organization*, 60 (3), 563–93.

Diez, Thomas, Mathias Albert and Stephan Stetter (eds) (2008) *The European Union and Border Conflicts: The Power of Integration and Association* (Cambridge: Cambridge University Press).

Dinan, Desmond (1999) *Ever Closer Union: An Introduction to European Integration* (Boulder, CO: Lynne Rienner; 2nd edn).

Donnan, Hastings and Thomas M. Wilson (1999) *Borders: Frontiers of Identity, Nation and State* (Oxford: Berg).

Donnelly, Jack (1986) 'International Human Rights: A Regime Analysis', *International Organization*, 40 (3), 599–639.

Donnelly, Jack (1992) 'Twentieth-Century Realism', in Terry Nardin and David R. Mapel (eds), *Traditions of International Ethics* (Cambridge: Cambridge University Press), 85–111.

Donnelly, Jack (2003) *Universal Human Rights in Theory & Practice* (Ithaca, NY: Cornell University Press, 2nd edn).

Donnelly, Jack (2006) 'Sovereign Inequalities and Hierarchy in Anarchy: American Power and International Society', *European Journal of International Relations* 12 (2), 139–70.

Donnelly, Jack (2008) 'The Ethics of Realism', in Christian Reus-Smit and Duncan Snidal (eds), *The Oxford Handbook of International Relations* (Oxford: Oxford University Press), 150–62.

Donnelly, Jack (2009) 'Realism', in Scott Burchill et al., *Theories of International Relations* (Basingstoke: Palgrave Macmillan, 4th edn), 31–55.

Doran, Charles F. (1971) *The Politics of Assimilation: Hegemony and its Aftermath* (Baltimore, MD: Johns Hopkins University Press).

Dos Santos, Theotonio (1970) 'The Structure of Dependence', *American Economic Review* 60 (6), 231–6.

Doyle, Michael W. (1983) 'Kant, Liberal Legacies, and Foreign Affairs', *Philosophy and Public Affairs* 12 (3), 205–35.

Doyle, Michael W. (1986a) 'Liberalism and World Politics', *American Political Science Review* 80 (4), 1151–69.

Doyle, Michael W. (1986b) *Empires* (Ithaca, NY: Cornell University Press).

Doyle, Michael W. (1997) *Ways of War and Peace* (New York: W. W. Norton).

Doyle, Michael and Nicholas Sambanis (2000) 'International Peacebuilding: A Theoretical and Quantitative Analysis', *American Political Science Review* 94 (4), 779–802.

Doyle, Michael and Nicholas Sambanis (2006) *Making War and Building Peace: United Nations Peacekeeping Operations* (Princeton: Princeton University Press).

Druckman, Daniel (1986) 'Stages, Turning Points, and Crises: Negotiating Military Base Rights, Spain and the United States', *Journal of Conflict Resolution* 30 (2), 327–60.

Dunn, David H. (1996) *Diplomacy at the Highest Level: The Evolution of International Summitry* (Basingstoke: Macmillan).

Dunne, Tim (1995) 'International Society – Theoretical Promises Fulfilled?', *Cooperation and Conflict* 30 (2), 125–54.

Dunne, Tim (1998) *Inventing International Society: A History of the English School* (Basingstoke: Macmillan).

Dunne, Tim (2005) 'Terrorism', in Brian White, Richard Little and Michael Smith (eds), *Issues in World Politics* (Houndmills: Palgrave Macmillan, 3rd edn).

Dunne, Tim (2007) 'Liberalism', in John Baylis, Steve Smith and Patricia Owens (eds), *The Globalization of World Politics* (Oxford: Oxford University Press, 4th edn), 110–22.

Dunne, Tim and Brian C. Schmidt (2007) 'Realism', in John Baylis, Steve Smith and Patricia Owens (eds), *The Globalization of World Politics* (Oxford: Oxford University Press, 4th edn), 92–106.

Dunne, Tim and Nicholas J. Wheeler (1999a) 'Introduction: Human Rights and the Fifty Years' Crisis', in Tim Dunne and Nicholas J. Wheeler (eds), *Human Rights in Global Politics* (Cambridge: Cambridge University Press), 1–28.

Dunne, Tim and Nicholas J. Wheeler (eds) (1999b) *Human Rights in Global Politics* (Cambridge: Cambridge University Press).

Eberwein, Wolf-Dieter and Sven Chojnacki (2001) 'Scientific Necessity and Political Utility: A Comparison of Data on Violent Conflicts', *WZB Discussion Paper* 01–304.

Edkins, Jenny (1999) *Poststructuralism and International Relations: Bringing the Political Back In* (Boulder, CO: Lynne Rienner).

Eilstrup-Sangiovanni, Mette (ed.) (2006) *Debates on European Integration: A Reader* (Basingstoke: Palgrave).

Elshtain, Jean Bethke (1981) *Public Man, Private Women: Women in Social and Political Thought* (Princeton: Princeton University Press).

Elster, Jon (2003) 'Marxism, Functionalism, and Game Theory: A Case for Methodological Individualism', in Derek Matravers and Jon Pike (eds), *Debates in Contemporary Political Philosophy: An Anthology* (London: Routledge), 22–40.

Enloe, Cynthia (1989) *Bananas, Beaches and Bases: Making Feminist Sense of International Politics* (London: Pandora Press).

Enloe, Cynthia (1996) 'Margins, Silences and Bottom Rungs: How to Overcome the Underestimation of Power in the Study of International Relations', in Steve Smith, Ken Booth and Marysia Zalewski (eds), *International Theory: Positivism and Beyond* (Cambridge: Cambridge University Press), 186–202.

Eriksen, Erik Oddvar and John Erik Fossum (2004) 'Europe in Search of Legitimacy: Strategies of Legitimation Assessed', *International Political Science Review* 25 (4), 435–59.

Escobar, Arturo (1984) 'Discourse and Power in Development: Michel Foucault and the Relevance of His Work to the Third World', *Alternatives* 10 (3), 377–400.

Escobar, Arturo (1995) *Encountering Development: The Making and Unmaking of the Third World* (Princeton: Princeton University Press).

Etzioni, Amitai (2006) 'Sovereignty as Responsibility', *Orbis* 50 (1), 71–85.

Falk, Richard (1970) *The Status of Law in International Society* (Princeton: Princeton University Press).

Farnham, B. (1990) 'Political Cognition and Decision Making', *Political Psychology* 11 (1), 83–112.

Fearon, James (1994) 'Domestic Political Audiences and the Escalation of International Disputes', *American Political Science Review* 88 (2), 577–92.

Fearon, James (1995) 'Rationalist Explanations for War', *International Organization* 49 (3), 379–414.

Fearon, James and Alexander Wendt (2002) 'Rationalism vs. Realism: A Skeptical View', in Walter Carlsnaes, Thomas Risse and Beth A. Simmons (eds), *Handbook of International Relations* (London: Sage), 52–72.

Feder, Stanley A. (2002) 'Forecasting for Policy-Making in the Post-Cold War Period', *Annual Review of Political Science* 5, 111–25.

Fierke, Karen M. (1998) *Changing Games, Changing Strategies: Critical Investigations in Security* (Manchester: Manchester University Press).

Finlayson, Jock A. and Mark Zacher (1985) 'The GATT and the Regulation of Trade Barriers: Regime Dynamics and Functions', in Stephen D. Krasner (ed.), *International Regimes* (Ithaca, NY: Cornell University Press), 273–314.

Finnemore, Martha (1996a) 'Constructing Norms of Humanitarian Intervention', in Peter J. Katzenstein (ed.), *The Culture of National Security: Norms and Identity in World Politics* (New York: Columbia University Press), 153–87.

Finnemore, Martha (1996b) *National Interests and International Society* (Ithaca, NY: Cornell University Press).

Finnemore, Martha (2003) *The Purpose of Intervention: Changing Beliefs about the Use of Force* (Ithaca, NY: Cornell University Press).

Finnemore, Martha and Kathryn Sikkink (1998) 'International Norm Dynamics and Political Change', *International Organization* 52 (4), 887–917.

Fisher, Roger and William Ury (1981) *Getting to Yes: Negotiating Agreement without Giving In* (Boston: Houghton Mifflin).

Fisher, Ronald J. and Loraleigh Keashly (1991) 'The Potential Complementarities of Mediation and Consultation within a Contingency Model of Third Party Intervention', *Journal of Peace Research* 28 (1), 29–42.

Fixdal, Mona and Dan Smith, 'Humanitarian intervention and just war', *Mershon International Studies Review* 42 (2), 283–312.

Forde, Steven (1992) 'Classical Realism', in Terry Nardin and David R. Mapel (eds), *Traditions of International Ethics* (Cambridge: Cambridge University Press), 62–84.

Forsythe, David P. (2006) *Human Rights in International Relations* (Cambridge: Cambridge University Press, 2nd edn).

Fortna, Virginia P. (2004) 'Does Peacekeeping Keep Peace? International Intervention and the Duration of Peace after Civil War', *International Studies Quarterly* 48 (2), 269–92.

Foucault, M. (1980) *Power/Knowledge: Selected Interviews and Other Writings* (New York: Pantheon).

Franck, Thomas M. (1990) *The Power of Legitimacy Among Nations* (New York: Oxford University Press).

Frank, Andre Gunder (1969) *Latin America – Underdevelopment or Revolution: Essays on the Development of Underdevelopment and the Immediate Enemy* (New York and London: Monthly Review Press).

Frank, Andre Gunder (1984) *Critique and Anticritique: Essays on Dependence and Reformism* (London: Macmillan).

Frank, Andre Gunder (1998) *ReOrient: Global Economy in the Asian Age* (Berkeley: University of California Press).

Friedman, George (1981) *The Political Philosophy of the Frankfurt School* (Ithaca, NY: Cornell University Press).

Galtung, Johan (1969) 'Violence, Peace, and Peace Research', *Journal of Peace Research* 6 (3), 167–191.

Galtung, Johan (1996) *Peace by Peaceful Means: Peace and Conflict, Development and Civilization* (Oslo: Prio).

Garrett, Geoffrey and Barry R. Weingast (1993) 'Ideas, Interests, and Institutions: Constructing the European Community's Internal Market', in Judith Goldstein and Robert O. Keohane (eds), *Ideas and Foreign Policy: Beliefs, Institutions and Political Change* (Ithaca, NY: Cornell University Press), 173–206.

Gavrilis, George (2008) *The Dynamics of Interstate Boundaries* (Cambridge: Cambridge University Press).

Gellner, Ernest (1983) *Nations and Nationalism* (Ithaca, NY: Cornell University Press).

George, Alexander L. (1967) 'The "Operational Code": A Neglected Approach to the Study of Political Leaders and Decision-Making', published as Memorandum RM-5427-PR prepared for United States Air Force Project Rand (Santa Monica, CA: Rand Corporation).

George, Alexander L. (1991) *Forceful Persuasion: Coercive Diplomacy as an Alternative to War* (Washington DC: United States Institute of Peace Press).

George, Jim (1994) *Discourses of Global Politics: A Critical (Re)Introduction to International Relations* (Boulder, CO: Lynne Rienner).

Giddens, Anthony (1986) *The Constitution of Society: Outline of the Theory of Structuration* (Oxford: Polity).

Gill, Stephen (ed.) (1993a) *Gramsci, Historical Materialism and International Relations* (Cambridge: Cambridge University Press).

Gill, Stephen (1993b) 'Gramsci and Global Politics: Towards a Post-Hegemonic Research Agenda', in Stephen Gill (ed.), *Gramsci, Historical Materialism and International Relations* (Cambridge: Cambridge University Press), 1–20.

Gill, Stephen (1995) 'Globalisation, Market Civilisation and Disciplinary Neo-Liberalism', *Millennium: Journal of International Studies* 24 (3), 399–423.

Gill, Stephen (2003) *Power and Resistance in the New World Order* (New York: Palgrave Macmillan).

Gilpin, Robert (1981) *War and Change in World Politics* (Cambridge: Cambridge University Press).

Gilpin, Robert (2000) *The Challenge of Global Capitalism* (Princeton: Princeton University Press).

Gilpin, Robert (2002) 'A Realist Perspective on International Governance', in David Held and Anthony McGrew (eds), *Governing Globalization: Power, Authority and Global Governance* (Cambridge: Polity), 237–48.

Glarbo, Kenneth (1999) 'Wide-awake Diplomacy: Reconstructing the Common Foreign and Security Policy of the European Union', *Journal of European Public Policy* 6 (4), 634–51.

Glaser, Charles L. (1997) 'The Security Dilemma Revisited', *World Politics* 50 (1), 171–201.

Glasl, Friedrich (1982) 'The process of conflict escalation and roles of third parties', in G. B. J. Bomers and R. B. Peterson (eds), *Conflict Management and Industrial Relations* (The Hague: Kluwer Nijhoff), 119–40.

Gleditsch, Nils Petter and Hårvard Hegre (1997) 'Peace and Democracy: Three Levels of Analysis', *Journal of Conflict Resolution* 41 (2), 283–310.

Gleditsch, Nils Petter, et al. (2002) 'Armed Conflict 1945–2001: A New Dataset', *Journal of Peace Research* 39 (5), 615–37.

Global Commission on International Migration (2005) *Migration in an Interconnected World: New Directions for Actions*, Report of the GCIM, www.gcim.org/attachements/gcim-complete-report-2005.pdf [7.05.2010].

Goffman, Erving (1969) *Strategic Interaction* (Philadelphia: University of Pennsylvania Press).

Goldblat, Jozef (1985) *Non-Proliferation: The Why and the Wherefore* (London: Taylor & Francis).

Goldstein, Judith and Robert O. Keohane (1993a) 'Ideas and Foreign Policy: An Analytical Framework', in Judith Goldstein and Robert O. Keohane (eds), *Ideas and Foreign Policy: Beliefs, Institutions and Political Change* (Ithaca, NY: Cornell University Press), 3–30.

Goldstein, Judith and Robert O. Keohane (eds) (1993b) *Ideas & Foreign Policy: Beliefs, Institutions and Political Change* (Ithaca, NY: Cornell University Press).

Goldstein, Judith, Miles Kahler, Robert O. Keohane and Anne-Marie Slaughter (2000) 'Introduction: Legalization and World Politics' *International Organization* 54 (3), 385–99.

Goldstone, Richard J. and Adam M. Smith (2009) *International Judicial Institutions: The Architecture of International Justice at Home and Abroad* (London: Routledge).

Gramsci, Antonio (1971) *Selections from the Prison Notebooks* (New York: International Publishers, ed. and trans. Quintin Hoare and Geoffrey Nowell-Smith).

Greig, Alastair, David Hulme and Mark Turner (2007) *Challenging Global Inequality. Development Theory and Practice in the 21st Century* (Basingstoke: Palgrave Macmillan).

Grieco, Joseph M. (1988) 'Anarchy and the Limits of Cooperation: A Realist Critique of the Newest Liberal Institutionalism', *International Organization* 42 (3), 485–508.

Grieco, Joseph M. (1997) 'Realist International Theory and the Study of World Politics', Michael W. Doyle and John G. Ikenberry (eds), *New Thinking in International Relations Theory* (Westview Press, CO: Boulder), 163–210.

Griffiths, Martin (1999) *Fifty Key Thinkers in International Relations* (London: Routledge).

Griffiths, Martin, Steven C. Roach and M. Scott Solomon (2009) *Fifty Key Thinkers in International Relations* (London: Routledge, 2nd edn).

Grotius, Hugo (2001) *The Law of War and Peace: De Jure Belli ac Pacis Libri Trea* (Kitchener: Batoche Books, orig. pub. 1625).

Gunning, Jeroen (2007) 'A Case for Critical Terrorism Studies?', *Government and Opposition*, 42 (3), 363–93.

Guzzini, Stefano (1993) 'Structural Power: The Limits of Neorealist Power Analysis', *International Organization* 47 (3), 443–78.

Guzzini, Stefano (2007) 'The Concept of Power: A Constructivist Analysis', in Felix Berenskoetter and M. J. Williams (eds), *Power in World Politics* (London: Routledge), 23–42.

Haas, Ernst B. (1964) *Beyond the Nation-State: Functionalism and International Organization* (Stanford: Stanford University Press).

Haas, Ernst B. (1968) *The Uniting of Europe* (Stanford: Stanford University Press, 2nd edn).

Haas, Richard N. (1988) 'Ripeness and the Settlement of International Disputes', *Survival* 30 (3), 232–51.

Habermas, Jürgen (1979) *Communication and the Evolution of Society* (Boston: Beacon Press).

Hall, Edward T. (1976) *Beyond Culture* (New York: Anchor).

Halliday, Fred (1988) 'Three Concepts of Internationalism', *International Affairs* 64 (2), 187–98.

Hamilton, Keith and Richard Langhorne (1995) *The Practice of Diplomacy: Its Evolution, Theory and Administration* (London and New York: Sage).

Hansen, Lene (2006) *Security as Practice: Discourse Analysis and the Bosnian War* (London: Routledge).

Hardt, Michael and Antonio Negri (2000) *Empire* (Cambridge, MA: Harvard University Press).

Hardt, Michael and Antonio Negri (2004) *Multitude: War and Democracy in the Age of Empire* (New York: Penguin).

Harvey, David (2005) *The New Imperialism* (Oxford: Oxford University Press).

Hasenclever, Andreas (2006) 'Liberale Ansätze zum "demokratischen Frieden"', in Siegfried Schieder and Manuel Spindler (eds), *Theorien der Internationalen Beziehungen* (Opladen: Barbara Budrich, 2nd edn).

Hasenclever, Andreas, Peter Mayer and Volker Rittberger (1997) *Theories of International Regimes* (Cambridge: Cambridge University Press).

Haslam, John (2002) *No Virtue Like Necessity: Realist Thought in International Relations* (New Haven: Yale University Press).

key concepts in international relations

Hay, Colin and David Marsh (eds) (2000) *Demystifying Globalization* (Basingstoke: Palgrave Macmillan).

Hedley, Bull (1977) *The Anarchical Society* (Houndsmills: Palgrave Macmillan).

Heinrich, Michael (2004) *Kritik der politischen Ökonomie: Eine Einführung* (Stuttgart: Schmetterling Verlag).

Heinrich, Michael (2006) 'Imperialismustheorie', in Siegfried Schieder and Manuela Spindler (eds), *Theorien der Internationalen Beziehungen* (Opladen: UTB, 2nd edn), 295–324.

Held, David and Anthony McGrew (2002) 'Introduction', in David Held and Anthony McGrew (eds), *Governing Globalization: Power, Authority and Global Governance* (Malden, MA: Blackwell), 1–24.

Held, David and Anthony McGrew (eds) (2007) *Globalization Theory: Approaches and Controversies* (Oxford: Blackwell).

Held, David, A. McGrew, D. Goldblatt and J. Perraton (1999) *Global Transformations: Politics, Economics and Culture* (Cambridge: Polity Press).

Henckaerts, Jean-Marie (2005) 'Study on Customary International Humanitarian Law: A Contribution to the Understanding and Respect for the Rule of Law in Armed Conflict', *International Review of the Red Cross* 857, 175–212.

Herbst, Jeffrey (1989) 'The Creation and Maintenance of National Boundaries in Africa', *International Organization* 43 (4), 673–92.

Hermann, Margaret G. (1980) 'Explaining Foreign Policy Behaviour Using the Personal Characteristics of Political Leaders', *International Studies Quarterly* 24 (1), 7–46.

Herrmann, Richard K., Thomas Risse and Marilynn B. Brewer (eds) (2004) *Transnational Identities: Becoming European in the EU* (Lanham, MD: Rowman & Littlefield).

Herz, John (1950) 'Idealist Internationalism and the Security Dilemma', *World Politics* 2 (2), 157–80.

Herz, John (1951) *Political Realism and Political Idealism: A Study in Theories and Realities* (Chicago: University of Chicago Press).

Herz, John (2003) 'The Security Dilemma in International Relations: Background and Present Problems', *International Relations* 17 (4), 411–16.

Hinsley, F. H. (1986). *Sovereignty* (Cambridge: Cambridge University Press, 2nd edn).

Hirst, Paul and Grahame Thompson (1996) *Globalization in Question* (Cambridge: Polity Press).

Hitchens, Christopher (2002) *The Trial of Henry Kissinger* (London: Verso).

Hobbes, Thomas (1996) *Leviathan* (Oxford: Oxford University Press, orig. 1651).

Hobden, Stephen and Richard Wyn Jones (2008) 'Marxist Theories of International Relations', in John Baylis, Steve Smith and Patricia Owens (eds), *The Globalization of World Politics: An Introduction to International Relations* (Oxford: Oxford University Press, 4th edn), 142–59.

Hobsbawm, Eric J. (1990) *Nations and Nationalism since 1780: Programme, Myth, Reality* (Cambridge: Cambridge University Press).

Hobsbawm, Eric J. and Terence Ranger (eds) (1992) *The Invention of Tradition* (Cambridge: Cambridge University Press).

Hobson, John A. (1988) *Imperialism: A Study* (London: Unwin Hyman, orig. pub. 1902).

Hocking, Brian (1999) 'Catalytic Diplomacy: Beyond "Newness" and "Decline"', in Jan Melissen (ed.), *Innovation in Diplomatic Practice* (Basingstoke: Macmillan), 21–42.

Höffe, Otfried (2007) *Democracy in an Age of Globalization* (Hamburg: Springer).

Hoffmann, Bruce (2006) *Inside Terrorism*, second edition (New York: Columbia University Press).

Hollis, Martin and Steve Smith (1990) *Explaining and Understanding International Relations* (Oxford: Clarendon).

Holsti, Kalevi J. (1992) 'Governance without Government: Polyarchy in Nineteenth-Century European International Politics', in James Rosenau and Ernst-Otto Czempiel (eds) (1992) *Governance Without Government: Order and Change in World Politics* (Cambridge: Cambridge University Press), 30–58.

Holsti, Ole (1962) 'The Belief System and National Images: A Case Study', *Journal of Conflict Resolution* 6 (3), 244–52.

Hopf, Ted (2002) *Social Construction of International Politics: Identities and Foreign Policies, Moscow, 1955 and 1999* (Ithaca, NY: Cornell University Press).

Hopgood, Stephen (2000) 'Reading the Small Print in Global Civil Society: The Inexorable Hegemony of the Liberal Self', *Millennium: Journal of International Studies* 29 (1), 1–25.

Horowitz, Donald L. (1985) *Ethnic Groups in Conflict* (Berkeley: University of California Press).

Howarth, David and Jacob Torfing (eds) (2005) *Discourse Theory in European Politics: Identity, Policy and Governance* (Basingstoke: Palgrave).

Howe, Stephen (2002) *Empire: A Very Short Introduction* (Oxford: Oxford University Press).

Hudson, Valerie M. (1998) *Culture and Foreign Policy* (Boulder, CO: Lynne Rienner).

Human Security Centre (2005) *Human Security Report: War and Peace in the Twenty-First Century* (New York: Oxford University Press).

Huntington, Samuel P. (1971) 'The Change to Change: Modernization, Development, and Politics', *Comparative Politics* 3 (3), 283–322.

Hurwitz, Roger (1989) 'Strategic and Social Fictions in the Prisoner's Dilemma', in James Der Derian and Michael J. Shapiro (eds), *International/Intertextual Relations: Postmodern Readings of World Politics* (New York: Lexington Books), 113–34.

Huysmans, Jef (2002) 'The European Union and the Securitization of Migration', *Journal of Common Market Studies* 38 (5), 751–77.

Huysmans, Jef (2006) *The Politics of Insecurity: Fear, Migration and Asylum in the EU* (London: Routledge).

Hyde-Price, Adrian (2000) *Germany and European Order: Enlarging NATO and the EU* (Manchester: Manchester University Press).

Ignatieff, Michael (2003) *Empire Lite: Nation Building in Bosnia, Kosovo, Afghanistan* (London: Vintage).

Ikenberry, John G. (2008) 'The Rise of China and the Future of the West: Can the Liberal System Survive?', *Foreign Affairs* 87 (1): 23–37.

International Commission on Intervention and State Sovereignty (ICISS) (2001) *The Responsibility to Protect: The Report of the International Commission on Intervention and State Sovereignty* (Ottawa: International Development Research Centre).

Jabri, Vivienne (1996) *Discourses on Violence: Conflict Analysis Reconsidered* (Manchester: Manchester University Press).

Jackson, Richard (2007) 'The Core Commitments of Critical Terrorism Studies', *European Consortium for Political Research* 6, 244–51, www.palgrave-journals.com/eps [9.05.2010].

Jackson, Robert H. (1990) *Quasi-States: Sovereignty, International Relations and the Third World* (Cambridge: Cambridge University Press).

Jackson, Robert H. (1993) 'Armed Humanitarianism', *International Journal* 48 (4), 579–606.

Jellinek, Georg (1922) *Allgemeine Staatslehre* (Berlin: Springer Verlag, 3rd edn).

Jervis, Robert (1976) *Perception and Misperception in International Politics* (Princeton: Princeton University Press).

Jervis, Robert (1978) 'Cooperation under the Security Dilemma', *World Politics* 30 (2), 167–214.

Joachim, Jutta (1999) 'Shaping the Human Rights Agenda: The Case of Violence against Women', in Mary K. Meyer and Elisabeth Prügl (eds), *Gender Politics in Global Governance* (Lanham: Rowman & Littlefield), 142–60.

Joerges, Christian and Jürgen Neyer (2002) 'From Intergovernmental Bargaining to Deliberative Political Processes: The Constitutional Challenge', *European Law Journal* 3 (3), 273–99.

Jönsson, Christer (2002) 'Diplomacy, Bargaining and Negotiation', in Walter Carlsnaes, Thomas Risse and Beth A. Simmons (eds), *Handbook of International Relations* (London: Sage), 212–34.

Jönsson, Christer (2008) 'Global Governance: Challenges to Diplomatic Communication, Representation, and Recognition', in Andrew F. Cooper, Brian Hocking and William Maley (eds), *Global Governance and Diplomacy: Worlds Apart?* (New York: Palgrave Macmillan), 29–38.

Journal of European Public Policy (1999) 'Review Section Symposium: The Choice for Europe', *Journal of European Public Policy* 6 (1), 155–79.

Kaldor, Mary (1999) *New and Old Wars: Organized Violence in a Global Era* (Stanford: Stanford University Press).

Kaldor, Mary (2007) *Human Security: Reflections on Globalization and Intervention* (Cambridge: Polity Press).

Kant, Immanuel (1991): 'Perpetual Peace: A Philosophical Sketch', in Immanuel Kant, *Political Writings* (Cambridge: Cambridge University Press, 2nd edn, orig. 1795), 93–130.

Kant, Immanuel (2003) *To Perpetual Peace: A Philosophical Sketch* (Indianapolis, IN: Hackett Publishing, orig. 1795).

Kaplan, Robert (2005) 'How We Would Fight China', *The Atlantic Monthly* 295 (5), 549–64.

Kapstein, Ethan B. and Michael Mastanduno (eds) (1999) *Unipolar Politics: Realism and State Strategies After the Cold War* (New York: Columbia University Press).

Katzenstein, Peter J. (ed.) (1996) *The Culture of National Security: Norms and Identity in World Politics* (New York: Columbia University Press).

references

Kaufman, Stuart J. (1996) 'Spiraling to Ethnic War: Elites, Masses and Moscow in Moldova's Civil War', *International Security* 21 (2), 108–38.

Kaul, Inge (2006) 'Exploring the Policy Space between Markets and States: Global Public Private Partnerships', in Inge Kaul and Pedro Conceiçao (eds), *The New Public Finance: Responding to Global Challenges* (Oxford: Oxford University Press), 219–68.

Kaul, Inge, Isabelle Grunberg and Marc A. Stern (1999) *Global Public Goods: International Organizations in the 21st Century* (Oxford: Oxford University Press).

Kemp, Tom (1967) *Theories of Imperialism* (London: Dennis Dobson).

Keohane, Robert O. (1984) *After Hegemony: Cooperation and Discord in the World Political Economy* (Princeton: Princeton University Press).

Keohane, Robert O. (1988) 'International Institutions: Two Approaches', *International Studies Quarterly* 32 (4), 379–96.

Keohane, Robert O. (2005) 'Global Governance and Democratic Accountability', in Rorden Wilkinson (ed.), *The Global Governance Reader* (London: Routledge), 120–38.

Keohane, Robert O. and Joseph S. Nye (1977) *Power and Interdependence: World Politics in Transition* (Boston: Little, Brown).

Keohane, Robert O. and Joseph S. Nye (1989) *Power and Interdependence* (New York: Harper Collins; 2nd edn).

Kinder, Donald R. and Janet A. Weiss (1978) 'In Lieu of Rationality: Psychological Perspectives on Foreign Policy Decision Making', *Journal of Conflict Resolution* 22 (4), 707–35.

Kindleberger, Charles P. (1976) 'Systems of International Economic Organization', in David P. Calleo and Harold B. van Cleveland (eds), *Money and the Coming World Order* (New York: New York University Press), 15–39.

Kiras, James D. (2008) 'Terrorism and Globalization', in John Baylis, Steve Smith and Patricia Owens (eds), *The Globalization of World Politics* (New York: Oxford University Press).

Kissinger, Henry (1957) *Nuclear Weapons and Foreign Policy* (New York: Harper).

Kissinger, Henry (1994) *Diplomacy* (New York: Simon & Schuster).

Kleiboer, Mareike (1994) 'Ripeness of Conflict: A Fruitful Notion', *Journal of Peace Research* 31 (1), 109–16.

Kohn, Margaret (2008) 'Colonialism', in Edward N. Zalta (ed.), *The Stanford Encyclopedia of Philosophy* (Fall 2008 Edition), http://plato.stanford.edu/archives/fall2008/entries/colonialism/ [9.02.2010].

Krasner, Stephen D. (1976) 'State Power and the Structure of International Trade', *World Politics* 28 (3), 317–47.

Krasner, Stephen D. (ed.) (1983) *International Regimes* (Ithaca, NY: Cornell University Press).

Krasner, Stephen D. (1991) 'Global Communications and National Power: Life on the Pareto Frontier, *World Politics* 43 (3), 336–66.

Krasner, Stephen D. (1995) 'Compromising Westphalia', *International Security* 20 (3), 115–51.

Krasner, Stephen D. (1999) *Sovereignty: Organized Hypocrisy* (Princeton: Princeton University Press).

Kratochwil, Friedrich and John Gerard Ruggie (1986) 'International Organization: A State of the Art on an Art of the State' *International Organization* 40 (4), 753–75.

Krause, Keith and Michael C. Williams (eds) (1997) *Critical Security Studies: Concepts and Cases* (London: Routledge).

Kriesberg, Louis (2007) *Constructive Conflicts* (Lanham, MD: Rowman & Littlefield, 3rd edn).

Kunz, Josef L. (1952) 'The Status of the Holy See in International Law', *The American Journal of International Law* 46 (2), 308–14.

Laclau, Ernesto and Chantal Mouffe (1985) *Hegemony and Socialist Strategy: Towards a Radical Democratic Politics* (London: Verso).

Laffey, Mark and Jutta Weldes (1997) 'Beyond Belief: Ideas and Symbolic Technologies in the Study of International Relations', *European Journal of International Relations* 3 (2), 193–237.

Landes, David (1961) 'Some Thoughts on the Nature of Economic Imperialism', *Journal of Economic History* 21, 496–512.

Lapid, Yosef (1989) 'The Third Debate: On the Prospects of International Theory in a Post-Positivist Era', *International Studies Quarterly* 33 (3), 235–54.

Lapid, Yosef and Friedrich Kratochwil (eds) (1995) *The Return of Culture and Identity in IR Theory* (Boulder, CO: Lynne Rienner).

Laqueur, Walter (1977) *Terrorism* (Boston: Little, Brown).

Laqueur, Walter (1987) *The Age of Terrorism* (Boston: Little, Brown).

Larner, Wendy and William Walters (2004) 'Globalisation as Governmentality', *Alternatives* 29 (5), 495–514.

Larsen, Henrik (1997) *Foreign Policy and Discourse Analysis: France, Britain and Europe* (London: Routledge).

Layne, Christopher (1993) 'The Unipolar Illusion: Why New Great Powers Will Rise', *International Security* 17 (4), 5–51.

Lederach, John Paul (1995) 'Conflict Transformation in Protracted Internal Conflicts: The Case for a Comprehensive Framework', in Kumar Rupesinghe (ed.), *Conflict Transformation* (Houndmills: Macmillan), 201–22.

Lederach, John Paul (1997) *Building Peace. Sustainable Reconciliation in Divided Societies* (Washington DC: United States Institute for Peace Press).

Lenin, Vladimir I. (2000) *Imperialism, the Highest Stage of Capitalism: A Popular Outline* (New Delhi: LeftWord Books, orig. 1917).

Lerner, Daniel (1968) 'Modernisation', in David L. Sills (ed.), *International Encyclopedia of the Social Sciences* 10 (New York: Free Press), 386–95.

Lewis, Arthur W. (1954) 'Economic Development with Unlimited Supplies of Labour', *The Manchester School of Economic and Social Studies* 22, 139–91.

Lindberg, Leon N. and Stuart A. Scheingold (1970) *Europe's Would-Be Polity: Patterns of Change in the European Community* (Englewood Cliffs, NJ: Prentice-Hall).

Linklater, Andrew (1982) *Men and Citizens in the Theory of International Relations* (London: Macmillan).

Linklater, Andrew (1990) *Beyond Realism and Marxism: Critical Theory and International Relations* (London: Macmillan).

Linklater, Andrew (1998) *The Transformation of Political Community: Ethical Foundations of the Post-Westphalian Era* (Cambridge: Polity Press).

Linklater, Andrew (2009) 'Marx and Marxism', in Scott Burchill, et al. (eds), *Theories of International Relations* (Basingstoke: Palgrave Macmillan, 4th edn), 111–35.

Lippmann, Walter (1943) *US Foreign Policy: Shield of the Republic* (Boston: Little, Brown).

Lipschutz, Ronnie D. (1995) *On Security* (New York: Columbia University Press).

Lipschutz, Ronnie D. (1996) *Global Civil Society and Global Environmental Governance: The Politics of Nature from Place to Planet* (Albany, NY: New York State University Press).

Little, Richard (2007) *The Balance of Power in International Relations* (Cambridge: Cambridge University Press).

Lose, Lars G. (2001) 'Communicative Action and the World of Diplomacy', in Karin Fierke and Knud Erik Jørgensen (eds), *Constructing International Relations: The Next Generation* (Armonk, NY: M. E. Sharpe), 179–200.

Lukes, Steven (1974) *Power: A Radical View* (Houndmills: Macmillan Education).

Lukes, Steven (2007) 'Power and the Battle for Hearts and Minds: On the Bluntness of Soft Power', in Felix Berenskoetter and M. J. Williams (eds), *Power in World Politics* (London: Routledge), 83–97.

Lumsdaine, David H. (1993) *Moral Vision in International Politics: The Foreign Aid Regime 1945–1989* (Princeton: Princeton University Press).

Luxemburg, Rosa (1971) *The Accumulation of Capital* (London: Routledge and Kegan Paul, orig. 1913).

Manners, Ian (2002) 'Normative Power Europe: A Contradiction in Terms?', *Journal of Common Market Studies* 40 (2), 235–58.

Mansfield, Edward D. and Jack Snyder (1995) 'Democratization and the Danger of War', *International Security* 20 (1), 5–38.

Maoz, Zeev and Bruce M. Russett (1993) 'Normative and Structural Causes of Democratic Peace, 1946–1986', *American Political Science Review* 87 (3), 624–38.

March, James G. and Johan P. Olsen (1989) *Rediscovering Institutions: The Organizational Basis of Politics* (New York: Free Press).

Marks, Gary, F. W. Scharpf, P. C. Schmitter and W. Streeck (1996) *Governance in the European Union* (London: Sage).

Martell, Luke (2007) 'The Third Wave in Globalization Theory', *International Studies Review* 9, 173–96.

Martin, Gus (2008) *Essentials of Terrorism* (London: Sage).

Martin, Gus (2010) *Understanding Terrorism* (London: Sage).

Martin, Lisa L. (1992) 'Interests, Power, and Multilateralism', *International Organization* 46 (4), 765–92.

Martin, Lisa L. (2007) 'Neo-Liberalism', in Tim Dunne, Milya Kurki and Steve Smith (eds), *Theories of International Relations: Discipline and Diversity* (Oxford: Oxford University Press), 111–25.

Marx, Karl (1977a) 'Theses on Feuerbach', in David McLellan (ed.), *Karl Marx: Selected Writings* (Oxford: Oxford University Press, orig. 1888), 98–100.

Marx, Karl (1977b) 'The Eighteenth Brumaire on Louis Bonaparte', in David McLellan (ed.), *Karl Marx: Selected Writings* (Oxford: Oxford University Press, orig. 1952), 187–208.

Marx, Karl and Friedrich Engels (1977) 'The Communist Manifesto', in David McLellan (ed.), *Karl Marx: Selected Writings* (Oxford: Oxford University Press, orig. 1948), 157–86.

Massey, Douglas S., et al. (1993) 'Theories of International Migration: A Review and Appraisal', *Population and Development Review* 19 (3), 431–66.

Mastanduno, Michael (1999) 'Preserving the Unipolar Moment: Realist Theories and US: Grand Strategy after the Cold War', in Ethan B. Kapstein and Michael Mastanduno (eds), (1999) *Unipolar Politics: Realism and State Strategies after the Cold War* (New York: Columbia University Press), 138–81.

Mayall, James (1990) *Nationalism and International Society* (Cambridge: Cambridge University Press).

McDonald, John W. (1991) 'Further Exploration of Track Two Diplomacy', in Louis Kriesberg and Stuart J. Thorson (eds), *Timing the De-escalation of International Conflicts* (Syracuse, NY: Syracuse University Press).

McRae, Rob and Don Hubert (eds) (2001) *Human Security and the New Diplomacy: Protecting People, Promoting Peace* (Montréal and Kingston: McGill-Queen's University Press).

McSweeney, Bill (1999) *Security, Identity and Interests: A Sociology of International Relations* (Cambridge: Cambridge University Press).

Mearsheimer, John J. (1990) 'Back to the Future: Instability in Europe after the Cold War', *International Security* 14 (4), 5–56.

Mearsheimer, John J. (2001) *The Tragedy of Great Power Politics* (New York: W. W. Norton).

Mearsheimer, John J. (2007): 'Structural Realism', in Tim Dunne, Milja Kurki and Steve Smith (eds), *Theories of International Relations: Discipline and Diversity* (Oxford: Oxford University Press), 71–88.

Melissen, Jan (ed.) (1999) *Innovation in Diplomatic Practice* (Basingstoke: Palgrave).

Miller, Jody (2001) *One of the Guys: Girls, Gangs and Gender* (New York, London: Oxford University Press).

Milliken, Jennifer (1999) 'The Study of Discourse in International Relations: A Critique of Research and Methods', *European Journal of International Relations* 5 (2), 225–54.

Mitchell, C. R. (1981) *The Structure of International Conflict* (London and Basingstoke: Macmillan).

Mitrany, David (1966) *A Working Peace System* (Chicago: Quadrangle Books).

Mitzen, Jennifer (2006) 'Ontological Security in World Politics: State Identity and the Security Dilemma', *European Journal of International Relations* 12 (3), 341–70.

Montgomery, Evan Braden (2006) 'Breaking out of the Security Dilemma: Realism, Reassurance, and the Problem of Uncertainty', *International Security* 31 (2), 151–85.

Moravcsik, Andrew (1997) 'Taking Preferences Seriously: A Liberal Theory of International Politics', *International Organization* 51 (4), 513–53.

Moravcsik, Andrew (1998) *The Choice for Europe: Social Purpose and State Power from Messina to Maastricht* (Ithaca, NY: Cornell University Press).

Morgenthau, Hans J. (1961) *Politics Among Nations: The Struggle for Power and Peace* (New York: Knopf, 3rd edn).

Morgenthau, Hans J. (1962) 'A Political Theory of Foreign Aid', *American Political Science Review* 56 (2), 301–9.

Müller, Harald (1993) 'The Internalization of Principles, Norms, and Rules by Governments: The Case of Security Regimes', in Volker Rittberger (ed.), *Regime Theory and International Relations* (Oxford: Clarendon Press), 361–88.

Müller, Harald (1995) 'Spielen hilft nicht immer: Die Grenzen des Rational-Choice-Ansatzes und der Platz der Theorie kommunikativen Handelns in der Analyse internationaler Beziehungen', *Zeitschrift für Internationale Beziehungen* 2 (2), 371–91.

Müller, Harald (1998) 'Regimeanalyse und Sicherheitspolitik. Das Beispiel Nonproliferation', in Beate Kohler-Koch (ed.), *Regime in den Internationalen Beziehungen* (Baden-Baden: Nomos Verlag), 277–14.

Müller, Harald and Jonas Wolff (2006) 'Democratic Peace: Many Data, Little Explanation?', in Lothar Brock, Anna Geis and Harald Müller (eds), *Democratic Wars: Looking at the Dark Side of Democratic Peace* (Houndsmills: Palgrave), 41–73.

Münkler, Herfried (2005a) *Imperien: Die Logik der Weltherrschaft – vom alten Rom bis zu den Vereinigten Staaten* (Berlin: Rowohlt).

Münkler, Herfried (2005b) *The New Wars* (Cambridge: Polity Press).

Murray, Alastair J. H. (1996) 'The Moral Politics of Hans Morgenthau', *The Review of Politics* 58 (1), 81–107.

Naím, Moisés (2000) 'Washington Consensus or Washington Confusion', *Foreign Policy* 118, 86–103.

Nardin, Terry (2002) 'The Moral Basis of Humanitarian Intervention', *Ethics and International Affairs*, 57–70.

Nardin, Terry and David R. Maple (eds) (1993) *Traditions of International Ethics* (Cambridge: Cambridge University Press).

Neumann, Iver B. (1999) *Uses of the Other: 'The East' in European Identity Formation* (Minneapolis: University of Minnesota Press).

Neumann, Iver B. (2003) 'The English School on Diplomacy: Scholarly Promise Unfulfilled', *International Relations* 17 (3), 341–69.

Neumann, Iver B. (2005) 'To Be a Diplomat', *International Studies Perspectives* 6 (1), 72–93.

Newman, David (2006a) 'The Lines That Continue to Separate Us: Borders in Our "Borderless" World', *Progress in Human Geography* 30 (2), 143–61.

Newman, David (2006b) 'Borders and Bordering: Towards an Interdisciplinary Dialogue', *European Journal of Social Theory* 9 (2), 171–86.

Newman, David and Anssi Paasi (1998) 'Fences and Neighbours in the Postmodern World: Boundary Narratives in Political Geography', *Progress in Human Geography* 22 (2), 186–207.

Newman, Edward S. (2004) 'The "New Wars" Debate: A Historical Perspective is Needed', *Security Dialogue* 35 (2), 173–89.

Nicolson, Harold (1939) *Diplomacy* (Oxford: Oxford University Press).

Niebuhr, Reinhold (1932) *Moral Man and Immoral Society: Study in Ethics and Politics* (New York: Charles Scribner's Sons).

Niemann, Arne with Philippe C. Schmitter (2009) 'Neofunctionalism', in Antje Wiener and Thomas Diez (eds), *European Integration Theory* (Oxford: Oxford University Press), 45 66.

Nye, Joseph S. (1990) 'The Changing Nature of World Power', *Political Science Quarterly* 105 (2), 177–92.

Nye, Joseph S., Jr. (2007) 'Notes for a Soft-Power Research Agenda', in Felix Berenskoetter and M. J. Williams (eds), *Power in World Politics* (London: Routledge), 162–72.

O'Brien, Conor Cruise (1993) 'The Wrath of Ages: Nationalism's Primordial Roots', *Foreign Affairs* 72 (5), 142–9.

O'Brien, Philip J. (1975) 'A Critique of Latin American Theories of Dependency', in Ivar Oxaal, Tony Barnett and David Booth (eds), *Beyond the Sociology of Development: Economy and Society in Latin America and Africa* (London and Boston: Routledge & Kegan Paul), 7–27.

O'Neal, John and Bruce Russett (2001) *Triangulating Peace: Democracy, Interdependence and International Organizations* (New York: W. W. Norton).

O'Neill, Onora (2000) 'Bounded and Cosmopolitan Justice', *Review of International Studies* 26 (Special Issue), 45–60.

Ohmae, Kenichi (1996) *The End of the Nation-State: The Rise of Regional Economies* (New York: HarperCollins).

Okur, Mehmet Akif (2007) 'Rethinking Empire After 9/11: Towards a New Ontological Image of World Order', *Perspectives: Journal of International Affairs* 12, 61–94.

Oren, Ido and Jude Hays (1997) 'Democracies May Rarely Fight One Another, but Developed States Rarely Fight at All', *Alternatives: Social Transformation and Humane Governance* 22 (4), 493–521.

Osborne, Martin J. and Ariel Rubinstein (1998) *A Course in Game Theory* (Cambridge, MA: MIT Press).

Palma, Gabriel (1978) 'Dependency: A Formal Theory of Underdevelopment or a Methodology for the Analysis of Concrete Situations of Underdevelopment?', *World Development* 6, 881–924.

Panitch, Leo and Sam Gindin (2004) *Global Capitalism and American Empire* (London: Merlin Press).

Paris, Roland (2001) 'Human Security: Paradigm Shift or Hot Air?', *International Security* 26 (2), 87–102.

Passavant, Paul A. (2004) 'Introduction', in Paul A. Passavant and Jodi Dean (eds), *Empire's New Clothes: Reading Hardt and Negri* (New York and London: Routledge), 1–20.

Payne, Tony (2005) *The Global Politics of Unequal Development* (Basingstoke: Palgrave).

Pedersen, Thomas (1998) *Germany, France and the Integration of Europe: A Realist Interpretation* (London: Pinter).

Petras, James and Henry Veltmeyer (2001) *Globalization Unmasked: Imperialism in the 21st Century* (London: Zed Books).

Phillips, David L. (2005) *Unsilencing the Past: Track Two Diplomacy and Turkish–Armenian Reconciliation* (New York and Oxford: Berghahn).

Piore, Michael J. (1979) *Birds of Passage: Migrant Labor in Industrial Societies* (Cambridge: Cambridge University Press).

Pogge, Thomas (2002) *World Poverty and Human Rights* (Cambridge: Polity Press).

Posen, Barry R. (1993) 'The Security Dilemma and Ethnic Conflict', *Survival* 35 (1), 27–47.

Power, Samantha (2008) *Chasing the Flame: Sergio Vieira de Mello and the Fight to Save the World* (New York: Penguin).

Prebisch, Raúl (1950) *The Economic Development of Latin America and its Principal Problems* (New York: United Nations).

Price, Richard (1998) 'Reversing the Gun Sights: Transnational Civil Society Targets Landmines', *International Organisation* 52, 613–44.

Prince, L (1998) 'The Neglected Rules: On Leadership and Dissent', in A. C. Coulson (ed.), *Trust and Contracts: Relationships in Local Government Health and Public Services* (Bristol: Polity Press), 95–126.

Prügl, Elisabeth (1999) *The Global Construction of Gender: Home-Based Work in the Political Economy of the 20th Century* (New York: Columbia University Press).

Pugh, Michael (2004) 'Peacekeeping and Critical Theory', *International Peacekeeping* 11 (1), 39–58.

Ramcharan, Bertrand G. (2008) *Preventive Diplomacy at the UN* (Bloomington, IN: Indiana University Press).

Ramsbotham, Oliver, Tom Woodhouse and Hugh Miall (2008) *Contemporary Conflict Resolution* (Cambridge: Polity Press, 2nd edn).

Rapaport, Anatol (1960) *Fights, Games and Debates* (Ann Arbor, MI: University of Michigan Press).

Rawls, John (1971) *A Theory of Justice* (Cambridge, MA: Harvard University Press).

Rawls, John (1999) *The Law of Peoples* (Cambridge, MA: Harvard University Press).

Reinicke, Wolfgang H. and Francis Deng (eds) (2000) *Critical Choices. The United Nations, Networks and the Future of Global Governance* (Ottawa: International Development Research Centre).

Reus-Smit, Christian (2001) 'Human Rights and the Social Construction of Sovereignty', *Review of International Studies* 27 (4), 519–38.

Reus-Smit, Christian (2003a) 'Introduction', in Christian Reus-Smit (ed.), *The Politics of International Law* (Cambridge: Cambridge University Press), 1–13.

Reus-Smit, Christian (2003b) 'The Politics of International Law', in Christian Reus-Smit (ed.), *The Politics of International Law* (Cambridge: Cambridge University Press), 14–44.

Reus-Smit, Christian (2008) 'International Law', in John Baylis, Steve Smith and Patricia Owens (eds), *The Globalization of World Politics: An Introduction to International Relations* (Oxford: Oxford University Press, 4th edn), 278–95.

Richardson, Louise (2006) *What Terrorists Want* (New York: Random House).

Richmond, Oliver P. (2005) *The Transformation of Peace* (Basingstoke: Palgrave Macmillan).

Risse, Thomas (2000) '"Let's Argue!": Communicative Action in World Politics', *International Organization* 54 (1), 1–39.

Risse, Thomas (2001) 'A European Identity? Europeanization and the Evolution of Nation-State Identities', in Maria Green Cowles et al. (eds), *Transforming Europe: Europeanization and Domestic Change* (Ithaca, NY: Cornell University Press), 198–216.

Risse, Thomas (2009) 'Social Constructivism', in Antje Wiener and Thomas Diez (eds), *European Integration Theory* (Oxford: Oxford University Press, 2nd edn).

Risse, Thomas and Kathryn Sikkink (1999) 'The Socialization of International Human Right Norms into Domestic Practices: Introduction', in Thomas Risse, Stephen C. Ropp and Kathryn Sikkink (eds), *The Power of Human Rights: International Norms and Domestic Change* (Cambridge: Cambridge University Press), 1–38.

Risse, Thomas, D. Engelmann-Martin, H.-J. Knopf and K. Roscher (1999a) 'To Euro or Not to Euro? The EMU and Identity Politics in the European Union', *European Journal of International Relations* 5 (2), 147–87.

Risse, Thomas, Stephen C. Ropp and Kathryn Sikkink (eds) (1999b) *The Power of Human Rights: International Norms and Domestic Change* (Cambridge: Cambridge University Press).

Risse-Kappen, Thomas (1995) 'Democratic Peace – Warlike Democracies? A Social Constructivist Interpretation of the Liberal Argument', *European Journal of International Relations* 1 (4), 491–517.

Risse-Kappen, Thomas (1996a) 'Collective Identity in a Democratic Community: The Case of NATO', in Peter J. Katzenstein (ed.), *The Culture of National Security: Norms and Identity in World Politics* (New York: Columbia University Press), 357–99.

Risse-Kappen, Thomas (1996b) 'Identity in a Democratic Security Community: The Case of NATO', in Peter J. Katzenstein (ed.), *The Culture of National Security* (New York: Columbia University Press), 357–99.

Rittberger, Volker (ed.) (1993) *Regime Theory and International Relations* (Oxford: Clarendon Press).

Rittberger, Volker and Bernhard Zangl (2006) *International Organization: Polity, Politics and Policies* (London: Palgrave).

Rittberger, Volker and Michael Zürn (1990) 'Towards Regulated Anarchy in East–West Relations', in Volker Rittberger (ed.), *International Regimes in East–West Politics* (London: Pinter), 9–63.

Rittberger, Volker, C. Huckel, L. Reith and M. Zimmer (2008) 'Inclusive Global Institutions for a Global Political Economy', in Volker Rittberger, Martin Nettesheim and Carmen Huckel (eds), *Authority in the Global Political Economy* (Basingstoke: Palgrave), 13–54.

Robertson, Roland (1995) 'Glocalization: Time–Space and Homogeneity–Heterogeneity', in Mike Featherstone, Scott Lash and Roland Robertson (eds), *Global Modernities* (London: Sage), 25–44.

Roe, Paul (1999) 'The Intrastate Security Dilemma: Ethnic Conflict as "Tragedy"?', *Journal of Peace Research* 36 (2), 183–202.

Roe, Paul (2005) *Ethnic Violence and the Societal Security Dilemma* (London: Routledge).

Rosamond, Ben (2000) 'Neofunctionalism', in B. Rosamond, *Theories of European Integration* (Basingstoke: Palgrave Macmillan), 31–42.

Rosato, Sebastian (2003) 'The Flawed Logic of Democratic Peace Theory', *American Political Science Review* 97 (4), 585–602.

Rose, G. (1998) 'Neoclassical Realism and Theories of Foreign Policy', *World Politics,* 51 (1), 144–72.

Rosenau, James N. (ed.) (1967) *Domestic Sources of Foreign Policy* (London: Collier-Macmillan).

Rosenau, James N. (ed.) (1969) *International Politics and Foreign Policy: A Reader in Research and Theory* (New York: Free Press).

Rosenau, James N. (1980) *The Scientific Study of Foreign Policy* (London: Pinter).

Rosenau, James N. (1992) 'Governance, Order, And Change in World Politics', in Rosenau, James N. and Ernst-Otto Czempiel (eds), *Governance Without Government: Order and Change in World Politics* (Cambridge: Cambridge University Press), 1–29.

Rosenau, James N. (1997) *Along the Domestic–Foreign Frontier: Exploring Governance in a Turbulent World* (New York: Cambridge University Press).

Rosenau, James N. and Ernst-Otto Czempiel (eds) (1992) *Governance Without Government: Order and Change in World Politics* (Cambridge: Cambridge University Press).

Rosenberg, Justin (1994) *The Empire of Civil Society: A Critique of the Realist Theory of International Relations* (London: Verso).

Rosenberg, Justin (2000) *The Follies of Globalisation Theory: Polemical Essays* (London: Verso).

Rosenberg, Justin (2006) 'Why is There No International Historical Sociology?', *European Journal of International Relations* 12 (3), 307–40.

Rostow, Walt (1960) *The Stages of Growth: A Non-Communist Manifesto* (Cambridge: Cambridge University Press).

Rubin, Jeffrey Z., Dean G. Pruitt and Sung Hee Kim (1994) *Social Conflict: Escalation, Stalemate, and Settlement* (New York: McGraw Hill, 2nd edn).

Ruggie, John Gerard (1983) 'Continuity and Transformation in the World Polity: Toward a Neorealist Synthesis', *World Politics* 35 (2), 261–85.

Ruggie, John Gerard (1993) 'Territoriality and Beyond: Problematizing Modernity in International Relations', *International Organization* 47 (1), 139–74.

Rumelili, Bahar (2008) *Constructing Regional Community and Order in Europe and Southeast Asia* (Basingstoke: Palgrave).

Rumford, Chris (2009) *Citizens and Borderwork in Contemporary Europe* (London: Routledge).

Rummel, Rudolph J. (1997) *Power Kills: Democracy as a Method of Nonviolence* (New Brunswick, NJ: Transaction Publishers).

Russett, Bruce (1993) *Grasping the Democratic Peace: Principles for a Post-Cold War World* (Princeton: Princeton University Press).

Russett, Bruce (1998) 'A Neo-Kantian Perspective: Democracy, Interdependence and International Organizations in Building Security Communities', in Emanuel Adler and Michael Barnett (eds), *Security Communities* (Cambridge: Cambridge University Press), 368–94.

Sachs, Wolfgang (1992) *The Development Dictionary: A Guide to Knowledge as Power* (London: Zed).

Said, Edward (1979) *Orientalism* (New York: Vintage).

Salem, Paul F. (1993) 'In Theory: A Critique of Western Conflict Resolution from a Non-Western Perspective', *Negotiation Journal*, 9 (4), 361–9.

Salem, Paul F. (ed.) (1997) *Conflict Resolution in the Arab World: Selected Essays* (New York: American University of Beirut).

Sanders, Douglas (1991) 'Collective Rights', *Human Rights Quarterly* 13 (3), 368–86.

Sassen, Saskia (1991) *Global City: New York, London, Tokyo* (Princeton: Princeton University Press).

Sassen, Saskia (1996) *Losing Control: Sovereignty in an Age of Globalization* (New York: Columbia University Press).

Schelling, Thomas C. (1960) *The Strategy of Conflict* (Cambridge, MA: Harvard University Press).

Schimmelfennig, Frank (2001) 'The Community Trap: Liberal Norms, Rhetorical Action, and the Eastern Enlargement of the European Union', *International Organization* 55 (1), 47–80.

Schlichte, Klaus (2002) 'Neues über den Krieg? Einige Anmerkungen zum Stand der Kriegsforschung in den Internationalen Beziehungen', *Zeitschrift für Internationale Beziehungen* 9 (1), 113–37.

Schmidt, Brian C. (1998) 'Lessons from the Past: Reassessing the Interwar Disciplinary History of International Relations', *International Studies Quarterly* 42 (3), 433–59.

Schmidt, Brian C. (2007) 'Realist Conceptions of Power', in Felix Berenskoetter and M. J. Williams (eds), *Power in World Politics* (London: Routledge), 43–63.

Scholte, Jan Aart (2005) *Globalization: A Critical Introduction* (Basingstoke: Palgrave Macmillan).

Schultz, Kenneth A. (2001) *Democracy and Coercive Diplomacy* (Cambridge: Cambridge University Press).

Schumpeter, Joseph A. (1951) *Imperialism and Social Classes* (Oxford: Blackwell, orig. 1919).

Schweller, Randall L. (1996) 'Neorealism's Status-Quo Bias: What Security Dilemma?', *Security Studies* 5 (3), 90–121.

Scott, Craig (1999) 'Reaching Beyond (Without Abandoning) the Category of "Economic, Social and Cultural Rights"', *Human Rights Quarterly* 21 (3), 533–60.

Scott, Shirley V. (1994) 'International Law as Ideology: Theorising the Relationship between International Law and International Politics', *European Journal of International Relations* 5, 1–14.

Sen, Amartya (1999) *Development as Freedom* (Oxford: Oxford University Press).

Senghaas, Dieter (1972) *Abschreckung und Frieden: Studien zur Kritik organisierter Friedlosigkeit* (Frankfurt am Main: Fischer).

Senghaas, Dieter (1995) 'Frieden als Zivilisierungsobjekt', in Dieter Senghaas (ed.), *Den Frieden denken: Si vis pacem, para pacem* (Frankfurt am Main: Suhrkamp), 196–223.

Seton-Watson, Hugh (1977) *Nations & States: An Inquiry into the Origins of Nations and the Politics of Nationalism* (London: Methuen).

Seybolt, Taylor B. (2007) *Humanitarian Military Intervention: The Conditions for Success and Failure* (Oxford: Oxford University Press).

Shapcott, Richard (2001) *Justice, Community and Dialogue in International Relations* (Cambridge: Cambridge University Press).

Shapcott, Richard (2008) 'International Ethics', in J. Baylis, S. Smith and P. Owens (eds), *The Globalization of World Politics: An Introduction to International Relations* (Oxford: Oxford University Press, 4th edn), 192–206.

Shapiro, Michael J. (ed.) (1984) *Language and Politics* (Oxford: Blackwell).

Sharp, Paul (1999) 'For Diplomacy: Representation and the Study of International Relations', *International Studies Review* 1 (1), 33–57.

Shepherd, Laura J. (2006) 'Veiled References: Constructions of Gender in the Bush Administration Discourse on the Attacks on Afghanistan post-9/11', *International Feminist Journal of Politics* 8 (1), 19–41.

Shepherd, Laura J. (2008) *Gender, Violence and Security: Discourse as Practice* (London: Zed Books).

Shorten, Andrew (2008) 'Nation and State', in Catriona McKinnon (ed.) *Issues in Political Theory* (Oxford: Oxford University Press), 33–55.

Shubik, Martin (1982) *Game Theory in the Social Sciences: Concepts and Solutions* (Cambridge, MA: MIT Press).

Silke, Andrew (ed.) (2004) *Research on Terrorism* (London: Frank Cass).

Silverman, Maxim (1992) *Deconstructing the Nation: Immigration, Racism, and Citizenship in Modern France* (London: Routledge).

Simmons, Beth A. and Lisa L. Martin (2002) 'International Organizations and Institutions', in Walter Carlsnaes, Thomas Risse and Beth A. Simmons (eds), *Handbook of International Relations* (London: Sage), 192–211.

Singer, J. David (1961) 'The Levels-of-Analysis Problem in International Relations', *World Politics* 14 (1), 77–92.

Singer, J. David and Melvin Small (1972) *The Wages of War, 1816–1965* (New York: Wiley).

Slaughter, Anne-Marie (1995) 'International Law in a World of Liberal States', *European Journal of International Law* 6 (1), 503–38.

Smith, Anthony D. (1986) *The Ethnic Origins of Nations* (Oxford: Blackwell).

Smith, Anthony D. (1998) *Nationalism and Modernism* (London: Routledge).

Smith, Steve, Ken Booth and Marysia Zalewski (eds) (1996) *International Theory: Positivism and Beyond* (London: Sage).

Snidal, Duncan (1985) 'The Game Theory of International Politics', *World Politics* 38 (1), 25–57.

Snidal, Duncan (1986) 'The Game Theory of International Politics', in Kenneth Oye (ed.), *Cooperation under Anarchy* (Princeton: Princeton University Press), 25–57.

Snyder, Jack L. (1985) 'Perceptions of the Security Dilemma in 1914', in Robert Jervis, Richard Ned Lebow and Janice Gross Stein (eds), *Psychology and Deterrence* (Baltimore: Johns Hopkins University Press), 153–79.

Sørensen, Georg (1999) 'Sovereignty: Change and Continuity in a Fundamental Institution', *Political Studies* 47 (4), 590–604.

Spruyt, Hendrik (1994) *The Sovereign State and Its Competitors* (Princeton: Princeton University Press).

Steans, Jill (2006) *Gender and International Relations* (Cambridge: Polity, 2nd edn).

Steans, Jill (2007) 'Debating Women's Rights as a Universal Feminist Project: Defending Women's Human Rights as a Political Tool', *Review of International Studies* 33 (1), 11–27.

Stein, Arthur A. (1983) 'Coordination and Collaboration: Regimes in an Anarchic World', in Stephen D. Krasner (ed.), *International Regimes* (Ithaca, NY: Cornell University Press), 115–40.

Strange, Susan (1996) *The Retreat of the State: The Diffusion of Power in the World Economy* (Cambridge: Cambridge University Press).

Sylvester, Christine (1980) 'UN Elites: Perspectives on Peace', *Journal of Peace Research* 17 (4), 305–23.

Sylvester, Christine (1992) 'Man, the State, and War: Gendered Perspectives on National Security', in Judith Ann Tickner (ed.), *Gender in International Relations – Feminist Perspectives on Achieving Global Security* (New York: Columbia University Press).

Sylvester, Christine (1994) *Feminist Theory and International Relations in a Postmodern Era* (New York: Cambridge University Press).

Taylor, Paul (1968) 'The Functionalist Approach to the Problem of International Order: A Defence', *Political Studies* 16 (3), 393–410.

Teschke, Benno (2003) *The Myth of 1648: Class, Geopolitics and the Making of Modern International Relations* (Verso: London).

Teschke, Benno (2008) 'Marxism', in Christian Reus-Smit (ed.), *The Oxford Handbook of International Relations* (Oxford: Oxford University Press), 163–87.

Thakur, Ramesh (2007) 'Humanitarian Intervention', in Thomas G. Weiss and Sam Daws (eds), *The Oxford Handbook on the United Nations* (Oxford: Oxford University Press), 387–403.

Tickner, Judith Ann (1988) 'Hans Morgenthau's Principles of Political Realism: A Feminist Reformulation', *Millennium: Journal of International Studies* 17 (3), 429–40.

Tickner, Judith Ann (ed.) (1992) *Gender in International Relations: Feminist Perspectives on Achieving Global Security* (New York: Columbia University Press).

Tickner, Judith Ann (2001) *Gendering World Politics: Issues and Approaches in the Post-Cold War Era* (New York: Columbia University Press).

Tickner, Judith Ann (2006) 'Feminist Perspectives on International Relations', in Walter Carlsnaes (ed.), *Handbook of International Relations* (London: Sage), 275–91.

Tickner, Judith Ann and Laura Sjoberg (2007) 'Feminism', in Tim Dunne, Milja Kurki and Steve Smith (eds), *International Relations Theories: Discipline and Diversity* (Oxford: Oxford University Press), 185–202.

Tilly, Charles (2004) 'Terror, Terrorism, Terrorists', *Social Theory* 22 (1), 1–9.

Todaro, Michael P. (1989) *Economic Development in the Third World* (New York: Longman).

True, Jacqui (2006) 'The Ethics of Feminism', in Christian Reus-Smit (ed.), *The Oxford Handbook of International Relations* (Oxford: Oxford University Press), 408–21.

True, Jacqui (2009) 'Feminism', in Scott Burchill et al. (eds), *Theories of International Relations* (London: Palgrave Macmillan, 4th edn), 237–59.

Truman, Harry S. (1949) *Inaugural Address*, www.trumanlibrary.org/whistlestop/50yr_archive/inagural20jan1949.htm [20.04.2010].

Turner, Frederick Jackson (1953) *The Frontier in American History* (New York: Holt, 2nd edn).

ul Haq, Mahbub (1995) *Reflections on Human Development* (Oxford: Oxford University Press).

United Nations (1945) *Statute of the International Court of Justice* (The Hague: ICJ).

United Nations (1948) *Convention on the Prevention and Punishment of the Crime of Genocide*, www.preventgenocide.org/law/convention/text.htm [12.11.2009].

United Nations (2008) *United Nations Peacekeeping Operations: Principles and Guidelines* (United Nations: New York).

United Nations Development Programme (2010) *The Human Development Concept*, http://hdr.undp.org/en/humandev/ [22.04.2010].

United Nations General Assembly (1974) *Declaration on the Establishment of a New International Economic Order*, A/RES/S-6/3201, www.un-documents.net/s6r3201.htm [20.04.2010].

United Nations General Assembly (2000) *United Nations Millennium Declaration*, A/RES/55/2, www.un.org/millennium/declaration/ares552e.htm [22.04.2010].

United Nations General Assembly (2005) *2005 World Summit Outcome* (A/RES/60/1).

United Nations General Assembly Resolution 60/288 (2006) www.un.org/terrorism/strategy-counter-terrorism.shtml#resolution [09.05.2010].

United Nations Security Council (1999) *Resolution 1272 on the Situation in East Timor*, S/RES/1272, http://daccessdds.un.org/doc/UNDOC/GEN/N99/312/77/PDF/N9931277.pdf?OpenElement [12.08.2009].

United Nations Security Council Resolution 1566 (2004) http://ods-dds-ny.un.org/doc/UNDOC/GEN/N04/542/82/PDF/N0454282.pdf?OpenElement [09.05.2010].

Van Crefeld, Martin (1991) *On Future War* (London: Brassey).

Van der Pijl, Kees (1998) *Transnational Classes and International Relations* (London: Routledge).

Väyrynen, Raimo (2000) 'Stable Peace Through Security Communities? Steps Towards Theory Building', in Arie M. Kacowicz, et al. (eds), *Stable Peace amongst Nations* (Boston: Rowman & Littlefield), 108–29.

Vincent, R. J. (1987) *Human Rights and International Relations* (Cambridge: Cambridge University Press).

von Clausewitz, Karl (1982) *On War* (London: Penguin Books, orig. 1832).

von Neumann, John and Oskar Morgenstern (1944) *Theory of Games and Economic Behaviour* (Princeton: Princeton University Press).

Wæver, Ole (1993) 'Societal Security', in Ole Waever, et al. (eds), *Identity, Migration and the New Security Agenda in Europe* (New York: St. Martin's Press), 17–40.

Wæver, Ole (1997a) 'Imperial Metaphors: Emerging European Analogies to Pre-Nation-State Imperial System', in Ola Tunander, Pavel K. Baev and Victoria Ingrid Einagel (eds), *Geo-Politics in Post-Wall Europe: Security, Territory, Identity* (London: Sage), 59–93.

Wæver, Ole (1997b) 'Figures of International Thought: Introducing Persons Instead of Paradigms', in Iver B. Neumann and Ole Wæver (eds), *The Future of International Relations: Masters in the Making* (London: Routledge), 7–37.

Wæver, Ole (2002) 'Identity, Communities and Foreign Policy: Discourse Analysis as Foreign Policy Theory', in Lene Hansen and Ole Wæver (eds), *European*

Integration and National Identity: The Challenge of Nordic States (London: Routledge), 20–49.

Wæver, Ole (2009) 'Discursive Approaches', in Antje Wiener and Thomas Diez (eds), *European Integration Theory* (Oxford: Oxford University Press, 2nd edn).

Wæver Ole, Ulla Holm and Henrik Larsen (1998) *The Struggle for Europe: French and German Concepts of State, Nation and European Union* (Copenhagen: unpublished MS).

Walker, R. B. J. (1993) *Inside/Outside: International Relations as Political Theory* (Cambridge: Cambridge University Press).

Wallensteen, Peter (2007) *Understanding Conflict Resolution* (London: Sage, 2nd edn).

Wallensteen, Peter and Margareta Sollenberg (1999) 'Armed Conflict 1989–1998', *Journal of Peace Research* 36 (5), 593–606.

Wallerstein, Immanuel (1979) *The Capitalist World Economy* (Cambridge: Cambridge University Press).

Wallerstein, Immanuel M. (1984) *The Politics of the World-Economy: The States, the Movements and the Civilizations* (Cambridge: Cambridge University Press).

Walt, Stephen M. (1987) *The Origins of Alliances* (Ithaca, NY: Cornell University Press).

Walter, Barbara F. (2002) *Committing to Peace: The Successful Settlement of Civil Wars* (Princeton: Princeton University Press).

Waltz, Kenneth N. (1959) *Man, the State and War: A Theoretical Analysis* (New York: Columbia University Press, 2nd edn).

Waltz, Kenneth N. (1979) *Theory of International Politics* (New York: Random House).

Waltz, Kenneth N. (1995) *Peace, Stability, and Nuclear Weapons* (Berkeley: Berkeley Institute on Global Conflict and Cooperation).

Walzer, Michael (2000) *Just and Unjust Wars: A Moral Argument with Historical Illustrations* (New York: Basic Books, 3rd edn).

Walzer, Michael (2004) 'Words of War: Challenges to the Just War Theory', *Harvard International Review* 26 (1), 36–8.

Walzer, Michael (2006) *Just and Unjust Wars: A Moral Argument with Historical Illustrations* (New York: Basic Books; 3rd edn).

Watson, Adam (1983) *Diplomacy: The Dialogue Between States* (New York: McGraw Hill).

Watson, Adam (1992) *The Evolution of International Society: A Comparative Historical Analysis* (London: Routledge).

Weale, Albert and Michael Nentwich (ed.) (1998) *Political Theory and the European Union: Legitimacy, Constitutional Choice and Citizenship* (London: Routledge).

Weber, Cynthia (1995) *Simulating Sovereignty: Intervention, the State, and Symbolic Exchange* (Cambridge: Cambridge University Press).

Weber, Max (1922) *Wirtschaft und Gesellschaft: Grundriss der Sozialökonomik* (Tuebingen: Mohr).

Weinberger, Naomi (2002) 'Civil-Military Coordination in Peacebuilding: The Challenge in Afghanistan', *Journal of International Affairs* 55 (2), 245–74.

Weiss, Thomas G. (2007) *Humanitarian Intervention: Ideas in Action* (Cambridge: Polity Press).

Wendt, Alexander (1990) *Social Theory of International Politics* (Cambridge: Cambridge University Press).

Wendt, Alexander (1992) 'Anarchy Is What States Make of It: The Social Construction of Power Politics', *International Organization* 46 (2), 391–425.

Wendt, Alexander (1995) 'Constructing International Politics', *International Security* 20 (1), 71–81.

Wendt, Alexander (1999) *Social Theory of International Politics* (Cambridge: Cambridge University Press).

Wendt, Alexander (2000) 'On the Via Media: A Response to the Critics', *Review of International Studies* 26 (2), 165–80.

Wendt, Alexander (2003) 'Why a World State is Inevitable', *European Journal of International Relations* 9 (4), 491–542.

Wheeler, Nicholas J. (1992) 'Pluralist or Solidarist Conceptions of International Society: Bull and Vincent on Humanitarian Intervention', *Millennium: Journal of International Studies* 21 (3), 463–87.

Wheeler, Nicholas J. (2000) *Saving Strangers: Humanitarian Intervention in International Society* (Oxford: Oxford University Press).

Wheeler, Nicholas J. (2004a) 'The Humanitarian Responsibilities of Sovereignty: Explaining the Development of a New Norm of Military Intervention for the Humanitarian Purposes of International Society', in Jennifer M. Welsh (ed.), *Humanitarian Intervention and International Relations* (Oxford: Oxford University Press), 29–51.

Wheeler, Nicholas J. (2004b) 'The Kosovo Bombing Campaign', in Christian Reus-Smit (ed.), *The Politics of International Law* (Cambridge: Cambridge University Press), 189–216.

Whelan, Daniel J and Jack Donnelly (2007) 'The West, Economic and Social Rights, and the Global Human Rights Regime: Setting the Record Straight', *Human Rights Quarterly* 29 (4), 908–49.

Whitworth, Sandra (1994) *Feminism and International Relations: Towards a Global Political Economy of Gender in Interstate and Non-governmental Institutions* (Basingstoke: Macmillan).

Whitworth, Sandra (2004) *Men, Militarism and UN Peacekeeping: A Gendered Analysis* (Boulder, CO: Lynne Rienner).

Whitworth, Sandra (2006) 'Theory and Exclusion: Gender, Masculinity, and International Political Economy', in Richard Stubbs (ed.), *Political Economy and the Changing Global Order* (Oxford: Oxford University Press, 3rd edn), 88–99.

Whitworth, Sandra (2008) 'Feminism', in Christian Reus-Smit (ed.), *The Oxford Handbook of International Relations* (Oxford: Oxford University Press), 391–407.

Wiener, Antje (2007) 'The Dual Quality of Norms and the Governance beyond the State: Sociological and Normative Approaches to "Interaction"', *Critical Review of International Social and Political Philosophy* 10 (1), 47–69.

Wiener, Antje (2008) *The Invisible Constitution of Politics: Contested Norms and International Encounters* (Cambridge: Cambridge University Press).

Wiener, Antje and Thomas Diez (eds) (2009) *European Integration Theory* (Oxford: Oxford University Press, 2nd edn).

Wight, Martin (1977) *Systems of States*, ed. Hedley Bull (Leicester: Leicester University Press).

Wight, Martin (1978) *Power Politics* (Leicester: Leicester University Press).

Wight, Martin (1991) *International Theory: The Three Traditions*, eds Brian Porter and Gabriele Wight (Leicester: Leicester University Press).

Wilkinson, Paul (2001) *Terrorism vs. Democracy* (London: Frank Cass).

Wilkinson, Rorden (2005) 'Introduction: Concepts and Issues in Global Governance', in Rorden Wilkinson (ed.), *The Global Governance Reader* (London: Routledge), 1–22.

Wilkinson, Rorden (2007) 'Global Governance', in Mark Bevir (ed.), *Encyclopedia of Governance* (Thousand Oaks, CA: Sage), 344–9.

William, Michael C. and Iver B. Neumann (2000) 'From Alliance to Security Community: NATO, Russia, and the Power of Identity', *Millennium: Journal of International Studies*, 29 (2), 357–87.

Williams, John (2002) 'Territorial Borders, Toleration and the English School', *Review of International Studies* 28 (4), 737–58.

Williams, Paul D. (ed.) (2008) *Security Studies: An Introduction* (London: Routledge).

Wohlforth, William C. (1999) 'The Stability of a Unipolar World', *International Security* 24 (1), 5–41.

Wolfe, Patrick (1997) 'History and Imperialism – A Century of Theory: From Marx to Postcolonialism', *American Historical Review* 102 (2), 388–420.

Wolfers, Arnold (1962) *Discord and Collaboration: Essays on International Politics* (Baltimore, MD: Johns Hopkins University Press).

Wolff, R. P. (1970) *In Defense of Anarchism* (New York: Harper and Row).

World Bank (2008) *World Development Indicators* (Washington DC: World Bank).

Wyn Jones, Richard (1999) *Security, Strategy, and Critical Theory* (Boulder, CO: Lynne Rienner).

Yee, Albert S. (1996) 'The Causal Effect of Ideas on Policies', *International Organization* 50 (1), 69–108.

Young, Oran R. (1989) *International Cooperation* (Ithaca, NY: Cornell University Press).

Zartmann, Ira William (1985) *Ripe for Resolution: Conflict and Intervention in Africa* (New York: Oxford University Press).

Zartman, Ira William (1989) *Ripe for Resolution: Conflict and Intervention in Africa* (New York: Oxford University Press).

Zehfuss, Maja (2002) *Constructivism in International Relations: The Politics of Reality* (Cambridge: Cambridge University Press).

index

key concepts in
international relations